AF469444

SHALL WE EVER KNOW?

BOOKS BY WILLIAM COOPER

Scenes from Provincial Life
The Struggles of Albert Woods
The Ever-Interesting Topic
Disquiet and Peace
Young People
Scenes from Married Life
Memoirs of a New Man
You Want the Right Frame of Reference

Rook's Farm, Stocking Pelham

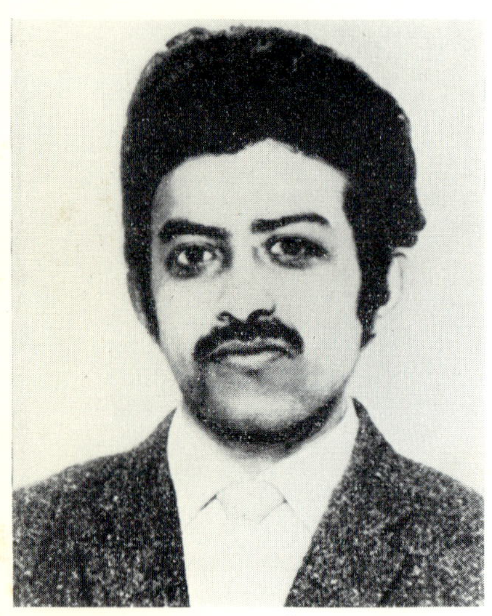

Arthur
Hosein

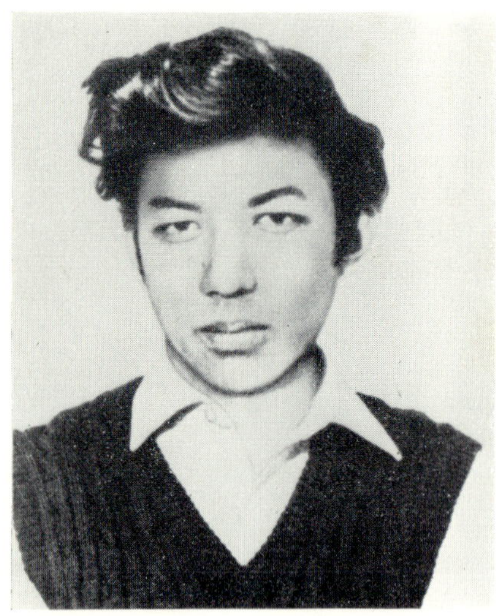

Nizamodeen
Hosein

SHALL WE EVER KNOW?

The trial of the Hosein Brothers for the murder of Mrs McKay

William Cooper

HUTCHINSON OF LONDON

HUTCHINSON & CO (*Publishers*) LTD
178–202 Great Portland Street, London W1

London Melbourne Sydney Auckland
Wellington Johannesburg Cape Town
and agencies throughout the world

First published 1971

This book has been set in Imprint type, printed in Great Britain on antique wove paper by Anchor Press, and bound by Wm. Brendon, both of Tiptree, Essex

ISBN 0 09 108270 6

Contents

THE ACCUSED

Arthur Hosein, aged 34, and
Nizamodeen Hosein, his brother, aged 22,
both of Rook's Farm, Stocking Pelham, Hertfordshire

THE JUDGE

The Hon. Mr. Justice Shaw

FOR THE PROSECUTION

The Attorney General, Sir Peter Rawlinson, Q.C., M.P.
Mr. E. J. P. Cussen, Senior Treasury Counsel
Mr. B. L. Leary, Junior Treasury Counsel

FOR THE DEFENCE

Mr. W. M. F. Hudson, Q.C. Mr. H. Dunn	for Arthur Hosein
Mr. D. P. Draycott, Q.C. Mr. L. Woodley	for Nizamodeen Hosein

ERRATUM

Page 220. Mr. Aubrey Rose was not the new solicitor for Arthur Hosein: he acted as solicitor for Nizamodeen Hosein throughout the whole case.

THE CHARGES

1 – That between December 29, 1969 and February 7, 1970 they murdered Mrs Muriel Florence McKay.

2 – That on December 29, 1969 they stole and unlawfully carried away Mrs McKay against her will.

3 – That between December 29, 1969 and February 7, 1970 they assaulted and imprisoned Mrs Muriel McKay against her will in some secret place.

4 – That on January 21, 1970 they sent an unwarranted demand for £1,000,000 with menaces.

5 – That on January 21 they sent a letter to Mr McKay threatening to murder Mrs McKay.

6 – That on January 26 they sent a letter addressed to Mr McKay making an unwarranted demand for £1,000,000 with menaces.

7 – That on January 26 they sent a letter to Mr McKay threatening to murder Mrs McKay.

CENTRAL CRIMINAL COURTS
OLD BAILEY

14 September 1970

COURT 1

R. v. Hosein & Anor

Thus reads the announcement outside the court on the morning of the trial's beginning—as near to a blank sheet as could be, given that it has to make an announcement at all.

But this happens to be a case where what is factually known already is nothing compared with what is publicly rumoured in London. In the first place Mrs McKay's disappearance from Wimbledon was given the widest publicity—she was the wife of a newspaper boss. And in the second place the accused men's arrest for kidnapping and murdering her was followed by hearings before a Lower Court which were public—and the facts that came out there were so incredible that, although the Press was not allowed to report them, word-of-mouth passed them outwards in all directions.

As I go up the steps of the Old Bailey, this unusually warm and sunny September morning, I wonder how many of the other people doing the same thing have already heard that:
(i) Mrs McKay was kidnapped in mistake for *someone else*,
(ii) The kidnappers demanded *£1,000,000* in ransom,
(iii) No trace of her has ever been found.

So incredible that just in themselves they offer the prospect of a *cause célèbre*. And added to them are the rumours, bizarre rumours, about how, if she really was murdered at Rook's Farm, the body was disposed of without a trace.

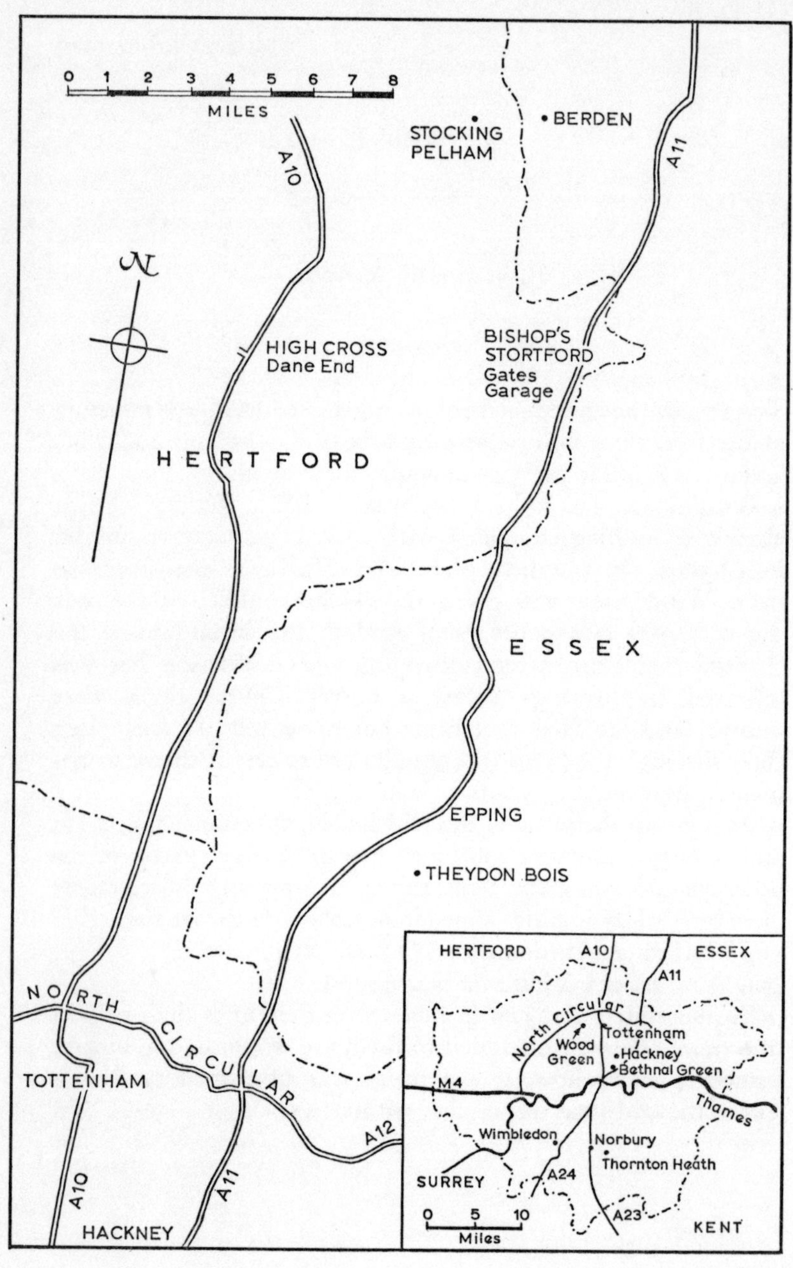
0 1 2 3 4 5 6 7 8
MILES
A10
STOCKING PELHAM
BERDEN
A11
N
HIGH CROSS
Dane End
BISHOP'S STORTFORD
Gates Garage
HERTFORD
ESSEX
EPPING
THEYDON BOIS
NORTH CIRCULAR
TOTTENHAM
A12
A10
A11
HACKNEY
HERTFORD
A10
ESSEX
A11
North Circular
Wood Green
Tottenham
Hackney
Bethnal Green
M4
Thames
Wimbledon
Norbury
Thornton Heath
SURREY
A24
0 5 10
Miles
A23
KENT

I

The ambience

'Put up Arthur Hosein and Nizamodeen Hosein!' So runs the formula with which the ritual of an English trial begins. At those words, uttered by the Clerk of the Court, the accused make their first, fateful appearance in the dock. Even the police officers who have previously spent hours interrogating them, and their counsel and solicitors who have spent hours conferring with them, glance up at them afresh. There they stand, come to trial—in this case for murder, for which the penalty, if they are convicted, now is imprisonment for life and only a few years ago would have been the gallows.

They stand, awaiting the beginning of a process in which they are presumed innocent until such time as the Crown may have proved beyond all reasonable doubt to a jury of twelve men and women drawn from the common public that they are guilty.

If 'putting them up' gives a first impression of the proceedings' being in any way awful or brutal, or even inconsiderate, it is totally misleading. Considerateness in every conceivable form, beginning above all with the presumption of innocence until guilt is proved, is the natural order—perhaps, foreigners might be thinking, the typical British order. The prosecution may interrogate formidably and the defence may retaliate with the most commanding arts of advocacy; yet voices are rarely raised beyond normal speaking tone and there are frequent pauses of sheer silence. If anyone were allowed to look into the court just *en passant*, he might see the proceedings as unbelievably calm, might even think there was scarcely anything going on.

The drama of the trial is going on, as it were, in the mind.

Every participant is exercising his wits to the full towards some end or other. It is particularly noticeable in the counsel, where one is frequently aware of that exercise going on even while they are on their feet: they frequently pause—that is when some of the dead silences occur—while thinking out the next question on the spot. (The silences are mystifying to the onlooker.) The drama of the trial is going on in the mind, yet all the time it is menaced from the immediate past and the immediate future by violent action in physical reality. These abstract, intellectual arguments spring from kidnapping and possibly murder, followed by investigating, pursuing, trapping. . . . And they may lead straight into the hideous physical rigours of punishment.

So it is with the trial of the Hosein brothers, two dark-skinned men from Trinidad, well-dressed, speaking English perfectly well (accent apart), brought to trial in Court 1, the 'star' court of the Old Bailey. Voices rarely raised above speaking tone; movement in court reduced to a minimum—very properly, as the acoustics of Court 1 are not as good as all that. (Nor, for that matter, are the heating arrangements: we frequently end a session with numbed lower limbs. The accused Trinidadians put on pullovers.) Actually the court itself is not very large—it would not hold much over a couple of hundred people if it were packed, which it practically never is. It is more or less square in shape, with walls panelled in nineteen-twentyish, board-room light oak. From the cornices rise moulded plaster arches, softly lit with concealed golden strip-lighting, which support the large, circular, ceiling window, in squared panes of frosted glass with daylight and 'day' strip-lighting behind them. Altogether not specially aweing—nor specially cosy, either.

The disposition of the participants in the trial has a geometrical formality that adds to the air of stately seriousness. Across the top end of the room, raised up, is the Bench, where sits only the Judge with a thin, wraithlike clerk in black tail-coat beside him—plus an occasional visiting City of London dignitary in robe or uniform. Just below the Judge sits the Clerk of the Court. At the bottom end of the room the corners are taken off for two vestibules, between which are benches used mainly for seating prospective jurors awaiting their call to service, and occasionally for witnesses who stay on after completing their evidence

—it is here that Arthur Hosein's German wife sits for most of the time.

The dock rises nearly in the centre of the room—large enough to hold a troop of conspirators—with steps leading up into it from the cells below, and plate-glassed rear- and side-walls. The Judge and the accused look straight across at each other on the same level. The jury sit in two rows of benches descending from that level on one side of the room, with the witness-box between them and the Judge.

Down below, in the well of the court, is a long table where the police officers connected with the case sit, together with solicitors and their clerks. On the other side, in ascending rows, are the benches which seat leading counsel on the front row, their juniors behind them in a row or two; and then benches for distinguished guests, under the public gallery which hangs out from the wall. The Press are fitted mainly into benches on either side of the dock—it is unobtrusively in the far corner of one of these benches that Mr McKay and his son frequently sit, listening, unable to tear themselves away from it all, no matter how unbearable, because they want to know what, what became of Mrs McKay. . . . Sometimes during the day the court seems to darken. And sometimes one notices, vertical on the wall behind the Judge, in direct line of the accused men's view, the long Sword of Justice.

And that reminds me again of what anyone glancing *en passant* into the court might notice, or rather might *not* notice. Without glancing at the dock he would have no idea that the complexion of the accused men differs in colour from that of Judge and jury.

'Put up Arthur Hosein and Nizamodeen Hosein!' The ritual opening. Already I have used the word 'drama'. And it would be impossible not to add, if one were to be completely frank, that time-honoured custom lends the proceedings, whether anyone finds the idea offending or not, a touch of the theatre. The scarlet robe and the black silk gowns; the grey wigs and whitish wigs, and the white collar bands; all the grave ceremonial bowing; and the usher's loud cries—the *only* loud cries ever heard—of 'Be upstanding!', etc., and 'God Save The Queen!'.

English justice is on the move. The brothers Hosein make

their appearance in the dock of Court 1. And a story is unfolded that sounds for most of the time like fantasy; sheer fantasy; and which, when it is over and the verdict given, remains still mystifying, still nearly incredible, still not telling us how, when and where death came—if it came—to Mrs McKay.

2

Opening speech for the prosecution

14 September, *morning*

The brothers Hosein look so different from each other that one would not guess at first sight that they are brothers.

'Do you understand English?' asks the Clerk of the Court.

'Yes,' says the elder brother. Softly the younger says: 'Yes, sir.'

English has been their language for generations. They come from a family of tailors at some remove from the lower classes. Their father is in court, a thin, spare, reflective-looking man, wearing a suit that looks too big for him. He is said to be very 'holy'.

These two sons of his are named Arthur and Nizamodeen, the latter being called Nizam in the family—pronounced with a short 'i'. (This does not prevent the pronunciation in court from fluctuating at will—shades of the British during the Raj—between Nizzam and Nigh-Zam.)

The Clerk of the Court reads the charges and asks if they plead Guilty or Not Guilty.

Arthur Hosein: 'Not Guilty.' Nizamodeen Hosein (softly): 'Not Guilty, sir.'

The brothers remain standing up while the jury, who have been sitting on the benches at the back of the court, behind the dock, are called.

Arthur is the smaller, plumpish, with the beginnings of an *embonpoint* that curves over his waistbelt, immaculately suited according to his lights—after all he is a tailor's cutter by profession. He has handsome large black eyes with dark circles round them and full cheeks, beautiful bushy black wavy hair, well cut, and a black moustache. He watches the jury-calling with intelligent, critical interest. He stands, feet planted firmly apart, with one hand behind his back and the other touching his chin—like Napoleon.

The jury, nine men and three women, appear to be mostly in their fifties, excepting one younger man seemingly in his late thirties: their facial expressions are appropriately serious, attentive, stolid. These are the twelve who will exercise the common sense, the common judgement, for all of us.

The younger brother Hosein does not watch the jury being called: he quietly, motionlessly, looks straight ahead. He is taller and more athletic in physique, yet his features are softish, amorphous, distinctly Chinesey. He wears spectacles, and has a wad of dark hair combed across his forehead. His main likeness to his brother is in the full-lipped, downward-turning mouth, which on occasion gives each of them a sullen, pettish look. There is a strange stillness about him: only rarely during the coming days of the trial does his glance flick sideways—and then never at his brother.

The jury are sworn in, with the usual stumblings over reading the oath. (I stumbled myself when I was once an Old Bailey juror.) With a nod the Judge tells the accused men to sit down and on the front bench of counsel the Attorney General prepares to rise and open the case for the prosecution. Arthur Hosein undoes his collar and loosens his tie.

The general rule in this country is that the Attorney General always prosecutes in cases of murder by poisoning. The decision that the Attorney General should prosecute in this case was made by Sir Peter Rawlinson's predecessor in office—there was a change in Government between committal and trial—but the decision has been maintained. The Director of Public Prosecutions is present, sitting in the row behind the Attorney General. One gets a feeling that the big guns are being brought up. Is that surprising?

This is the first trial in contemporary legal history in this country for kidnapping for ransom. (Our nearest example would appear to be a case in Australia, R. *v.* Bradley, in 1960.) Furthermore it is an offence under Common Law here, but not statutory—as it is, for example, in France and the U.S.A.—which means that there is no prescribed punishment laid down.

And it is a trial for murder in which the Crown can produce no *corpus delicti*. Everyone outside the legal profession wants to know one thing: How can a jury find someone guilty of murder when there's no body?

The front bench of leading counsel shows the newspapers to have been wrong. They gave correctly Mr Barry Hudson, Q.C., and Mr Hubert Dunn for Arthur Hosein: but in giving only Mr Leonard Woodley for Nizamodeen, they omitted Mr Douglas Draycott, Q.C. Each brother has a leading counsel. So each brother has a separate defence. The charges are the same —are the defences going to be different? How? And why?

'On the evening of the 29th December, last year,' the Attorney General begins, 'Mrs McKay disappeared from her home at 20 Arthur Road, Wimbledon.' He pauses. 'She has never been seen again.'

It is a dramatic opening; but although his manner is admirably polished, it is not in the least showy or theatrical. He is tall and handsome like a rowing Blue, with a short nose and the first lines of age deepening down his cheeks. His tone of voice is never higher than man-to-man, and sometimes sounds almost restrained. The Crown alleges:

'This was a brutal and ruthless scheme to kidnap a wife, and by menaces to extort from her husband a vast sum of money.'

(A million pounds—we know that already. A million!)

The Attorney General speaks of days and weeks in which Mr McKay was subjected to a systematic series of threats by telephone and by letter, threats to execute his wife, threats to kill her. He leans forward a little towards the jury as he delivers straight away what sounds as if it is going to be the essence of the Crown case for alleging murder.

'We may infer that those who threatened to kill *did* kill.'

The Attorney General then launches the statement that the real intention of the kidnappers was to take *another woman*! She was Mrs Rupert Murdoch, wife of the Chairman of *The News Of The World* group of newspapers. Mrs McKay's husband, Mr Alick McKay, is deputy chairman.

Both Mr McKay and Mr Murdoch are Australian, and in the middle of December Mr Murdoch and his wife went to Australia for a visit: in his absence Mr McKay was acting chairman, and as such had use of the Chairman's Rolls-Royce, ULO 18F, travelling to and fro in it between 20 Arthur Road and the newspaper offices. The kidnappers, tracing the car, thought they were going to take the wife of the Chairman. Arthur Hosein, the Attorney General now tells the jury, had spoken to neighbours, telling them of his desire to become a millionaire.

The Attorney General switches to the Hoseins, since 1968 at Rook's Farm, Stocking Pelham, a farmhouse in which a large room at the front is converted into a work-room where Arthur Hosein practises his profession. The Farm is guarded by two exceptionally fierce and frightening Alsatian dogs kept in a rough shed. There are other outbuildings for the stock, including a place where calves are slaughtered and skinned, he says. And there are two cars, a Morris Minor out of commission, and a dark blue Volvo saloon, now registered in the name of Arthur's wife. The Attorney General gets down to reconstructing the events as the Crown alleges them to have occurred: he does it, naturally enough, in chronological order.

(I suppose almost everyone's first response to the opening speech for the prosecution in any trial is to think, 'They've done it!' One is the more persuaded by presentation of the relevant events, and the allegedly relevant events, in chronological order. One has repeatedly to remind oneself that the events were not discovered in that order. Indeed they may in real life have been much less ordered, less dependent and consecutive upon each other, than the hand of man, i.e. the prosecution, has made them.)

The story begins, the Attorney General says, on the 19th December—the actual date on which, unbeknownst to the brothers, Mr and Mrs Rupert Murdoch left for Australia—when Mr McKay began to use the Rolls-Royce. A dark-skinned man appeared at County Hall, saying his car had been in minor collision with a Rolls-Royce, ULO 18F, and he wanted to contact the owner. The Greater London Council records showed the owner as *The News Of The World*. The enquirer was far from satisfied with that reply, saying he wanted the home address of the user. He filled in an enquiry form, giving an address in Norbury Crescent and the signature Shariff Mustapha. The latter name was unknown at Norbury Crescent, which is the address of some friends of Nizamodeen Hosein, and the address he had given previously on a form of application for entry into the Royal Air Force. It is possible to say that the handwriting on the two forms is that of one and the same person.

'You may suppose,' says the Attorney General, 'that Nizamodeen and Arthur Hosein traced the user by following the car. So they got to the McKays' house.'

So we come to the 29th December, the day of Mrs McKay's disappearance for ever. Mr McKay left for the office in the Rolls: Mrs McKay went in her own car to fetch the daily help, went shopping, visited her dentist, and then, at 5 p.m., drove the daily help home. The daily help was the last person ever to see Mrs McKay alive—or dead. At that time Mrs McKay was wearing a green jersey suit, a black and white check topcoat, and cream-coloured leather driving shoes. (The clothing is important.)

The Attorney General now interpolates evidence of persons driving by, locally, in their cars; a man passed a Volvo at 4.40 p.m. cruising round the area at 15/20 m.p.h., containing two persons, one of whom looked like an Arab; a woman neighbour noticed all the McKay house lights on at 6 p.m. and a dark saloon car in the drive.

At 7.45 p.m. Mr McKay came home, got no answer to his ring on the doorbell, found the outer door to his surprise *not* on the chain, opened the inner door, and saw a desolating sight... Furniture disarranged; the telephone off the hook, the disc giving the number (ex-directory) having been removed; his wife's open handbag with its contents scattered; and some alien objects.... The Attorney General suggests their purpose:

A billhook, such as might have been used for intimidating;

A strip of 2½in. adhesive tape, for gagging;

Some baling twine, for trussing...

There were also sheets of newspaper on the floor, *The People* for the 28th December: additional sheets had already been noticed by Mr McKay outside. On one of the latter sheets is a palmprint—of, the Crown says, Arthur Hosein.

Mrs McKay's jewellery was gone; together with a reversible fawn and black topcoat, warmer than the black and white check coat, which was still there. Mr McKay seized the billhook to arm himself, rushed through the house—Mrs McKay's dachshund was sitting by the fire and the television was on—and through the outbuildings. His wife was gone. On his own telephone he couldn't call the police so he ran from house to house to find a neighbour's telephone. In ten minutes the Wimbledon police arrived and a search was begun with dogs. One of Mr McKay's two married daughters, Diane Dyer, joined him at 11.15 p.m., with her husband David. Shortly afterwards his other daughter, Jennifer Burgess, arrived with her husband, Ian.

'At 1.15 in the morning of the 30th December, five hours later, the first approach from the kidnappers reached the house.'

The call was from a public box at Epping—and it was overheard by the operator! The first baleful words:

'Tell Mr McKay it is the M3, the Mafia.'

A detective, listening on another extension, the Attorney General says, took the conversation down.

'This is the Mafia Group 3. We are from America. Mafia M3. We have your wife.' And then: 'You will need £1,000,000 by Wednesday.' Today was Tuesday. 'We have your wife. You will need £1,000,000 to get her back. You had better get it. You have friends. Get it from them.' And then: 'We tried to get Rupert Murdoch's wife. We could not get her, so we took yours instead. Have £1,000,000 by Wednesday night or we will kill her.'

How on earth could Mr McKay find a million? Suppose one were asked to find it oneself? . . . It is just simply too much. One looks across at the two brothers Hosein in the dock, allegedly having left a palmprint on a newspaper, having made a traceable telephone call, and having announced it was really somebody else they had planned to kidnap. It takes a strong effort of one's imagination to realise that in the circumstances the police, Scotland Yard *et al.*, must have had to take seriously the idea that a professional organisation was at work, the Mafia, or even some terrorist group.

The Attorney General resumes the story: the second telephone call from M3 came just before 5 p.m. on the 30th. It was taken by David Dyer: the police had by now attached a tape-recorder to the McKays' telephone. The Attorney General quotes from a transcript.

'This is M3 speaking again. 'Your wife just posted a letter to you.' Warning: 'For heaven's sake, for her sake, don't call the police!' Too late. 'Did you get my message?' (Why, one wonders, should he have asked that, if he made the first call himself?)

That evening at 8.50 p.m. Mrs Diane Dyer was interviewed on B.B.C. television about her mother's disappearance. (This is important in connection with the process of detection. It also stirs one's recollections of the enormous publicity in the newspapers, on radio and television. Instinctively Mr McKay, in his first shock and desolation, turned to friends and colleagues in the Press, as well as to the police. *HAVE YOU SEEN THIS WOMAN?* headlines immediately appeared everywhere. One imagines that as many journalists as policemen thronged 20 Arthur Road—presumably not making the policemen's job any easier.)

The Attorney General points out that Diane appeared on television again, including ITV on the 31st December, but on those occasions she did *not* speak. (Another important fact.)

On the 31st December there duly arrived at Arthur Road a letter, a heart-rending appeal in handwriting identified without doubt as Mrs McKay's, written in irregular lines diagonally across a sheet of cheap blue airmail paper. The Attorney General reads it aloud.

Alick darling, I am blindfolded and cold. Please do something and get me home. Please co-operate or I cannot keep going. I think of you all constantly and have kept calm so far. What have I done to deserve this treatment?

The letter had been posted in Tottenham, N.17; and the sheet of paper bears two fingerprints—of, the Crown says, Arthur Hosein.

On the 1st January Mr McKay's son, Ian, arrived at Arthur Road from Australia. That evening there was the next call, ending at 7.45 p.m., in which the caller asked to speak to Diane—he took to using the family's Christian names, it seems, without the least inhibition. The Attorney General reads from the transcript. 'Try and remember the M3,' the caller tells her; 'I wanted to speak to your Daddy.'—'He is not well.' M3: 'Where is your mother?'—'Do you have any idea?' M3: 'You've gone too far. It has gone too far now.'

A few minutes later he rings again and demands to speak to Diane. 'Now you tell them they've gone too far,' he says to Diane. 'They've gone to the police.' He goes on. 'They've got to get a million, in tenners and fivers.' When Ian takes over the call and asks how they are to raise such a sum of money he says: 'That's your business, not mine.'

Listening now in the dock, Arthur Hosein momentarily smiles. Nizam looks impassively ahead. The Attorney General reconstructs the situation for the kidnappers. 'They must have realised the effect of the hue and cry. Retention, undetected, of the victim alive had become impossible.'

The Attorney General mentions several letters from Mrs McKay received at later dates; but, he suggests, they could have been written earlier and posted by degrees. 'Perhaps it is not insignificant that a letter to Diane, received three weeks later, says *I heard you on TV*. During that period, he says, proofs repeatedly demanded by the family that Mrs McKay was *alive* were refused.

Turning to the situation at Rook's Farm, the Attorney General notes that Arthur Hosein's wife had taken the children on a visit to her relations in Germany on the 13th December and did not return until the 3rd January. But on the 31st December, only 48 hours after the kidnapping, a girl-friend of Nizam's came to stay overnight at the Farm: in his, the Attorney General's, submission Mrs McKay must even then already be dead.

At 20 Arthur Road, called St Mary House, there was silence from M3 for eight days. The next thing was a letter received by the then editor of *The News Of The World*, written in capital letters—disguised—on white, lined paper torn from an exercise book. It complained that the writer couldn't get through to Alick McKay and the telephone was bugged. (As a result of the publicity the McKay's telephone was often jammed with calls, and of course it was bugged.) The letter said Mrs McKay was being treated by a doctor from abroad, and that when Alick McKay sent the police away, he, the writer, would give proof that she was still alive. He suggested taking the million pounds in two instalments of half a million each time. *IF HE CO-OPERATES HE SHALL SEE HIS WIFE.* Then menacing: *IF HE DONT COOPERATE . . . HIS WIFE WILL BE DISPOSED OFF.* Concluding with two peculiar sentences:

OFF SAINT MARYS

HE HAS NOT PAID ∧ *FOR* ∧ *HOUSE* and *SHE SAID HE HASNT THE MONEY BUT HE CAN BORROW FROM FIRMS HE KNOW.*

The Attorney General says detectives found similar paper torn from an exercise book in a cardboard box in Nizamodeen's bedroom at Rook's Farm; and exhibits are handed to the jury. One consists of a photograph of the *News Of The World* letter overlaid by a positive transparency of a photograph of one of the sheets found in Nizam's room. On the transparency the staple mark is in the same place as on the letter and the profiles of the tear are similar. On the other exhibit some indentations on the sheet from the box in Nizam's roon have been treated to show up on the transparency: particularly clear are the inverted *V*s under the words *OFF* and *SAINT MARYS*, which exactly fit those on the letter.

Another silence of four days.

On the 14th January M3 telephoned the editor of *The News Of The World*, telling him to tell Mr McKay that he has proof of Mrs McKay's existence. Later in the day he rang Arthur Road, and speaking to Mr McKay's other son-in-law, Ian Burgess, referred to Mrs McKay's wearing the fawn and black coat, as proof. And for the first time he mentioned Mrs McKay's writing another letter.

On the 19th January came the next call ending at 3 p.m. 'Hello, Alex! We contacted you last week concerning Muriel.' It is a very long conversation, and although the Attorney General deliberately reads extracts from the transcript in a moderate tone, it makes unbearable hearing, in the anguish of Mr McKay and the boasting of the blackmailer. 'We got a tip from the C.I.D. that she contacted them. Now we've got men in the C.I.D. That's why they will never be able to solve this case.' More about how Mr McKay asks for proof that his wife is alive —such as her writing out the full names of the children, or what she got for a Christmas present. M3 evades him. 'You are to be blamed, for going to the police.' Leading to, 'We are looking for a place where you should meet us to bring the money.' He demands the first half, £500,000. Mr McKay cries: 'Look, bring a gun here and shoot *me*, rather than ask unreasonable situations!' (In his agonising emotion, grammar fails him.) Again he asks for proof.

Saying she *is* alive and will speak as soon as the first delivery of the money is made, M3 goes on: 'This is not one person, group. This is world-wide, international.' And, 'I run this branch in England, you see. Don't take any telephone calls from anyone else unless they say M3. The Mafia, M3.' Then he talks about 'The Boys'. 'They traced the car ULO 18F. They went there. They got her instead.' Mr McKay cries: 'What have I done to deserve this?' M3: 'I don't know. But your wife is such a nice person.'

Mr McKay suggests a reasonable sum—he can raise £20,000. 'Over here? No use. Accept or reject. Half a million.' And, 'You got to do something about it.' Mr McKay says: 'I could kill myself! That would solve the problem!'

M3: 'My taxi is waiting. I've got to go to the airport to receive one of The Boys. You've got to get half a million.'

Mr McKay: 'It's no good asking for half a million! Take *me* instead!' M3: 'This is my order and that is final.'

In the dock Arthur Hosein is listening attentively, Nizam looking straight ahead. The Attorney General goes on to the next call, on the 21st January, taken by Ian McKay, who says his father is now ill. M3: 'I wanted to get your Dad. He'll like this call.' He explains he is M3. 'We've got a doctor from abroad to take care of her. She's been offering herself to the doctor to get away.' Horrible.

The first discussions of a rendezvous take place. The Attorney General says Ian had a police officer beside him helping to suggest probing questions and to keep M3 on the line. (One presumes that M3 was making his calls on the automatic system, S.T.D., on which it is said to be extremely difficult to trace calls while they are in progress.) M3 promises proof that Mrs McKay is alive—two more letters, one to Mr McKay and one to Diane, which he has just posted, in one envelope, a few minutes ago. M3: 'She was trying to tell you all where she was, so we had to clip a few pieces off.'

Ian asks what his mother says that proves that she is alive, but all he gets is M3's ranting on about the letter: 'I'm doing business. I want business to be like business.'

A few minutes later another call, this time about the date of the rendezvous. Ian has said his father was too ill to come—the police were determined, in case an international gang was at work, to protect Mr McKay now. The date is to be the 1st February. 'We want a million, but the first delivery has got to be half a million!'

On the following day, the 22nd January, the two promised letters arrived in one envelope posted at Wood Green, N.22. Letters undoubtedly in Mrs McKay's handwriting. To her husband:

Dear Alick, I am deteriorating in health and spirit. Please co-operate. Excuse writing. I am blindfolded and cold. The earlier you get the money the quicker I may come home or you may not see me again darling. Negotiate with gang as quickly as possible. The gang is too large to fool.

And to her daughter:

I heard you on TV. If only you would persuade Daddy to co-operate with the gang. Please keep the police out of it if you want to see me.

Enclosed with these two letters, the Attorney General tells us, was another sheet of paper—the first ransom note. It warned the family not to inform the police and reiterated the demand for £1,000,000. It then gave Mr McKay his instructions—on the 1st February to place £½ million in a black suitcase, drive his wife's car along the North Circular Road to the A10 Cambridge road, where he would see a public telephone box: to enter it and wait for a call at 10 p.m. There is a P.T.O. More menaces—if Mr McKay co-operates over the first half million, the gang will decide on the next stage. The black suitcase is to be locked as it will be collected by a stranger who is paid to do the job: if he is caught he will not be able to help the police. Finally—*Any error on your part will only take two minutes and you will never see your wife again. You will see her dead and delivered at your door.*

The prosecution alleges that the Hosein brothers possessed writing-paper similar in colour, thickness, weight, line-spacing, margins: handwriting experts will say that Mrs McKay wrote her two letters; and that the ransom note was probably written in disguised handwriting by Arthur Hosein. On the ransom note is a palmprint—of, the Crown says, Arthur Hosein.

At that the Attorney General signifies to the Judge that he is prepared for the morning session to be adjourned for lunch.

14 September, *afternoon*

At 10.30 a.m. on the 23rd January the telephone calls to Arthur Road resumed with growing agitation. On the McKay family side they were handled by Ian, demanding proof that his mother was still alive; M3 sounding pressed and relapsing into menaces. The Attorney General reads more from the transcripts.

M3: 'Did you get the letters?' Ian: 'Yes, we have. But there's no proof in the letter that she's alive and well. This letter could have been written weeks ago. Why the hell should we give you the money unless we know she's alive?' He says he has the money. But, 'You haven't got her. She's dead!' and to M3's denial: 'Why not get her to write something?' Obviously harassed, M3 makes a ludicrous speech: 'If we're doing business, we don't want to sell rotten stuff. We want to sell good stuff.'

There follows an argument about whether a description of what Mrs McKay is wearing is proof. Ian points out that every police station in the country has a description. The argument reaches an impasse, M3 saying, 'Blame yourself,' and Ian saying, 'The gang will blame you!' M3 rings off.

But less than two hours later M3 is on the line again.

M3: 'I've just contacted Head Office and this is final.' Going on, 'If you don't intend to co-operate we shall drop the matter there. We won't be needing the money and you won't be seeing your Mum.'

Ian says they have a quarter of a million; but they need proof, another letter. M3 introduces a paranoiac note about somebody being seen trying to interfere with the letter at the Post Office. As for another letter—they are not going to get one.

Ian: 'It's because you haven't got her! You've got a corpse, you've got a corpse, you've got a corpse! . . .'

M3: 'We've got her.' Ian: 'You've got a dead person! You haven't got her at all. You know she's not alive so you're just trying to trick us, you're trying to trick us, you're trying to trick us!' M3: 'Look, if you want to stick we've got plenty of jobs.' Ian: 'How many kidnaps have you done, then?' M3: 'We've never murdered anyone as yet. But there's always got to be a first time.' Ian: 'O.K. then. But you get no money!'

M3 then says—of all things—'We deal with honesty!' At Ian's jeering he rings off.

Fifteen minutes later he is back on the line again. Mrs McKay is saying, he says to Ian, 'Why have they forsaken me?' Back to proof again. Ian: 'Buy tonight's *Evening Standard* and get her to write out the headlines and the date!' M3: 'I'm not going to ask her to write out anything again.' Ian repeats his demand. M3: 'We don't have to co-operate with you.' Ian makes his terms: 'The headlines on tonight's paper and the date in full!'

On the 26th January, a letter addressed to Mr McKay and posted in N.22 was received at 20 Arthur Road. It contained two letters written by Mrs McKay. The Attorney General says the lines are diagonal, indicating that she was blindfolded.

Alick darling—If I could only be home. I can't believe this thing has happened to me. Tonight I thought I see you. But it seems hopeless. That is all I can say at the moment. You betrayed me by going to Police, not co-operating with the M3 gang Love Muriel

The other:

Darling Alick—You don't seem to be helping me. Again I beg of you to co-operate with the M3 gang. You do understand that when the

There is something cut from the letter. The Attorney General reminds us that M3 said this *weeks* ago. The envelope also contained a letter from M3: he reads extracts—the whole of it is later printed in a newspaper.

I am sending you final letter for your wife reprieve. She will be executed on the 2nd February 1970 unless you keep our business date on the 1st February without any error. We demand the full million pound in two occassions, when you deliver the first half million you wife life will be saved and I personally shall allow her to speak to you on telephone. We will not allow you to tell us how to run our organisation. We are telling you what to do you cannot eat the cake and have it this is our 4th blackmail we have absorb 3½ million pound we did not murdered any one, because they were wise to pay up and their family were return to them. You do the same and she will return safely. My next blackmail will be in Australia some time this year. Looking forward in settling our business on the 1st February at 10 p.m. as stated on last letter in a very discreet and honest way, and you and your children will be very happy to join Muriel Mackay and our organisation also will be happy to continue our job elsewhere in Australia we shall look forward to see you son Ian when we visit Australia.

You see we dont make our customer happy we like to keep them in suspence in that way it is a gamble that is why we don't accept you IAN telling us what to do

We give the order and you must obey

M3

Also enclosed in the letter were three pieces of material: one piece of green woollen jersey material, one piece of fawn and black reversible material, one piece of cream-coloured leather.

The implications sink in—M3 must have actually had Mrs McKay, and not merely have been cashing in on the news that somebody else had kidnapped her.

The writing-paper, the Crown alleges, is again similar to the earlier pieces; on the letter beginning *Alick Darling* is a thumbprint and fingerprint, on the envelope a thumbprint – of Arthur Hosein.

Three days later, the 30th January, M3 was on the telephone to Ian McKay again, about the ransom-collecting. M3: 'Any error will be fatal.' Ian said he couldn't come in his mother's car because it was in the garage. He proposed to come in the Rolls and to be driven by the chauffeur—he had hurt his hand and had it in a sling. (This was part of a police plan.)

On the 1st February M3 telephoned Ian McKay to say that if everything went smoothly that night, he would see his 'Mum'.

But he must assure him, M3—'You got to give me your solemn word!'—that when she returned she would not be interrogated by the Press or the police. (As if she could come back without—and into a newspaper family, at that!). And he stipulated that the Rolls should not have a telecommunications set. (Of course it would—what would the police be doing to let it go out without one?)

The Attorney General now removes his spectacles, as if to project his narrative more intimately, and he gives it greater immediacy by using the present historic tense.

At 9 p.m. on the 1st February the Rolls leaves Arthur Road, driven by Detective Inspector John Minors dressed as the chauffeur and Detective Sergeant Street disguised as Ian McKay. In the car they have a black suitcase containing bundles of false banknotes, each bundle having a genuine banknote on the top—half a million pounds! The Rolls drives to the telephone box on the A10. 'Ian' duly receives the M3 call, which directs him to another box about forty minutes' drive down the Cambridge road. In the second box a call comes through quite soon. 'Look on the floor! You'll see a Piccadilly cigarette packet with your instructions.'

The instructions written on the packet are to go to a place called Dane End—about fifteen miles further—in High Cross, Hertfordshire. There, at the road corner, they will see two paper flowers stuck in the bank as markers for the depositing of the suitcase. About midnight 'Ian' and 'the chauffeur' see the paper flowers. (The Attorney General suddenly holds them up, rather crushed-looking paper carnations, one a primrosy yellow and the other a sagey green.) The suitcase is deposited and the Rolls drives back to the first telephone box, following M3's instructions, to hear from Mrs McKay. . . .

Further down the road from Dane End there is a café where police (presumably working on information steadily radioed from the Rolls) are watching. At 2.30 a.m. the suitcase is still there and Mr Minors is instructed to collect it, together with the paper flowers.

In the meantime a dark-coloured Volvo saloon has passed the café, where two police officers are watching from a taxi. In the Volvo are a driver and a passenger with bushy hair. (One cannot help looking up at the dock, at Arthur's beautiful wavy black bushy hair.)

The rear nearside light of the car is observed not to be working. The Hoseins' car, the Attorney General reminds us, is a Volvo, and when it was examined by detectives ten days later, the nearside rear light was found not to be working. Furthermore, Dane End is quite close to Stocking Pelham.

Still furthermore—the Attorney General anticipates some of the evidence to come—Nizamodeen's girl-friend, Liley Mohammed, a nurse, had seen patients in her hospital making such flowers from Kleenex tissues and paper-clips. (Everybody was making them around that time—my own daughters decorated the Christmas tree with them.) Liley had taken six of the flowers to Rook's Farm when she went to stay on the 1st January and later she had taught the Hoseins' children how to make them. On the police visit to Rook's Farm, similar flowers were found in the children's bedroom, in Nizam's waste-paper basket, and in the Volvo.

A handwriting expert considers, the Attorney General says, the writing on the cigarette packet to resemble Arthur Hosein's. A packet of Piccadilly tipped cigarettes had been given to Arthur on the morning of the 1st February by someone called Rosenthal. And the packet picked up in the telephone box bears a thumbprint—of, the Crown says, Arthur Hosein.

The Attorney General returns to February the 3rd. There were two calls from M3 to Ian McKay. In the first M3 says he is going to a meeting of the bosses, 'the semi-intellectuals', to settle the time at which 'your Mum' should be executed. As for the suitcase: 'You know why I didn't even touch it? My boss, the Head Boy, was there. All The Boys were there. We saw cars parked all round there. Did you know they were all police?' He goes on. 'This organisation's got money.' And, 'I'm going to this meeting of the semi-intellectuals to plead for your Mum. I'm fond of her, your Mum, because she reminds me of my Mum, you see.'

Two hours later came the second call. Another attempt to collect the ransom is on the tapis. 'The Boys' insist on delivery being made by Mr McKay and Diane. The Attorney General observes that M3 seemed to regard Ian as responsible for the police being there.

Then on the 5th February there is a first call: Mr McKay himself takes it, says the Attorney General, and attacks M3 for not being smart enough on the previous occasion. 'You gave us a Cook's tour round the country,' says Mr McKay—a speech that shows his own spiritedness and at the same time gives a frightening insight into how the crime had by now brought the criminals and their prey into a sort of intimacy.

A second call. 'You must bring Diane. The day will be tomorrow.' M3 proposes they should bring the money this time in two briefcases. Not big enough for half a million, Mr McKay points out, and they agree on two white suitcases, one each for the father and daughter. They must go in the Rolls, driven by Mr McKay, first to a telephone kiosk in Church Street, Tottenham, at 4 p.m.

So on the 6th February, Detective Inspector Minors, made-up as Mr McKay, and a woman police officer disguised as Diane set off in the Rolls. At the first kiosk 'Mr McKay' is directed to a second kiosk at Bethnal Green—M3 demands to speak to 'Diane' to make sure she is there. They are told to take the Tube down to Epping, then go to a specified telephone kiosk there. They drive to Theydon Bois, park the Rolls and get in the Tube—a member of the Flying Squad is in the same compartment.

At Epping they are told by M3 to take a taxi to Bishop's Stortford, stopping at Gates Garage, where in the used-car lot they will see a Minivan, UMH 587F. Beside it they are to drop the suitcases. 'We deal,' says M3, 'with high-powered telescopic-sighted rifles. Anyone illegal that attempts to interfere with the cases, we shall just let them have it, you see.'

The Attorney General describes the scene that follows at Gates Garage. There is snow on the ground—it is a bitterly cold night. Already there are police everywhere, some hidden in cars, some behind fences. When the taxi drives up 'Mr McKay' and 'Diane' get out and deposit the white suitcases—actually another police officer, hidden on the floor of the taxi, crawls out and conceals himself behind the hedge. 'Mr McKay' and 'Diane' get back into the taxi and return to the telephone box to await the next call from M3 about Mrs McKay's being returned.

Five minutes after the two suitcases have been deposited, the watching police officers see a dark blue Volvo, XGO 994G, driven slowly past the used-car lot with neither of the near-side obligatory lights working. The driver is alone. He looks out and drives slowly on. The Attorney General says he has subsequently been identified as Nizam.

At 9.35 p.m. the Volvo, allegedly driven by Nizam, returns from Bishop's Stortford, circles round the garage again, the driver slowing down to look at the suitcases. Then it circles again, 'like a crow round its meat', as the Attorney General puts it. It slows down almost to a halt, when a car behind it hoots and it drives on. Then it disappears in the direction of Bishop's Stortford, near the village of Berden where Arthur Hosein is at this time in a public house.

At 10.47 p.m. the Volvo comes back yet again, but now with a man in the passenger seat—a man who has been subsequently identified, according to the prosecution, as Arthur Hosein.

At 11 p.m. two well-meaning members of the public drive by: they see the apparently abandoned suitcases, and stop: one gets out to stand guard, while the other telephones the local police, who immediately come and take the suitcases away!

The Attorney General goes back a few hours in time, to when a Volvo had come to Gates Garage, and the driver, a coloured man, had asked for air for his tyres—and then remained there, stationary, for some quarter of an hour. Both garage attendants had seen the Volvo circling round later and had reported it to the local police.

Then he moves the story to the public house, called The Raven, at Berden, Essex—near to Rook's Farm—where Arthur Hosein had appeared, the only customer in the public bar, just after 7 p.m. At 7.30 a television actor with two girl friends came into the saloon bar and Arthur joined them, saying he was waiting for Nizam to collect him. Nizam came in at 10 p.m. and the two of them left at 10.30 p.m.

As time in the court is getting towards four o'clock, the Attorney General concludes this part of the story. After the suitcases were taken away the Volvo was not seen again. On the following morning, the 7th February, the police, having traced the owners of the Volvo, went to Rook's Farm with a search warrant.

The Attorney General glances at the Judge, who nods, signifying the end of the day. The usher recites his formula in a ringing voice. 'Be upstanding!—ending with 'God Save The Queen!' Ceremonial bowings to and from his Lordship, who goes out. In the dock the warders take the two accused men downstairs out of sight. And the rest of us in the court trail out into the spacious flagged lobby from which a double curving staircase leads down to the open doors on the street.

So that's that. 'They've done it!' is what one feels. But what an incredible thing to do, if they did it—with what a fantastic mixture of ingenuity and incompetence! For the moment the incompetence eclipses the ingenuity with which the victim must have been kidnapped and the body disposed of. Fingerprints on everything—by the time we got to the Piccadilly cigarette packet I should have been surprised if it had *not* borne the fingerprints allegedly of Arthur Hosein. But isn't that eclipsed by going to 20 Arthur Road thinking it was Mrs Murdoch they were going to kidnap? As for the craziness, almost childish in its combination of unreality with greed, of demanding a million pounds—a million! . . .

It seems that the Crown consider Mrs McKay was murdered very soon after being kidnapped. This tallies with statistics brought out in the Australian case I referred to, that in cases of kidnap for ransom in the U.S.A. 70% of the victims were murdered within seventy-two hours, and most of those within forty-eight hours. But how far does it all go beyond that? Are we one iota nearer to knowing what actually happened to Mrs McKay?

15 September, *morning*

What looks like unaccustomed agitation on the front bench of counsel before the Judge comes in: Mr Barry Hudson, counsel for Arthur Hosein, is in particularly animated conversation with his junior in the row behind him. Like his colleague, Mr Douglas Draycott, defending Nizam, he is one of the foremost advocates in the country—perhaps there as counterpoise to the Attorney General? (Both brothers' defence counsel are provided under the scheme for Legal Aid: if the trial goes on for a month, as expected, the fees will run the country up a bill of between £10,000 and £20,000, I should think. As for the cost of the whole process, investigation and trial combined, with hundreds of policemen engaged over months before the courts get to work—it must be of the odrer of £100,000, I guess. I wonder if anyone has ever costed it?)

The agitation goes on. Mr Hudson is a large man, broad-cheeked, with eagle-like eyes and nose. In the lobby he chain-smokes; then, in his floating black silk gown, he sails into court like a galleon. 'Barry Hudson's a wise old owl,' commented a thoughtful young detective yesterday evening in the café across the road. Mr Hudson's junior, Mr Hubert Dunn, to whom he is, talking is an active-looking young man—and equally animated.

Mr Leonard Woodley, Mr Draycott's junior, himself a Trinidadian, is finding a place in court for the Hoseins' father. The jury are having their names called, like children before class. 'Be upstanding!' The Judge comes in and Mr Hudson's discussion is ended. The Judge nods to the Clerk of the Court, who nods to the warder in the dock, who transmits the message to down below, from whence the brothers and their two accompanying warders come up into view. The Attorney General rises to complete the prosecution's story.

On the 7th February, a party of police, led by Detective Chief Superintendent Wilfred Smith, who has been in charge of the investigation with Detective Inspector Minors as his second-in-command, went to Rook's Farm with a search warrant for stolen jewellery, Mrs McKay's jewellery. Even at this stage it appears that the most the police could justifiably take out a warrant for was search for stolen jewellery.

The police party included the Detective Sergeant who had travelled in the boot of the Rolls to Dane End and on the floor of the taxi to Gates Garage—where he had watched from behind a hedge. At the Farm he identified the Volvo, XGO 994G, which was standing outside; and he identified Nizam as the man who circled round the garage in it on the preceding evening. Another detective identified Arthur as the passenger on the Volvo's last appearance at 10.47 p.m.

'When he was shown the search warrant,' the Attorney General says, 'Arthur Hosein replied: "I know nothing. I earn £150 a week. I'm a wealthy man. I don't deal in stolen property. You can look where you like." '

During the search which followed the police discovered:

an empty Elastoplast tin of the size to hold 2½in. tape,

six paper flowers in various places—home-made like those used as markers,

an empty Piccadilly tipped cigarette packet.

'On further search, six days later,' the Attorney General adds with devastating effect, 'the police found a pair of trousers belonging to Nizam, in the left hand-pocket of which was a piece of paper giving the number of the Minivan, UMH 587F at Gates Garage used-car lot.' In the search of Arthur's workroom, Chief Superintendent Smith took possession of two pairs of tailor's shears: in the kitchen he found a billhook.

The Attorney General then goes over ensuing interrogations by Chief Superintendent Smith, with Inspector Minors at his side, alternately of Arthur Hosein and Nizam.

First Arthur. On being shown the paper flowers from the house: 'I've never seen the flowers before.' The writing-paper from Nizam's bedroom: 'I've never seen paper like that before, I never do my own correspondence. As it was in Nizam's bedroom, you'd better ask him!' The Piccadilly tipped cigarette packet: he and Nizam smoke other brands – this packet was given to them by Mr Rosenthal.

The billhook—Arthur says it was borrowed from a farmer friend of his, for chopping up a calf that died, and Nizam did the chopping up. Nizam confirms this. Mr Smith to Nizam: 'What did you do with the calf afterwards?' Nizam: 'I fed it to the dogs.' Mr Smith: 'What happened to the bones and the head?' Nizam: 'They were put out with the rubbish for the refuse men.'

The brothers were taken in separate police cars to Kingston Police Station. On the way Arthur pointed out Sleepy Hollow Farm, home of the farmer friend who, he says, lent the billhook to chop up the calf.

But there are two billhooks. The other one is the one left at 20 Arthur Road, and it has been traced, the Crown alleges, to Arthur's home. A farmer, Mr Len Smith, will say he saw the brothers at an auction sale for furniture, and brought the brothers' purchases back in his car, in which he always kept his billhook. To get the furniture in he had to move his spare wheel and billhook. After delivering the furniture he found he had left the spare wheel and billhook behind. The Hoseins returned the spare wheel but *not* the billhook. Mr Len Smith will identify it.

The Attorney General now moves on to the interrogations at Kingston Police Station. By this time the police had disclosed that the jewellery in question was Mrs McKay's and that they were looking for *her*.

The Attorney General reports the interrogations. In a dialogue with Mr Smith, Nizam says: 'Somebody says I've been seen driving the Volvo on Friday night,' meaning the 6th. He is deeply upset. 'Oh my God, what has Arthur done to me? . . . I had a date with Susan.' Mr Minors asks him about Susan. She works, Nizam says, on the sausage counter at Tesco's. He has never been to her home. She is not on the telephone. In due course he breaks down into weeping and moaning. He cries: 'Kill me! Kill me! Arthur always gets me into trouble. Kill me now!'

Next Mr Smith is questioning Arthur about his movements on December the 29th. The Judge interrupts for a moment to instruct the jury: what one of the defendants says about the other is not evidence against the other. 'I went to the finishers,' says Arthur to Mr Smith. (He means the people who 'finish' the trousers that he has cut.) Mr Smith asks him about when he got home. 'I think Nizam was there.'

Mr Smith says: 'Were you ever in Wimbledon?' Arthur: 'Where *is* Wimbledon?'

Mr Smith: 'Have you ever heard of Mrs McKay?' Arthur: 'I never read the newspapers or watch TV.' Soon after that he says: 'I'm very tired.' He refuses to read through his statement.

Next Nizam. Chief Superintendent Smith asks him where he was on the 29th December. He begins to tremble and shake his head. 'Where did Arthur say I was? I was with my brother, Arthur.'

'Did you go to Wimbledon?' says Mr Smith. Nizam fails to reply, and Mr Smith asks him what is the matter. 'I want to die. Let me die!' Mr Smith: 'What is troubling you?'—'My brother Arthur will kill me. He beats me.'—'Why should he kill you?'—'I can't speak. I mustn't speak. Let me see Arthur!'

Mr Smith: 'Where were you? Nizam: 'Why don't you kill me?'

More interrogations on the 8th February. Mr Smith questions Nizam about what he did on the 1st February, the date of the first ransom-collecting attempt. The scene has begun with Nizam saying: 'When can I speak to Arthur? What has he said? Has he blamed me for something?'

'Wimbledon?' Mr Smith suggests. 'I don't know the names of places,' says Nizam.

'Were you there with Arthur?'—'No. Not Wimbledon.'

'If you don't know the names of places, how do you know you *weren't* there?'

In due course they get to the 1st February. Nizam: 'I was out at the Farm.' Mr Smith: 'Did you go out?' Nizam: 'Yes, with Arthur.' Mr Smith: 'What time?' Nizam: 'It was getting dark.' Mr Smith: 'Where did you go?' Nizam: 'To London. To the finishers.' He adds: 'Arthur drove the car.' Mr Smith: 'Which finishers?' Nizam gives him a list of names and addresses. He says Arthur stayed in the car while he, Nizam, did the deliveries.

Then there was a row between them. Arthur sent Nizam into a pub to buy some cigarettes and Nizam stopped there to have a drink. Arthur hit him. Mr Smith: 'What time did you get home?' Nizam: 'Late. The pubs had closed.'

Mr Smith now shows Nizam the paper flowers from the road bank near Dane End. Nizam does not reply. He is shaking his head, his eyes closed. And he cries again: 'Let me die! I want to die!' When Mr Smith speaks to him he shows no sign of having heard.

Chief Superintendent Smith now turns his attention back to Arthur, who says: 'I want to help you all I can. I realise you have a very difficult case.' Questioned about his movements on Sunday, the 1st February, Arthur says he was in the Farm all day, visited by a friend, Gerry Gordon, who left at 5.30 p.m., at which time Arthur Rosenthal arrived—a trimming merchant. At this point Arthur was getting ready to go on his trip to the finishers. He gives Mr Smith the list of names and addresses—he took Nizam to teach him where the finishers live. He did no telephoning.

When shown the paper flowers from Dane End, Arthur knows

nothing about paper flowers, either in his house or in his car. He admits that he took *The People*, but stopped three weeks ago. He agrees to do a handwriting test. He is shown the billhook from Arthur Road: he has not seen it before. 'But it is like one I borrowed from George to chop up the calf.' The sticking plaster: 'What is it?' And he is then asked about Mrs McKay.

Arthur: 'I am sorry for that poor lady and her family.'

Mr Smith shows him the three pieces of material, sent to Mr McKay. 'I know nothing at all.'

Mr Smith: 'Have you written to Mr McKay?' Arthur: 'No. I don't write letters to anyone.'

Still more reported interrogations. Chief Superintendent Smith asks Nizam about his movements on February the 6th, the night of the second ransom-collecting attempt. Nizam says he went to London with Arthur in the Volvo, to a list of places, tailors etc., finishing about seven o'clock. Mr Smith asks what time he got home. 'After the pubs closed. Eleven o'clock.' He accounts for the time in between by the date he had with Susan at Bishop's Stortford: Arthur let him have the Volvo. Then he went to The Raven for a drink and Arthur was there. Arthur said he wanted to go for a drive, so they went to Bishop's Stortford. Mr Smith: 'What did you do there?' Nizam: 'Nothing. We drove home.'

Nizam gives handwriting specimens. He is shown the billhook from Arthur Road, and starts to shake, closes his eyes; the baling twine, more shaking of the head; then the sticking plaster—he suddenly cries: 'Let me die!' In the court now, having been motionless throughout, Nizam shakes his head, as if to deny something.

The Attorney General tells us that house-to-house enquiry has located no Susan. He reminds the jury of the piece of paper in Nizam's trouser pocket that night giving the number of the Minivan in the used-car lot.

Next day Chief Superintendent Smith asks Arthur about the 6th February. 'That is all right, Mr Smith. You have a very difficult case and I am genuinely sorry for you.' Arthur tells Mr Smith he left the Farm at 9 a.m., taking Nizam and also Liley, who had been staying overnight. They dropped Liley off; then they delivered clothes to tailors, finishing at 4.30 p.m. or later. It was dark when they got to Bishop's Stortford, when Arthur let Nizam have the car and himself took a taxi to The Raven. The Raven is about one mile from Rook's Farm. 'Nizam has told me he met you in The Raven and you asked him to take you to Bishop's Stortford,' says Mr Smith. 'Nizam's a fool,' retorts Arthur, 'to have told you that!' And, 'We did not go!'

Mr Smith asks Arthur to speak into a telephone—connected to Arthur Road, where it is recorded in the police tape-recorder. (This is to enable comparisons to be made between M3's voice and Arthur's recorded under similar conditions.)

Finally Mr Smith tells Arthur his fingerprints have been found on the letter to Mr McKay, *The People*, and the Piccadilly cigarette packet. . . .

'That is impossible!' says Arthur. 'You are just trying to trick me, Mr Smith.' Then he sits with his head bent, shaking from side to side; and he feels his pulse—'Do you want to see a doctor?' says Mr Smith. In the court, now Arthur smiles sardonically: in due course we shall find out why.

Then another scene between Mr Smith and Nizam. At the pieces of material from Mrs McKay's clothing—again cries of 'Let me die! Let me die! Why don't I die?'

Mr Smith asks: 'Why are you behaving like this?' Nizam looks at the ceiling.

Mr Smith asks: 'Is Mrs McKay dead?' Nizam appears to be in a trance.

Later that day Mr Smith taxes Arthur with writing letters to St Mary House, to *The News Of The World*. He also taxes Arthur with attempting, in the handwriting test, to disguise his hand. Arthur denies it all.

Mr Smith: 'What happened to Mrs McKay, Arthur? Where is she?' Arthur: 'I can't tell you any more. When can I go back to the Farm?'

Mr Smith: 'That will be all for now.' Arthur refuses to sign the record.

Later Arthur's solicitor, Mr David Coote, arrives and says to Nizam: 'If there is a possibility that Mrs McKay is alive, and if you have any knowledge of where she is, then you must tell the officers.' Nizam hangs his head as if he has not heard.

Next day, 10th February, Chief Superintendent Smith asks

Nizam to speak into the telephone. He refuses. 'It's a trick!' he cries. 'Has Arthur done it? I don't believe it. I don't want to do it!' And he does *not* do it.

That night there is a final confrontation between Arthur and Chief Superintendent Smith, in which Arthur furiously says: 'If you've got anything on me, then book me!' A little later the brothers Hosein are formally charged with the murder of Mrs McKay and with demanding a million pounds by menaces from Mr McKay.

There is only one addition to the story. The Attorney General tells of Nizam being visited in Brixton Prison by another of his brothers, called Adam. Nizam pressed a piece of paper against the partition which separated him from Adam, for Adam to read it.

Don't say anything to no one not even solicitor that I was down by you on Monday night. Some farmers are saying Arthur was with them.

The piece of paper was confiscated afterwards. The Attorney General remarks, as if by the way, that Adam's house is three or four miles from Wimbledon. The Judge enquires, for the benefit of the jury, if the note was in Nizam's hand. It was.

At that the Attorney General concludes the prosecution's opening speech by touching finally on the main Crown allegations; that it was:

Nizam who pretended to be Shariff Mustapha at County Hall in order to trace the home of the woman they meant to kidnap;

Nizam who drove the Volvo frequently and who drove it round and round the suitcases;

Nizam who tried to excuse his presence in the car on the 6th February by talking of Susan;

Nizam who had the number of the Minivan and the name of the garage written down;

Nizam who was in daily contact with his brother.

Furthermore that it was:

Arthur whose fingerprint or palmprint was on *The People* and on the envelopes and letters from the imprisoned woman;

Arthur whose thumbprint was on the Piccadilly cigarette packet;

Arthur from whose house the billhook found at 20 Arthur Road was taken, also the writing-paper which matched in indentations, etc., the ransom letters;

Arthur whose disguised handwriting on the ransom letters gave the ransom instructions.

'Point by point the two brothers,' the Attorney General says, 'are linked to the telephone caller M3, who admitted that he had seized Mrs McKay, and demanded £1,000,000 in ransom, sending pieces from her clothes and letters threatening to kill her.' He pauses. 'Altogether there were eighteen telephone calls* and five letters. Since the day before the police came to Rook's Farm, there has been complete and utter silence from M3.'

He counsels the jury that once they are satisfied with the identity of M3, the verdict is clear. (Instinctively one puts oneself in a juryman's position—*would* it be clear? After the excitement of the story's being told, detail by detail, the closing list of allegations has somehow come as a bit of an anti-climax. Would it be clear? When the case ends, *will* it be clear?)

The speech has lasted five and a half hours, and a gruelling time it has been, because of the detail. But it is by the detail that the jury will have to satisfy themselves about who was where, when, and what did he do? For the brothers Hosein it may be possible in the course of the coming days to sort that out. But for Mrs McKay, after 5.30 p.m. on the 29th December? . . .

*The Attorney General was referring only to calls to Arthur Road.

3

The bombshell

Mr Draycott, leading counsel in the defence of Nizam, stands up and, addressing himself respectfully to the Judge, says that before evidence is called for the prosecution he wishes to make certain admissions on behalf of his client.

'I should like to emphasise,' he says—he is a smallish, sturdy, healthily pink-faced man with an extraordinarily courteous and measured delivery of speech—'that the admissions do not involve any knowledge of or intention to commit the offences in the indictment.'

Nizam's admissions are:

1. That he made the application on the 19th December 1969 to the Greater London Council.
2. That on the 1st February he placed two paper flowers where they were subsequently found by the police near the junction of Dane End and the Cambridge road.
3. On the 6th February at about 8 p.m. he drove the Volvo, XGO 994G to Gates Used Cars; that he did so in order to look for two suitcases, that he drove around and waited for about an hour, that he saw the two white suitcases on the pavement opposite the Minivan.
4. On the 6th February he drove the Volvo to The Raven public house, arriving about 10 p.m.
5. At 10.47 p.m. on the 6th February he returned in the Volvo to Gates Used Cars.
6. That the note (exhibit 83), the small note referring to the Minivan, is in his handwriting.
7. That the note found by the prison officer when he was searched is in his handwriting.

Immediately Mr Hudson protests. 'I understand that m'-learned friend Mr Draycott is admitting these documents to make them admissions of fact. There is certainly one item that on behalf of Arthur Hosein I am not prepared to admit.'

The Judge says one accused cannot prevent another from making admissions. Mr Hudson registers a caveat that Item 5 is not admitted by his client. The Judge says that Arthur Hosein had made no admissions. 'They are not in any sense evidence so far as the brother is concerned.' He makes sure that the jury understands—Nizam's admissions are not to be attributed to Arthur.

So one brother has ratted, at least partially, on the other! Some things begin to fall into place—the change from joint defence to separate defences, Mr Draycott's appearance on the scene for Nizam; and Mr Hudson's very animated conversation first thing this morning with his junior—how long has he known? one wonders.

The Judge is instructing the jury about the next stage in which certain written evidence will be read to them: it is evidence about which there is no controversy. In the dock Arthur seems thoughtful—his rounded cheeks are sallowish. He is wearing a different suit from yesterday's. Nizam as usual is looking straight ahead. (Perhaps I should say that there is nothing trance-like about this look—one does not for a moment associate it with either stupor or stupidity. Something is going on in his mind, and it is probably quite a quick mind, at that: in fact I'm not at all sure, if I were asked to decide by the look of them which is the cleverer of the two, I should not put my money on Nizam.)

Now the Attorney General and the two leading counsel for the defence have agreed between themselves the legal admission of various photographs, plans, maps, etc., that are going to be used. Arthur Hosein has had a note passed down to his counsel. The proceedings are ready to go on again. Mr Draycott is turning sideways in his seat to make, in contrast to his extraordinarily stylised manner of address to the court, seemingly very unstylised ironic comments to his junior sitting behind him: he appears to be in the highest of spirits. Mr Hudson is thoughtfully passing his eagle-like glance across the rows of jury.

What is going to happen after all this? Apart from the fact that nobody, however little he already knows about the case, can possible think after this that the brothers Hosein are *not* connected with the kidnapping.

4

Interlude

The proceedings start up again. The Clerk of the Court reads out the testimonies referred to by the Attorney General at the beginning—people who saw a Volvo, a pair of dusky gentlemen, and so on, in Wimbledon on the 29th December.

The first witness to be called to the witness-box is Mr Alick McKay. He arrives in the box and there is another stir on the front bench of counsel. The Attorney General indicates that he wants to address himself to his Lordship about a matter in the absence of the jury. The jury is sent out.

The Attorney General tells his Lordship about Mr McKay's tape-recorded conversations with M3 and asks for them to be played for the jury to hear—also, he says, so that Mr McKay can swear, 'That's me.'

His Lordship asks if it isn't enough, so far as authentication is concerned, for Mr McKay to say 'That's me', without the tapes being played.

Mr Hudson joins in immediately. 'Mr Draycott and I agree with this course. We are prepared to admit the transcripts of the tape-recordings. Why play the tapes before the jury? This *may*, though it hasn't been suggested, be a temptation to amateur detection by the jury, recognising the voices.' He produces a law book and reads extracts—the gist of them being that there is no difference in principle between the admission of tape-recording and photographs, provided their accuracy is proved and *the voices identified.*

An argument ensues. The prosecution want the tapes played: the defence don't. The transcripts of the conversations will be in the hands of the jury. The Judge is coming down in favour of their not being played.

'When all the evidence is on the documents, why play the

recordings?' he asks, having suggested previously to the Attorney General that the playing would contribute dramatic effect. His Lordship, it appears, is out to keep dramatic effect down. Mr Hudson, having drawn a parallel with handwriting identification, has been saying that one of the police officers may say he is sure that the voices he heard on the tapes are those of the defendants—'But that officer is not an *expert*!' It occurs to me that if voice-identification had been technically developed far enough to be useful in this context, any hope of validating such identification scientifically in the case of these two defendants was neatly punctured by the quiet introverted Nizam simply refusing to speak into the telephone. For comparison with the telephone voice of M3 on tape the experts have got the telephoned voice of Arthur on tape using the same recorder; of Nizam, only his voice in life, which won't do.

So far, the Judge has made few interventions during the proceedings, but in this intermission he is quite naturally demonstrating who is in charge of them. A rather small man, sitting up on an extra leather cushion in his leather-upholstered, high-backed chair with its coat-of-arms, he looks rosy and acute in granny-spectacles. 'I see no point in playing the recordings over, unless a situation arises where . . .' The tapes are banished.

Mr Hudson and Mr Draycott assent enthusiastically. Not so the Attorney General, who still sees reason for the evidence being conveyed by a hearing of actual taped voices rather than a reading of the transcripts. But his Lordship says to him: 'Anyone hearing your opening would scarcely have wanted more inflection.' At that the Attorney General says he has no objection to the transcripts being used. Nizam is seen, for the first time, to speak to the warder beside him.

So we shall never hear the tapes played in court. There is to be no amateur detection in the court, no undue drama. But the lobby outside the court and the public house across the road are pullulating at lunchtime with crime-reporters and policemen, that joint army of takers-in each other's washing, who have heard extracts from the tapes played before the Lower Court at Wimbledon. 'That was Nizam's voice.' 'That was Arthur's voice.' Mostly, to my surprise at this stage in the trial, 'That was Nizam's voice.'

5

The prosecution witnesses

It has already been mooted around in the Press that both sides are to call astronomic numbers of witnesses—twenty-nine for the prosecution, thirty-nine for the defence. One doesn't expect the figures to be correct, but one does take it that there are going to be quite a lot of witnesses.

The first witness is the central person in the tragedy, Mr Alick McKay. One is glad that the tapes are not to be played to him in public. 'Take *me*, instead!' A tall, heavily-built man, his features as he stands back in the shadow of the canopy over the witness-box look pale and heavy with oppression.

The Attorney General examines him, bringing out more detail of the familiar story. His return home, on the evening of the 20th December. Photographs of the scene in the hall, as he saw it, are passed round to the jury .The process of identifying the exhibits is begun concurrently with eliciting the story—the strip of Elastoplast, twisted over on itself. There is a moment at which the oppression is lifted from Mr McKay, as he identifies his wife's handbag. 'It has a special catch.' As he finds it and it springs open he looks up with a triumphant smile, as if taken out of himself, perhaps taken back to the time when his wife first showed it to him. He identifies the baling twine, the billhook—he can hardly look at it in his hands, though he watches it being passed round the jury.

Mr McKay goes on with his story. The fire built up, the dog sleeping in front of it. (Nizam smiles at the yellow-haired warder beside him.) Then his rush through the house: the missing jewellery, valued for insurance at £600. Mrs McKay had lost most of her jewellery in a burglary the previous September. That was why she was nervous and kept the chain on the front door always. Mr McKay rang a special code on the doorbell when he came home. He describes calling the police, the arrival of his two daughters and their husbands, friends coming round to the house as the news spread. . . . The first call at 1.15 a.m. from M3.

The Judge says: 'Must we go through all this?' He, like counsel on both sides, seems concerned to spare Mr McKay—and perhaps also to keep a long trial moving.

The telephone calls of the next day; then the receiving of the letters. Exhibits appear. In the dock Arthur Hosein takes what looks like a white tablet or sweet. Mr Draycott asks for Mr McKay's distress to be spared: Mr Hudson agrees subject to necessary intervention.

More telephone calls and the question of identifying the kind of voice, or voices. 'Sometimes softer and deeper,' says Mr McKay, 'with a stronger American accent.' The conclusion: that they were West Indian. 'When,' asks the Judge, 'did you identify them as West Indian? Before February?'—'Yes. In January.' (This means before anyone dusky was seen in a Volvo circling round suitcases.)

More letters; sheets of writing-paper; those pieces of material . . . horrifying.

Then the first ransom-collecting attempt. The procedure laid down for examination has its *longueurs,* probably for the participants as well as the listeners. The Attorney General is compelled by it to ask such questions as:

'A few days later, did you look out two white suitcases for a certain purpose?' Mr McKay says: 'Yes, they were my wife's.'

And so on to final questions. 'Was there a great deal of publicity?' And, 'All your children were very close to their mother?' Mr McKay nods. The Attorney General sits down.

Mr Hudson cross-examines. 'Would it be true to say that you've had *several* people trying to get money out of you?' Mr McKay: 'Yes.'

Mr Hudson: 'One man was prosecuted and convicted?'—'Yes.'

'A large number of people offered spurious information?'

Mr McKay: 'I don't know if it was spurious.'

'People have written offering to help?'—'Yes.'

We now hear of hoaxes, other police traps and all the rest of it, giving intimations of mountainous detail behind the scenes, from which what we have heard in the prosecution case has been selected and set in order. After questions about Mrs McKay's tablets for rheumatism, Mr Hudson ends with the most mysterious question of the day.

'Do you remember some trees being cut down or clipped in Arthur Road about four years ago?'

Mr McKay: 'They're always cutting down the trees.'

Mr Hudson sits down. And solitarily, almost unceremoniously, Mr McKay leaves the witness-box. As he passes the long table in the well of the court, Detective Chief Superintendent Smith speaks to him, but with a wave of the hand he goes on, apparently to the door. (It is only some time later that one realises he has stowed himself in a distant corner of the court, now looking greyly hatchet-faced, to listen. . . .)

The next witness is Mrs McKay's daily help, Mrs Nightingale. Following the examining procedure, the Attorney General's junior, Mr Brian Leary, asks in a clear, resonant voice:

'Is it Mrs Marjorie Nightingale?'

It is. Her examination is largely about Mrs McKay's precautions after the burglary and about her clothes at the time she was last seen. Mrs Nightingale is handed the three pieces of material sent by the kidnapper. (I must say that in the distance they look to be neatly cut rectangles, like tailor's samples.) Mr Draycott cross-examines about Mrs McKay's always being very careful over fastening the chain on the outer door.

'I think so,' says Mrs Nightingale, very small-voiced but not got down. 'I wasn't there always.'

Mr Draycott has difficulty in hearing her. '*I* heard it,' says his Lordship, and tells him what the witness said. Mr Draycott sits down.

We now see a couple of policemen; first the inspector who arrived after Mr McKay's call. He is examined about the inner door, of which the lock had been forced—photographs are passed round. While counsel waits the Judge asks technical questions about the type of lock. Could it be pushed open by bodily pressure from the outside and then shut again from

D

inside? The hypothesis dawns on me: the intruders got into 20 Arthur Road while Mrs McKay was taking Mrs Nightingale home. While she was out the chain was necessarily off the outer door, so they had only to force the inner door as lightly as possible from outside, and then shut it with themselves inside—and wait for her to let herself in. . . .

The second policeman is the detective sergeant who was listening on the extension of the McKays' telephone when the first call came through from M3 at 1.15 a.m. on the 30th December. He says the caller's voice appeared to have a West Indian accent, also a trace of American, North American. After the end of the call he spoke to the telephone exchange operator at Epping.

We now see the exchange operator, a young man with marvellous mutton-chop sidewhiskers, a bright green trendy tie, and a matching up-to-date 'cool'. Mr Leary examines him. He was on the night shift, 11 p.m. to 8 a.m. entirely alone. About the call; first of all, what time was it? Between two o'clock and three. 'When you're working by yourself you have no idea of the time. It may have been before. Or after.'

The caller asked for assistance because he had trouble in dialling. 'And was the number 01–946–2656?' enquires Mr Leary, rattling off the McKays' number. 'Have you got the ticket there?' the young man asks Mr Leary.

The witness thinks the caller was American or coloured. 'And did you ask him anything?' enquires Mr Leary. 'I told him to put the money in the box. He had no sixpence, so he put in a shilling.'

Pause. Fancy, if you are a kidnapper, going to the telephone to make your first ransom demand without equipping yourself with the right coin for the box, and into the bargain asking for the assistance of an operator who may listen!

Wearing his head-set the operator dialled, and then checked that caller and called were speaking. The caller asked for Mr McKay and got Mr McKay's son-in-law, Mr Dyer. The operator went on listening:

'I thought I was in trouble for getting the wrong number! I heard him say "This is M5"—or M3. It sounded like a motorway.'

'And did you hear anything,' enquires Mr Leary, 'that made you prick your ears up?'—'He was demanding one million pounds by Wednesday, or he wouldn't see his wife again alive.'

Mr Hudson cross-examines mainly from the witness's written statement made the following day. *The American was speaking very softly in a deep drawl, making me think he was a Negro.*

Mr Hudson: 'This telephone caller kept using the word "man". Every other word was "Yeh, man"?'

(Arthur Hosein has been living in England since 1955; but Nizam only since 1968.)

The young man gives *dégagé* assent.

And that is the end of the day. 'Be upstanding!' With formal bows and a small swirl of robes the Judge goes out.

When he has gone one reflects on what a wonderful time Judges must have, sitting alone up there, robed in scarlet like the repository of ancient wisdom, scribing away in their big book, simply inviting cool young persons down below to think they are old and past it—and in perfect position to strike at any moment with some indication that they are not missing a single trick. Correcting an error, spotting a crucial detail; explaining to a witness what counsel is asking and to counsel what a witness is saying. (In the latter case counsel look pained.)

Today is seems to me that Mr Justice Sebag Shaw has begun to play a livelier part in the proceedings—a distinctly illuminating, independent part—than many judges do. Rosy and acute and granny-spectacled . . . What does *he* think so far of Arthur and Nizamodeen Hosein?

The crime-reporters disperse to the telephones, the policemen to cups of tea across the road.

16 September, *morning*

We begin with the other members of the McKay family; the two daughters, Diane and Jennifer, with their respective husbands, David Dyer and Ian Burgess; and the son, Ian, who flew in from Australia on the 31st January. The young women have the well-dressed, affluent look one would expect. Their father has an Australian accent: they have not. Their husbands are apparently English. So far as physical resemblance goes, it is only strong between father and son—and there it is very strong. They both have the same heavy build, the same rather pale complexion and small light eyes, the same thinning dark hair.

David Dyer goes into the witness-box first. He took M3's first call: like Mr McKay he has heard the tapes so often since that he has to pause and think which is which. Mr Hudson cross-examines him about whether he thinks call No. 2 and call No. 3 from M3 were made by different voices from that of the call he took. 'Similar,' he says.

Diane Dyer, slender and nervous, with her hair drawn back into a high bunch of curls, has to identify her mother's clothes, the letters, the pieces of material. But the essential part of her evidence is about when she *spoke* on television, as well as being seen.

'I do remember,' she says to the Attorney General. 'I do remember speaking on Monday, the 9th.'

Mr Hudson has his diary open. The Judge intervenes for her—the 9th was not a Monday. Mr Hudson explains.

'It is very important, because of Mrs McKay's writing *I heard you on television* in the letter received by Mr McKay on the 22nd January.'

The evidence so far is that Diane was heard to speak only on the transmission of the 30th December: she appeared on others, but any parts of the recorded interviews in which she may have spoken were not transmitted.

Mrs Dyer's mouth quivers as she says: 'It was a very confusing time.' And: 'We were besieged by TV men.' Mr Hudson says consolingly: 'Then you spoke on quite a number of occasions,' and lets it go at that.

(It seems now that both prosecution and defence must believe that the last moment at which they can be certain Mrs McKay was still alive was shortly after her daughter last spoke on TV.)

Ian McKay makes a brief appearance, alert and businesslike—he knows the telephone calls by their numbers and does not need to refer to the transcripts. He vouches for switching on the tape-recorder at Arthur Road when Arthur Hosein spoke into the telephone for the purpose of making the test-recording.

The Attorney General: 'After the 6th February, were there any more calls from M3?'

'No.'

Jennifer Burgess, sun-tanned and subdued-looking under a big white felt safari hat, took one of M3's telephone calls. 'I gave my sister's name because he usually spoke to her.' Another vista into the repulsive Christian-name intimacy forced by the blackmailers on the family. 'I wanted to negotiate as quickly as possible.'

Next the then editor of *The News Of The World*. He took the call from M3 which followed the letter, keeping M3 hanging on till he became angry and abusive: 'Tell McKay I want a million! I will prove his wife is in existence.' Mr Hudson finds that the newspaper received over a hundred letters and many telephone calls, some giving information, some asking for money. The reason M3 got through direct to the editor was that the editor had an acquaintance who gave the code-name M!

Now two young detectives—young detectives nowadays tend to have nice long hair growing down into sideboards and the nape of the neck. First a handsome young man who impersonated Ian McKay on the first ransom-collecting police-trap which led them to the paper flowers at Dane End at midnight on the 1st February. Mr Hudson establishes that he was not wearing gloves when he opened the Piccadilly tipped cigarette packet, the packet that allegedly bears Arthur Hosein's thumbprint.

Then a detective who, with Inspector O'Hara, was watching Dane End from a plain-clothes police car. He saw the Volvo, with two passengers, one with bushy hair, and noticed the nearside obligatory light unlit. Mr Hudson asks if the index plate was lit. (This was the night when nobody took the Volvo's registration number.) He also establishes that there were so many plain-clothes vehicles around that the detective and the inspector did not know which of the cars passing by were police cars and which were not. (No wonder M3 noticed them!)

Mr Draycott asks the witness when he first began to attach importance to the Volvo. Some days later. After the police went to Rook's Farm on the 7th February? Following some argie-bargie they settle for the 4th or 5th—which is when, Mr Draycott artlessly points out, he had to cast his mind back to describe the passengers of the Volvo as it went by in the dark on the 1st.

Next a marked change of atmosphere. Mr Rosenthal, a very large, portly fellow who puts on a Jewish cap to take the oath. He wears thick spectacles, and has a small, cheerful, smiling mouth. He might have spent his life in witness-boxes, for all the awe he displays. He is manager of a tailor's trimming business, a monthly customer of Arthur Hosein's for years. It is he who, while visiting Arthur at Rook's Farm—for the purpose of getting an order, he says—on the evening of the 1st February, presented him with a packet of Piccadilly tipped cigarettes before he, Arthur, left with Nizam in the Volvo for London, to go to the finishers, at about 6.50 p.m. Mr Rosenthal stayed on with Mrs Hosein and the children till 9 p.m., when the brothers had not returned.

Mr Hudson rises, and within two minutes they are in collision. Mr Rosenthal says he went to get an order: Mr Hudson suggests he has not quite told the truth—he went for the purpose of delivering goods. If it was only for an order, why did he not telephone? Mr Rosenthal is confronted with a large exhibit, a parcel of pocketing material, tailor's wax, etc., which Mr Hudson alleges he delivered to Mrs Hosein.

'Definitely a lie.'

Mr Hudson produces evidence of a bill, dated the 9th February, and an invoice. He suggests Mr Rosenthal has been ringing up Mrs Hosein for payment. He gets Mr Rosenthal to laugh unkindly at Arthur's expense. He then turns to the packet of Piccadilly tipped cigarettes.

'I suggest you gave Arthur only one cigarette?' Mr Rosenthal: 'Do I have to agree with everything you say?'

The Judge: 'There is no need to get into a tizzy. You don't have to agree. All you have to say is "It's not right." Can you say something about the packet?'—'It was unused.'

Mr Hudson plugs away again about Mr Rosenthal's going to Rook's Farm for delivery, not an order. Mr Rosenthal is tempted to say: 'I was there, and you weren't!'

The Judge: 'Are you certain he wasn't?' (Laughter in court.)

Mr Rosenthal makes a retort ending: 'He's a free member of society, like you or I.'

Mr Hudson goes back: 'I suggest you're lying.' Mr Rosenthal: 'That's your prerogative. I'm not.'

Mr Hudson returns to his main charge. 'You don't smoke?' he asks. 'No. Nor drink, either.'

'We're on cigarettes. You offered Mrs Hosein some cigarettes before you left. They weren't Piccadilly?'—'Not the ones I gave her. It will come back to me what they were.'

Mr Hudson: 'We'll wait.' Mr Rosenthal: 'I'll think of it and let you know.'

With that Mr Rosenthal leaves the box. But by this time the Judge has studied the bill and the invoice. He has Mr Rosenthal called back. Looking at the invoice, he says to him: 'At the top corner is written the word *Verbal*. Might that mean that the order was made over the telephone?'

'Yes.'

(Very neat!)

Mr Rosenthal finally disappears from the case. As for the Piccadilly tipped cigarette packet—who knows what, as a result of it all?

Something very different again—the beginning of the forensic evidence against Arthur Hosein. (From the Attorney General's opening we know there is none against Nizam.) Detective Chief Inspector Brine, who has served in the Fingerprint Branch of Scotland Yard for twenty-two years. He is a biggish man with a large pointed nose that he lifts into the air, slightly fussy movements, and the sort of near-godlike confidence that encourages (in me) counter-suggestibility—no man ought to be *so* confident about *anything*.

Attorney General: 'Have you ever known prints not to conform to a sequence of ridge-patterns?'

Mr Brine (in ringing tones): 'Never!' He points his nose upwards.

Under the Attorney General's examination we all set ourselves laboriously to learn about the technique of fingerprintery; the remarking of ridge-characteristics in detail and in their sequence; and the basis for identifying one print with another. Eight characteristics in common are declared by Mr Brine to be 'satisfactory', ten 'good', eighteen 'beyond doubt'. Two fingers of a 'good' ten apiece apparently count as a stunning twenty. (Would four fingers of five apiece equally count as a stunning twenty, or ten fingers of two apiece?) Frequently in the case of Arthur Hosein, Mr Brine announces, the score is sixteen. Pause.

Mr Brine: 'Want any more, sir?' Nose upwards.

The Judge asks a question I should like to ask myself: 'Do you get any help from general pattern?' (Computers are being developed to do certain types of pattern-recognition.)

Mr Brine: 'Well, sir, we just concentrate on characteristics as they appear in the same sequence.' (Shades of a sergeant-major's answer!) 'When you get sixteen, you stop.'

In like manner we get clear the difference between professionally taken fingerprints and those left accidentally, between what is visible at life-size and at photographic enlargement. And the scores to be totted up against Arthur Hosein on the various documents.

Mr Hudson rises.

'I hope you'll bear with me when I say with all humility, addressing an expert like yourself—I hope you'll bear with me . . .' (I don't know how he has the nerve to say it, as he is clearly opening a forensic duel in which Mr Brine is going to have to bear with him, with or without all humility, probably for several hours.)

Mr Hudson slips his spectacles down his nose so as to look through them at the piles of photographs and over them at Mr Brine.

We go over the question of prints fading, and of documents being handled by a lot of people—such as policemen without gloves—before they are examined for prints. We learn that whem Mr Brine examined the thumbprint on the Piccadilly cigarette packet he found no corresponding master-print in the Criminal Record Office. (So Arthur presumably has no criminal record, which is an interesting fact to learn.) We go on to the number of points of identification.

Mr Hudson: 'The Crown invites conviction on sixteen?'

Mr Brine 'The courts accept ten.'

The Judge: '*You* accept ten?'

Mr Brine says he is satisfied with eight.

Mr Hudson turns to the palmprint on *The People.*

'I suggest you attribute sixteen. I suggest that only six are acceptable.' (So those are his tactics!) 'I've got to do this, I'm afraid, so that everybody finds it acceptable.' (In the dock Arthur suddenly laughs: it is obvious that he has enormous confidence in his counsel.) Mr Hudson goes on to enumerate his six acceptable points of characterisation, most telling when they are grouped together—'They are then called an "island"?' he suggests.

'Lake, or island.' The nose points upwards with satisfaction.

'I think I shall be able to show differences due to photography, not to reality,' says Mr Hudson.

'We always do it by photographs.'

Mr Hudson begins on a lengthy process of taking the documents one by one, challenging individual points of characterisation (which are numbered on the photographs). He selects one particular point. 'Again, I'm only an ignoramus, but I'd like to hear what you say about it. It doesn't show that junction.'

Mr Brine: 'It does to me.'

Mr Hudson: 'Again, I'm in the hands of an expert.' He laughs in a friendly, rueful way. 'You'll agree it's not obvious to the naked eye?' He laughs a little again. 'That's what makes the difference?' He looks at the photograph. 'It's not very clear, I suggest.'—'It is to me.'

The jury are attentively and stolidly looking at the photographs. Mr Hudson says to the expert, apologetically: 'You appreciate I'm doing this on instruction by somebody else who has already examined the documents.' (The defence expert, Dr Julius Grant, will appear later.) And on it goes. Mr Hudson challenges the certainty of a particular ridge-ending. 'Where there are gaps all over the place, it does not say that a ridge has ended.'

'I say it does.'

'Forgive me! I must pursue this a bit further.' We come to the effect of the pressure with which a print is made making a difference.

The Judge keeps up, scribing it all in his big book. He intervenes from time to time. Mr Hudson persists. He has in effect been taking advantage of technology at the expert's expense. He turns to another print.

'Over on this side . . . it's very difficult for me to see anything but a blank space. But I don't matter.' Two members of the jury laugh together.

The expert retaliates.

Mr Hudson: 'Could you speak a little more slowly?'

The expert is tempted to make a score.

Mr Hudson: 'If you please! . . . This is much too serious a matter.'

It still goes on. Mr Hudson now sets about scoring the scientific point that Mr Brine is sometimes interpreting *imperfect* points of identification in terms of *perfect* ones.

In the dock Nizam looks round the court over his spectacles. The impression of it all on me, at least, is a feeling that fingerprintery is much more open to argument than I had previously imagined.

The Attorney General sees fit to re-examine.

'You have a reputation for fingerprint evaluation. You're conscious of it, you're a chief inspector. . . . Before giving evidence in court you have to have seven years' training. How many fingerprints do you assess in a month? Thousands?'

Mr Brine assents.

'Does speculation ever enter into it? Do you speculate?' Answer: 'No.'—'Are you satisfied?' Answer: 'Yes.'

The Judge: 'By what standards?'

Mr Brine: 'I'm sure of it.'

The Attorney General comes in again: 'Do you accept that there are any points that can be challenged?'—'No, sir!'

'Thank you, Chief Inspector!'

The day now comes to its close with the detective chief inspector who was the passenger in the plain-clothes police car on the 1st February at Dane End, driven by the detective sergeant who has already given evidence. He saw the Rolls drive up, the black suitcase deposited beside the paper flowers, the Rolls drive away again. Then the Volvo with *two* men in it went by.

After Mr Hudson, Mr Draycott rises—his client is involved. He asks to read Mr O'Hara's note. *Volvo car, two up, nearside lights out.*

Mr Draycott's point is that the witness saw two *figures*, and only settled for two *men* when the police went to Rook's Farm on the 7th February, saw the Volvo and the two brothers.

'It is abundantly apparent that what he is saying now is *not* what he put in the note. I am suggesting to the detective chief inspector that if that's what he saw, he would make an accurate note.'

With that the day ends. It must be the sort of thing that detective chief inspectors are used to in court—in fact it is not all that easy to imagine the sort of note-taking that would defeat the efforts of defence counsel.

But it is the forensic duel over fingerprints that lingers in the mind. It was brilliant: gaps in the Crown's case were brought to light. Yet human nature is such that I'd bet on most people in the court thinking, just the same, that the fingerprints are in all probability Arthur Hosein's.

On the way home, having got right away from the court, I reflect more generally on how, as the trial gets under way, everyone in court—including, I think, even the men in the dock—is tending to become absorbed in the minutiae of evidence at the expense of the major way the trial is moving. It reminds me of how, when someone is suffering from a fatal illness, their day-to-day recoveries and minor relapses tend to obscure the fact that the illness itself can lead only to one end.

17 September

The day begins with four police witnesses, involved in the second ransom-collecting police-trap set on the 6th February. (Actually, can it be called a 'police-trap' when M3 devised it himself?) First the young woman detective who posed as Diane Dyer with Detective Inspector Minors disguised as Mr Alick McKay. They drove down to Bethnal Green in the Rolls for the second telephone call. 'Any error will be fatal to your Mum.' Then to Epping and finally by taxi to Gates used-car lot, where she and Mr Minors deposited the two white suitcases beside the Mini-van. Second the detective who rode on the floor of the taxi and scuttled out behind the hedge to watch the suitcases. Maps and photographs of the spot are circulated to the jury. This witness saw the Volvo circulating between 9 p.m. and 9.45 p.m. with

Nizam at the wheel—Nizam now admits it: and again at 10.47 p.m.—which Mr Hudson on behalf of Arthur does not admit—with two men. On the 7th February he went with the police to Rook's Farm and identified the brothers as the two men.

(One can't help being stopped in one's tracks by the thought that it was not until the early hours of the morning when the Volvo disappeared leaving the white suitcases, that the police seem to have had any idea *whom* they were going to arrest!)

Third a detective who was watching the Minivan, kneeling down and looking through gaps in slats of a fence, on the bitterly cold night. Both Mr Hudson and Mr Draycott have a go at him, especially Mr Hudson over his being able to see that the passenger was the man whom on the following day he identified with Arthur Hosein.

Fourth another detective who was watching behind the fence and gives evidence that he saw that the passenger in the Volvo was Indian-looking, had a moustache and bushy hair.

Next the Gates Garage attendant who early in the evening of the 6th February gave Nizam the air-line, saw him reading a piece of paper about the size of a telegram. (Was it the paper with the Minivan number?) After twenty minutes he asked Nizam to move on and reported him to the local police. He saw the two white suitcases beside the Minivan as he went off duty at 10 p.m. Mr Draycott cross-examines him.

'When Nizam drove the Volvo into the petrol station it was well lit.' His speech becomes even more measured for emphasis. 'He made no attempt to conceal himself.' Nizam spoke to both attendants. 'He made no attempt to conceal himself: he hung about for twenty minutes in the lighted area.' And: 'You wondered why he was hanging about so long?'

'I was thinking about our money.'

'He made no attempt to conceal his identity? Just the opposite?' (We are having it rubbed in. Incredible as it sounds, it must in fact be Nizam's *defence*.)

We move to The Raven, the public house at Berden where that night Arthur allegedly turned up as the first customer just after 7 p.m. and left with Nizam just after 10.30 p.m. The licensee appears first in the witness-box, a bearded man with a vaguely piercing glance. He is wearing a beige fisherman's-knit cardigan with a leather front. He looks the way middle-aged poets used to look in the fifties.

One recalls the story as it can be pieced together so far. Arthur came to the pub from Bishop's Stortford in a taxi, where he left Nizam with the Volvo. There were two M3 telephone calls that evening, one to Bethnal Green at 6 p.m., which could have been made by either Arthur or Nizam; the other to Epping at 7.30 p.m. Could Arthur have made the second call?

The licensee tells his story. Arthur, the first customer of the evening, arrived at just after 7 p.m. when the licensee and his wife were playing shove ha'penny in the public bar. He ordered a double scotch and ginger for himself, stood the licensee a drink, and chatted with them till the television actor and his two girl friends arrived in the saloon bar. Arthur joined them till Nizam came at 10 p.m. Then Arthur and Nizam stayed talking, after the actor and the girls had departed, till 10.30 p.m.

Mr Hudson cross-examines. The point at issue is what time Arthur went to the lavatory and how long he took. The Raven is a small pub, entered by a porch with a door to the public bar on one side, to the saloon on the other, saloon and public being separated by a partition wall ending at the counter which serves both bars. From the public there is a corridor, with on one side a door labelled *TOILET*, and on the other side a door to the living quarters, where there is a telephone. The living quarters are visible through the doorway behind the counter and there is a dog there. Arthur went to the lavatory shortly before the actor and the girls arrived. 'Only there for two or three minutes,' says the licensee.

Mr Hudson ascertains that there is a telephone box down the street. 'A hundred yards away at least.'

Mr Draycott's turn. 'Why do you say he was going to the lavatory?'—'If he goes through the door labelled *TOILET*, you assume . . .' Mr Draycott: 'He could have gone into the living quarters, or into the street. You draw the obvious conclusion. That's what you've done.'

The licensee tells the Judge that from where he and his wife were serving behind the counter, they could have seen Arthur go into the living quarters.

The licensee's wife recalls the evening: Arthur's two visits to the lavatory at about 7.30 p.m. and 9.30 p.m., Nizam's appearance at 10 p.m. and Arthur's asking shortly afterwards for six pennies to be included in change for two shillings. The public box in the street is not S.T.D. but of the old-fashioned kind requiring four pennies.

Mr Hudson says Arthur has no recollection of asking for the change at 10.20 p.m. Arthur had been drinking double scotches all night. Mr Draycott returns to the charge over the 7.30 trip to the toilet, which means, if Arthur did telephone, his either risking being seen in the living quarters or sprinting 100 yards and back. 'Just to get it clear,' says Mr Draycott. 'You don't time people going to the toilet?' It seems that Mr Draycott is keen on leaving the jury with some idea that M3's call might have been made by Arthur and not Nizam—assuming for the moment that either of them made it. (So far, neither of the brothers has been proved to be M3.)

We now come to the evidence of the television actor with two girl friends. He wears his hair over his collar, and is dressed in a suède jacket and open-necked yellow shirt with cravat. It is he to whom Arthur has made the headline-catching remark about wanting to be a millionaire. Mr Leary asks him about the conversation, and the actor gives his answers.

'He spoke about life in Trinidad. He spoke about money. He said he wanted to be a millionaire like his father.' (Like his father, indeed!)

Mr Leary: 'And did he speak about Nizam?'—'He said Nizam was coming from London to collect him. In a car.'

Mr Hudson: 'You remember Nizam arriving. And after Nizam arrived, Arthur pressed you and the two ladies to have *another* drink?'—'Yes.'

Mr Hudson (later): 'It's true, isn't it, that Arthur talks a lot? He's often boasting about money?'—'Yes.'

'And *you* said you'd like to be a millionaire as well?'

'I said yes. I would like to be comfortably off.'

Mr Draycott rises to emphasise Arthur's saying he was waiting for Nizam: 'You remember because Arthur made a little point of it, saying why he was there? That's why you remember it?' Mr Draycott is obviously engaged in building a case.

The Judge, presumably in an effort to keep the trial moving, wonders whether one of the actor's girl friends need be called. The prosecution stick to it, and she appears—a pretty girl with fine flaxen hair flowing from a centre parting down over her shoulders, and make-up that gives her the up-to-date washed-out look. She smiles at the court. We add to our picture of social life in Stocking Pelham. Some of the edge has gone off the millionaire story, but more edge has come on to the ransom-collecting story—Arthur pressing the actor to stay and drink, when a million pounds was waiting unattended!

Another Detective Chief Superintendent—Mr Harvey, who led the police expedition to Rook's Farm at 1.45 p.m. on the 7th February. Mr Hudson cross-examines him directly. We get a description of the sitting-room at Rook's Farm—photographs are passed round to the jury. A biggish room with beams across the ceiling, and a style of furnishing appropriate to what would be called a 'lounge'—an open fireplace, a curved bar with a couple of stools, some sofas, a radiogram, a television set. Incidentally, there is nothing either cheap-looking or inappropriate-looking to contemporary dormitory belt society about Rook's Farm. It is pretty from the outside, eighteenth century, painted white. (Worth £15,000 or more?)

Mr Hudson cross-examines about the extensive searches of Rook's Farm in February and March, also others in June, July, and as recently as the 10th August. Police officers galore, police dogs galore. (Rook's Farm has fourteen acres.)

Mr Hudson fixes on the 2½in. Elastoplast tin, referred to in the opening speech of the Attorney General. Mr Harvey saw it on the 7th February? 'Yes.' But he did not collect it until the 21st February? 'Yes.' Mr Harvey, though he must have been supported by numerous policemen, nobly takes the responsibility. He is the sort of man who, when he makes a mistake, looks so reliable that he gets praise for admitting it instead of blame for making it.

Mr Hudson: 'There was no difficulty in getting it on the 21st—Mrs Hosein was asked for it and she gave it?' Mr Harvey: 'Her son gave it.'

Mr Hudson rubs it in: 'A fortnight later there was no difficulty in getting it from Mrs Hosein, who had frequently visited her husband in Brixton Prison in the meantime?'

Mr Draycott rises to lead up to the *dénouement.*

'Is it right to say Rook's Farm has been searched as scrupulously as it is possible to search anything?'—'Yes.'

'Every skill has been employed?'—'Yes.'

'And there is no trace of Mrs McKay having been on that Farm?' Mr Harvey: 'No trace whatsoever.'

No trace whatsoever.

Mr Draycott keeps on: 'Everything gone over with a toothcomb?'—'The whole place was searched.' Mr Draycott suggests that the forensic side can pick up things not seen by the naked eye. Also there were the dogs.

Still—no trace whatsoever.

(One thinks how, with a single fibre of green jersey material, a sliver of cream-coloured leather, let alone a spot of blood or a hair, the game would have been up. But instead, nothing. No trace whatsoever of Mrs McKay's ever having been at Rook's Farm.)

The Attorney General re-examines about the sheds, the dark outhouses with bales of straw, the calves and the pigs; the surface of the passage—hard—to where the rubbish was dumped by a stream. (The bizarre rumours hover, unspoken, in the air.)

There is an intermission in police evidence while Mrs McKay's doctor testifies to her having been in good health, cheerful, stable and strong-minded. One presumes that this must be to dispose of what was implied by some of the newspapers in the first *HAVE YOU SEEN THIS WOMAN?* publicity, that Mrs McKay's disappearance was being regarded as a menopausal incident.

Mr Hudson cross-examines about the drugs with which Mrs McKay was being treated, the possibility of side-effects—gastro-intestinal disturbances, peptic ulcers leading to haemorrhages and so on. (A possibility recurrently canvassed outside the court is that Mrs McKay may not have been murdered by her kidnappers but, for one reason or another—cold, exposure, shock—have *died on their hands.*)

The police evidence now comes to the two chief men in the case, Detective Chief Superintendent Smith, who led the whole investigation, and Detective Inspector Minors, who assisted him—also chauffeuring the Rolls in the first ransom-collecting expedition and disguising himself as Mr Alick McKay in the second. It is mainly due to these two men that the brothers Hosein are now in the dock. 'Joint army' gossip forecasts for them a grilling by Mr Hudson and Mr Draycott.

Detective Inspector Minors comes first. By coincidence both he and his chief were air-crew members during World War II. Mr Smith was a W.Op/Air-gunner and Mr Minors a W.Op/Navigator. On the ransom expeditions—Mr Smith was always on the spot—they must have thought, if there was an international gang at work, that they stood a chance of being shot up again.

Mr Minors is a big chap, full-cheeked, very fresh-complexioned and blue-eyed, with smooth darkish hair and a moustache. The Attorney General takes him through what is now the familiar story. Mr Minors is invited to compare the M3 voices he has heard in the telephone boxes during the ransom attempts with those recorded in conversation with Ian McKay at 20 Arthur Road. He says that in the box at Church Street, Tottenham, M3's voice seemed to be the voice he had heard on the tape-recorder.

The Judge: 'The same voice?'—'Very similar.' This was where M3 said: 'If the police are about this time we will execute Muriel and no one will ever see her again.'

The Judge: 'You can't swear it?' Mr Minors (sensibly): 'No, my Lord.'

At Epping at 7.30 p.m. the voice sounded muffled. A West Indian accent, as previously heard, but not the same voice—slightly different. This is where M3 said: 'You're being watched.' And he threatened with telescopic-sighted rifles, etc. 'If you don't drop the money, she'll be dead.'

We come to the 7th February at Rook's Farm, the search and the findings. Then the drive to Kingston Police Station, Arthur continually discoursing on his universal popularity, his intention of standing for the local Council, the influence 'in high places' of his wealthy father. And at the police station the first questions about the 29th December and Wimbledon. The Hoseins' fingerprints were taken that evening at Brixton.

During interrogation on the following day about the 1st

February, Nizam described the expedition to the finishers in Tottenham. He was shown the paper flowers and started to cry. On the other hand, Arthur said: 'You've got a very difficult case, Mr Smith. I want to help you.' Arthur gave a specimen of handwriting, was shown the baling twine, the billhook from 20 Arthur Road—'Like one I borrowed from George to chop up a calf'—and the adhesive tape—'What is it?' Asked about Mrs McKay, he said: 'That poor lady. I'd like to help.'

18 September

Mr Minors's examination-in-chief continues. We hear again about the continuing interrogations at Kingston Police Station of Arthur and Nizam alternately about the events of the 6th February.

First Nizam, who described the visit to the tailors, ending up at Percy Chaplin's in Bethnal Green at about 6.15 p.m.; followed by the drive to Bishop's Storftord and the date with Susie; and finally the drive to The Raven. Nizam gave a specimen of his handwriting. He was shown the twine and the Elastoplast . . . 'Let me die!'

Next Arthur, who was asked to speak into a telephone for a recording test; and then told the fingerprints were his. 'Impossible! You're trying to trick me!' The interrogations closed in on the subject of Mrs McKay. Arthur's solicitor, Mr Coote, came to see them and said to Nizam: 'If Mrs McKay is alive and you know anything, you must tell.'

On the following day Nizam refused, like Arthur, to sign his statements; and furthermore refused to speak into the telephone. At a later interrogation Arthur said: 'What, more questions, Mr Smith?' And, 'If you think that you've got anything on me, then book me!' In the evening of that day Mr Smith and Mr Minors told Arthur and Nizam they were going to be taken to Wimbledon Police Station where they would be charged. Arthur: 'I have nothing to say, Mr Smith. You have your job to do.' Nizam just made no reply at all.

Then there were the extraordinary scenes, we hear, resulting from Nizam's asking to see Mr Smith and Mr Minors without his legal representatives present. At the first Nizam said: 'Is anyone stopping Liley from coming to see me? Has my brother Adam told her not to? Could I speak to her?' To which Mr Smith said, not surprisingly: 'Is that all?'

But at the second came Nizam's extraordinary statement:

'I could get out of 90% of this trouble if I put my cards on the table.'

Mr Smith: 'What do you want to tell us?' After a silence Nizam replied: 'I want to think . . . I'll leave it till another day.'

The Attorney General ends at that point and Mr Hudson rises.

Mr Hudson first points out that the brothers were held in custody from Saturday, the 7th February, to Tuesday, the 10th February, 'assisting the police' without being charged with anything. (When shall we get rid of that mealy-mouthed expression? We all know that half the time it means being kept in custody while the police try to collect evidence for a charge.) The information about the fingerprints being identified as Arthur Hosein's was telephoned to the police by Mr Brine very late on Saturday night or early Sunday morning.

Mr Hudson: 'Having got this information you didn't charge them till Tuesday because you wanted to see if there was a chance, if they were connected with the affair, to find out where Mrs McKay was?'—'Yes.'

Mr Hudson next gets Mr Minors's assent to Arthur's complete denial of all knowledge of the crime—he is putting questions to cover what Arthur is likely to say in the witness-box. Mr Hudson claims that the police did not mention Mrs McKay to Arthur. 'We did.'

'You showed Arthur three sheets of paper from Nizam's bedroom, and your evidence is that he said: "I've never seen the paper before. You must ask Nizam." Hadn't he told you he'd written to Ipswich County Court on it? And you could have got a specimen of his handwriting?'

'Absolutely incorrect.' Later Mr Minors concedes that amongst some papers they found a summons.

Mr Hudson: 'I suggest Arthur Hosein never said 'Where *is* Wimbledon?" He told you he'd been dog-racing there.'

Mr Minors: 'I think he made reference to dog-racing. I have a feeling he mentioned Clapton.'

Mr Hudson comes to the last of his questions raised by what

Arthur may say in the witness-box—that Mr Smith slapped him across the face.

Mr Minors: 'No, sir. That's news to me.'

Mr Hudson (menacingly): 'I'll leave that to your senior officer.'

Now Mr Draycott slides smoothly and sweetly into a quite different line. 'I have no quarrel with your evidence,' he says: 'I want you to assist me about Nizam. At Wimbledon Police Station, when he was seen on the 12th June, he was on the brink of telling you something. He *wanted* to, but something held him back.' Mr Minors: 'We felt it did.'

Mr Draycott: 'Many times during the interview he showed marked signs of feeling afraid, did he not?'—'Yes.'—'He was certainly afraid.'—'Yes.'—'Very distressed?'—'Yes, we called the doctor.'—'What seemed to be holding him back was *fear*?' Mr Minors: 'Fear, sir.'

Mr Draycott: 'Would you agree with me that, having seen these two brothers over a long period, it is abundantly clear, abundantly plain, that Nizam's relationship with his brother is unusual, in that it is based not on brotherly affection but fear?'

(This is it. Now we begin to see the line plain.) Mr Minors: 'That would appear to be the case.'

Mr Draycott, still with most amicable courtesy—why should they quarrel?—says: 'Nizam's fingerprints have been taken. You agree with me, do you not, that there is no evidence of fingerprints to connect Nizamodeen Hosein with Mrs McKay's home at Arthur Road, Wimbledon?' He eyes the jury sagely. Mr Minors: 'No, sir.'

(Very nice, too, one thinks.) Mr Draycott sits down shortly after that. In a few minutes he is sitting sideways again in profile to the jury, high-spiritedly exchanging his comments with his learned Trinidadian junior.

Detective Chief Superintendent Smith is called. The grilling of Inspector Minors has not taken place. Perhaps this is going to be the big moment. He's the biggest man in the case, anyway. Mr Smith is shortish and very strongly built: he has a tough complexion and thinning wavy hair sprucely combed back from his forehead—spruceness characteristically epitomised by a neatly tied bow-tie that he constantly wears. He puts on horn-rimmed spectacles and promptly slips them half way down his nose, so as to read and to look over them.

The Attorney General examines Mr Smith on substantially the same story as Mr Minors's, since the two men worked together all the time. (I began by saying that the element of drama, the element of theatre, is endemic to a trial, whether anybody likes the idea or not. So is the element of repetition. It bears down on one. Perhaps it contributes to the weight of justice.)

All over again, the 29th and the 30th December, the 6th February, and the police going to Rook's Farm on the 7th. Mr Hudson, addressing Mr Smith as the senior officer in charge of the case, establishes that Arthur Hosein has no previous convictions for violence or dishonesty. (That was a question we wanted answered.) He has convictions for speeding offences and was court-martialled for desertion in 1960. (Not offences to be held against any man according to current *mœurs*, it would appear.)

Mr Hudson points out that after the charges being made on 10th February, there were seventeen remands until the hearings began at Wimbledon on 8th June, that is to say after being taken into custody on the 7th February no evidence was produced in court against them until the 8th June. During that time there were further searches; if there was anything to be found there was a better chance if the brothers were not in possession. (Obviously so, to me.)

Mr Hudson goes through some of the details of the investigation for Mr Smith's agreement. The Aga was dismantled. An architect and builder were consulted about possible secret compartments. Ponds were drained by the Fire Brigade. The hedges and ditches in surrounding fields were searched, Sleepy Hollow . . .

'Also Epping Forest,' says Mr Smith wryly.

Finally: 'I now put this to you, personally. I suggest that during some parts of the investigation at Kingston Police Station, you punched Arthur Hosein and slapped him across the face.'

'That is not true.'

From Mr Draycott, no questions.

(So the grilling has not taken place! The army of takers-in of each other's washing turn out to be not always right.)

Next, two television men to say that Mrs Diane Dyer spoke only once on a transmitted programme, on the night of the 30th December. This settles the last night on which everybody now takes it as certain that Mrs McKay was still alive.

The proceedings, which have been having more *longueurs*, are now enlivened by Farmer Leonard Smith, brought in to identify the billhook from Arthur Road. An elderly man, seventyish, who hobbles rheumatically. He has fair hair with a white badger streak, and rough withered cheeks; and a strong country accent.

The Attorney General begins to examine him about the auction sale, from which he used his truck to transport the brothers' purchases to Rook's Farm, there leaving behind, he says, his spare wheel and his bill. The Attorney General appears to be unaccustomed to its being called anything other than a billhook. Farmer Smith puts him right.

'It's a bill! B, I, double L. For hedging. . . .' He shows the Attorney General how you swipe a hedge with it. 'I lost *this*. Had to buy another.'

The Attorney General asks him if he remembers what happened to the bill when he got to Rook's Farm. 'No.'

The Judge asks him if the bill might have fallen out on the way. Farmer Smith: 'No. It was impossible for it to fall out.'

Attorney General (according to examining procedure): 'And when you got to Rook's Farm did you have a cup of tea?'

Farmer Smith (settling down): 'I'll tell you the whole story. Nizam came down with more stuff on a wheelbarrow. There was a pig got out and was running about. I run after this pig, went in and out, to get the pig in again. I'd nearly unloaded . . .'

The Attorney General courteously tries to get on with his procedure—his Lordship says to him:

'I'm not sure Mr Smith doesn't put it more picturesquely.'

In the long run we get to the end of the whole story—Farmer Smith could teach the Ancient Mariner a thing or two. The Hoseins returned the spare wheel but *not* the bill.

Attorney General: 'You saw the Hosein brothers on December the 27th?'—'I waved them goodbye. I couldn't find them any time. I was . . .'

Attorney General: 'On February the 17th did Detective Sergeant Simpson show you a certain hedging bill?' (The "certain bill"—it is the one from Arthur Road—is handed up to him.)

Farmer Smith: 'That's *my* billhook! I defy anybody to say it's not. I'm left-handed.' He looks at it. 'It's nothing near so sharp as it was when I lost it.'

Attorney General: 'Show us how you sharpen it.' The matter at issue is that a left-handed man and a right-handed man blunt different sides the more. Farmer Smith shows us. In the dock even both Hoseins laugh. The court breaks up for lunch.

After lunch Mr Hudson begins. He refers to an occasion on which Farmer Smith, in order to help Nizam to get a permit to go on staying in England, went with the Hoseins to vouch for his intention of employing Nizam on his farm, though, Mr Hudson suggests, Nizam had enough work to do on the Farm anyway. Mr Hudson: 'I suggest you got £20 from Arthur Hosein for that?'

Farmer Smith: 'I did not. All I got was a pint of beer and lunch in a Chinese restaurant. And then he borrowed £1 off me to pay the bill!'

The Judge: 'Did you get the £1 back?'—'Yes.'

Mr Hudson goes on to the brothers' calling to see Farmer Smith on the 27th December. Farmer Smith was at that time in a pub, doing a deal with a man with a cow. His wife telephoned him to say the brothers were waiting to see him in his caravan sixty yards away from the house. Arthur had come to drink some brandy with him as he was not well. (We thus hear for the first time about Arthur's allegedly having 'flu over Christmas.) According to his evidence Farmer Smith went back to his house and spoke to nobody. 'They came down from the caravan. I said I hadn't got time. They said Cheerio.'

'You got the message at The Jolly Waggoners. I suggest you went to the caravan to see who it was?'—'I wanted to let my cows in.'

'I suggest you said you had a cold, were not feeling very well. Perhaps your memory is hazy.'—'I did.'

'I suggest your memory is at fault.'—'I'll bring my wife! I'm here to tell the truth, not lies.'

'I'm not suggesting you're telling lies. Don't worry about that!' Mr Hudson now gets to the loss of the billhook. 'I suggest you never discussed the billhook at all!'

On 10th February a detective came with the billhook and Farmer Smith made a statement, claiming it as his by describing it.

Mr Hudson: 'I suggest you gave that description *after you'd been shown it.*'

Farmer Smith: 'The detective came the evening before. I said I was too busy, he'd have to wait. In the morning I finished one or two jobs, then made the statement.'

So much for the billhook. (So much also for the toil of a farmer's life.)

Mrs Liley Mohammed, Nizam's girl friend, is called next. We know already from the Attorney General that she spent the night of the 31st December at Rook's Farm. She is a hospital nurse, a bit short, dressed in a brown and white striped suit. She looks frightened. Her face is oval, her hair being drawn back from it into a high double bunch of curls like a more African version of Mrs Diane Dyer's.

The Attorney General examines. Mrs Mohammed—she soon becomes known as Liley—says she first spent the night at Rook's Farm on the 26th December. Nizam had invited her on Christmas Eve to come for Christmas, but night duty had prevented her from going before the 26th. After it she telephoned Nizam on the 27th and again on the 29th December.

The Attorney General asks more about the calls on the 29th. About 8 p.m. no reply; 9 p.m. no reply; but at 10.30 p.m. she was answered by Arthur and she left a message for Nizam. (In the early hours of the following morning came M3's first call to Arthur Road.) She spoke to Nizam on the telephone on the 30th. She next saw Nizam and Arthur in the Volvo in London on the evening of the 31st, when she did not want to go to the Farm; but she was finally persuaded, arriving there at about 9 p.m. She stayed till the 2nd January, preparing meals for the brothers. Mrs Hosein and the children were in Germany and not due to return till the 3rd.

Attorney General: 'Did Nizam leave the Farm during that period?'—'On the 1st January, in the afternoon. To get something for stomach-ache.' Nizam was away for about an hour and a half, she says.

Attorney General: 'What were you mainly doing?'—'Watching television and cooking.'

'When Nizam returned the three of you watched television?' They watched most of the time: she did not pay much attention.

The Judge asks if she remembers what she saw—the News? (The News was constantly referring to the disappearance of Mrs McKay.) She does not remember.

Liley visited the Farm, just for the day, in the early part of January, and then about a week later. Mrs Hosein and the children were there.

Mrs Mohammed is now shown a box of coloured tissues with some paper clips. 'It belongs to me.' She is questioned about how the paper flowers are made. 'In a special way?' the Judge says encouragingly: 'You have to know it?' Liley says timidly yes, though goodness knows how many people, including me, know it.

The Attorney General asks about the visit, when she took some flowers, ready-made, in her hand and gave them to Nizam—with the exception of some she fixed by the handle on the dashboard of the car.

The Judge: 'They looked prettier there?' Liley (smiling for the first time, sadly): 'I just felt like it. . . .'

Mr Hudson cross-examines, beginning with her visit on Boxing Day, when at first she did not want to go.

'Did Nizam ask you to speak to Arthur?'—'Yes.'

'Was it Arthur who persuaded you to go, to do the cooking?'—'Yes.'

While she was at the Farm she saw only Nizam and Arthur: she did not leave the Farm. Mr Hudson: 'You told us about several subsequent visits to the Farm. Did you get the impression on any of those visits that there was anything there to hide?'—'No.'

Mr Hudson pauses. 'As far as you were concerned, madam, you felt free to visit any of the farm buildings you wanted?'—'Yes.'

'At the Farm did you sometimes go out with Nizam while he was looking after the animals?'—'Yes.'—'You helped him to skin the calf?'—'Yes.'

Mr Hudson checks that Arthur answered the telephone at 10.30 p.m. on the night of the 29th and Nizam was out. And that on the 1st January Liley never went out and she is sure that Arthur did not go out. (On the 1st January there were M3 telephone calls to Arthur Road.)

Then Mr Draycott gets more surprising revelations. Referring to Boxing Night, he says:

'I am not going to ask for the details, but I believe there was some trouble between Arthur and Nizam that night. In the course of that trouble did Nizam get very frightened?'—'He did.'—'And run out?'—'Yes.'—'And when he came back did he say he'd made a complaint to the police?'—'He did.'

Mr Draycott pauses. Less than seventy-two hours before they were allegedly going to kidnap Mrs McKay, Nizam called in the police!

Mr Draycott now asks about the calf. 'When it died, what was his attitude?'—'He was very upset.'—'He was quite emotional?'—'Yes.'

Mr Draycott refers to Nizam's homesickness over Christmas, and his wanting to get into the Air Force.

'During the whole time you have known him has he been quite gentle and kind to you?'—'Yes.'

The Attorney General re-examines. Liley was free to go where she liked on the 31st. 'Did you know about the workshop?' he asks. Liley did not, not until Mrs Hosein came back.

'What was the calf cut up with?' 'A long knife. It looked like a chopper.'

'I don't suppose you went to the shed where the dogs were kept.' Liley (firmly): 'No, I did not.'

(We may guess again what these questions are getting at. The bizarre rumours hover once more.)

The next three witnesses are 'finishers' from Tottenham and Shoreditch, middle-aged ladies who do part-time work at home. They are questioned about when they first saw Arthur Hosein after Christmas. The first, upset by it all, finds it hard to remember what she has said in her statements: she thinks the 5th January, when he told her he had been unwell over Christmas; and next—she is more confused now—the 1st February. The other lady thinks the 12th January; on the 1st February Nizam asked if she had a sixpence for a telephone call; she did not see either of the brothers on the 6th February. The third lady saw neither on the 29th December; both on the 1st February; neither on the 6th February.

The Judge asks the third lady how much she gets for finishing a pair of trousers.

'Eight shillings.'

Another vista into how the world lives. And then suddenly another vista into how Arthur Hosein lives. . . . Eight shillings makes sense with the out-of-court view that Arthur probably gets thirty shillings profit on each pair of trousers he cuts. If he earns his £150 a week he must have to cut at least a hundred pairs of trousers a week! Even if one were to assume uncharitably that a lot of the transactions are casual, like this one, and may go undeclared for Income Tax purposes, it still does not make sense. A new mystery comes into the picture. Where has Arthur Hosein's money been coming from? How did he manage to keep up Rook's Farm; to pay the mortgage, to entertain, to run a Volvo, to spend whole evenings on double scotches? *How?*

Such speculations are cut short by a police constable appearing in the witness-box. As a result of Nizam's call in the early hours of the 27th December, he went to Rook's Farm at eleven o'clock on the morning of Sunday, the 28th, and said he might call again. The morning of the 28th, and he might call *again*!

Lastly we have the hairdresser in N.17 who cuts Arthur's hair. Examination-in-chief by Mr Edward Cussens, who ascertains that while Arthur was having his hair cut the one o'clock News was on the radio, mentioning Mrs McKay's disappearance. The barber wondered what had become of her, and Arthur said, 'Who knows?' Then Mr Hudson: 'During that period when Arthur Hosein was having his hair cut, I believe you introduced him to another customer, a policeman, saying Arthur had a farm? The subject of shooting arose. The police constable asked if he could come and shoot over the Farm. Arthur said: "Certainly"?'—'Arthur gave him his name and the address of the Farm.'

Mr Hudson: 'And it was an invitation to come at any time?' Answer: 'Yes.'

The day is coming to an end. There is some written evidence, which nobody disputes, read by the Clerk of the Court. And the prospect of witnesses no longer having to be called, because of Nizam's admissions.

The Judge: 'How much is left of the Crown case?'

(That is something which he is not the only person in the court to be wondering. The law, it seems, takes a long time.)

The Attorney General says there is the handwriting expert. The Judge decides to hold it over to the next day.

We have all had enough.

21 September

The law seems to take a long time, and the impression is not mitigated by the order in which witnesses are called. As we begin the last day of witnesses for the prosecution, it is difficult to see what order there has been. No doubt they were in the first place put down in an order that matched the development of the prosecution case. But that, for one reason or another—we have been told from time to time that a witness was not available—is not the order in which they turned up.

In fact to me they seem to have turned up higgledy-piggledy, presenting one with random bits of a mosaic that might suit a McLuhanite or the producer of trendy radio or television programmes, but does not suit anyone, e.g. me, trying to find his way through the case. Finding one's way through a case is a 'linear' activity—and extremely hard work into the bargain.

However, there has been a weekend in which to freshen up. And in parallel with diminishing excitement from the stream of prosecution witnesses—though, goodness knows, even the last one produced a surprising fact—there has been an augmenting excitement. What *is* the defence going to be? What on earth *can* it be?

The handwriting expert is a Principal Scientific Officer from the Metropolitan Police Laboratory, Mr Fryd. Ten years' experience. More damning forensic evidence against Arthur Hosein, no doubt. We bend our minds to learning how handwriting characteristics are identified, so far as they can be, by comparison of 'authentic' documents with 'questioned' documents. As this must have a weaker scientific basis than fingerprintery, we can hope—as it turns out, rightly—for less godlike confidence.

Mr Fryd talks of 'considerable probability'. However, he begins by making a modest score with his opinion, independently expressed in advance, that the handwriting of Shariff Mustapha at County Hall was Nizam's. Mr Fryd has only just returned from the U.S.A. and been made aware that Nizam has now admitted it. He laughs with amusement. He is a straight-backed middle-aged man with very arched eyebrows and a long nose. He holds his spectacles in his hands, waiting.

Examined by Mr Leary, Mr Fryd goes through the documents and passes incidental comments that make sense as soon as one thinks about it: that everybody's handwriting shows some variations whose extent, on a sort of statistical basis, can be categorised as normal and abnormal. The latter can be involuntary, due to the emotional state of the writer at the time, or voluntary, as in the case of deliberate disguising.

In the angry letter to the editor of *The News Of The World*—
OFF SAINT MARY
HE HAS NOT PAID ∧ FOR ∧ HOUSE—Mr Fryd is quite sure of persistent disguise. There are sufficient traces of the natural handwriting for him to compare it with Arthur's. 'There is so much careful, slow, deliberate disguise,' he says, 'that I couldn't compare it with anyone's handwriting.'

Mr Leary: 'So the disguise was successful?' Mr Fryd: 'Yes.'

(This means there may be a degree of privacy still left for the rest of us—but not for Arthur Hosein, because of the ingenious exhibit which consists of a normal photograph of the letter overlaid by a transparent photograph of indentations on a sheet of paper from the cardboard box in Nizam's bedroom.)

In cross-examining the expert Mr Hudson adopts a technique parallel with the one that paid dividends with the fingerprint expert, eroding the prosecution's case by reducing the degree of probability with which the handwriting on a 'questioned' document can be identified with that on an 'authentic' document. Again Mr Hudson takes up x points and challenges y of them. However, he begins with a semantic gambit.

'I notice that the words you used when you gave an opinion were "considerable probability". My suggestion is that the opinion should be put: "There is *reasonable doubt* that the same person wrote the authentic document and the questioned documents, but one cannot exclude the *possibility* that they were written by the same person." '

Mr Fryd: 'A very peculiar way of putting things. When one begins putting documents together there's always a reasonable doubt.'

'That is so,' says Mr Hudson, and repeats his suggestion.

Mr Fryd protests: 'It still puts the cart before the horse. Always reasonable doubt comes first. If reasonable doubt is increased . . .'

'Of course there is reasonable doubt when you start. *After* you've compared the documents, the reasonable doubt may be reduced.'

'If you've said there's a reasonable probability, there must be reasonable doubt.'

Mr Hudson: 'If there were no reasonable doubt I should not have said there was reasonable probability; as, for example, in the case of certain documents written by Mrs McKay and Nizam.'

Mr Hudson goes further with a question about comparison of Nizam's handwriting with the handwriting 'on certain documents', a question whose gist I do not gather—it is explained by the Judge to Mr Fryd, whose answer makes Mr Hudson's gambit only too clear.

'I didn't think anyone could possibly suggest, knowing Nizam's handwriting, could suggest he'd written the ransom notes and the instructions.'

(Nizam's admissions, through his counsel, have obviously put Arthur in the cart. To me it looks as if they have put both of them in the cart, come to that. I was wondering if Arthur, through his counsel, would try to put Nizam in the cart—and what protocol between the two defending counsel would govern it.)

The Judge says to Mr Fryd: 'You exclude Nizam's having written the ransom notes, and the instructions?' Mr Fryd is strongly inclined to do so.

Mr Hudson: 'Could they possibly have been written by Nizam?' The Judge intervenes: 'I know nothing of Nizam as a man. In making that writing (on the application form and on the note for Adam) Nizam was making no effort to disguise his handwriting. If he has practised writing his brother's handwriting, then it is possible that as a skilled forger he could deceive a handwriting expert.'

Mr Fryd looks neutral. At such times he has a habit of twiddling his spectacles between his fingers. Mr Hudson points out: 'You have agreed that the ransom notes were written by someone trying to disguise his handwriting.' Mr Fryd: 'To disguise, not to simulate.'

Mr Hudson returns to Arthur: 'You have not expressed an opinion that Arthur Hosein wrote those questioned documents?'

'I've said there is a considerable probability that he did.'

'There is a great difference.'—'Oh, yes.'

(It occurs to me that in all these discussions of probability and doubt, only a literary assessment, 'considerable', is used. Probability is a mathematical concept: is it possible for handwriting experts to go in for at least some quantification—or for the court to be prepared to listen to assessment even in the laymans terms of 'odds'? Or would that lead to more dangerous arguments from a legal point of view?)

Mr Hudson is going on about the absence of specimens of Arthur's handwriting *not* under strained circumstances, i.e. in the police station. Mr Fryd points out that under conditions of crime a man is writing under stress: therefore it is useful to see specimens of writing under stress as well as under normal conditions.

At this point Mr Hudson gets down to detail, as he did with the fingerprint expert. It goes on for ages. He floats the idea of a handwriting's being 'nondescript' or 'characterless', and therefore not indicative. He takes to comparing the thickness of strokes, the width of loops, the shape of tails. At last he concludes:

'I don't want to go through another number of letters. I'm not likely to get you to change your opinion.' Mr Fryd: 'I'd change it if I saw cause to.'

As Mr Hudson sits down, his Lordship gives him a passing smile and then says:

'It's so obvious that nobody has asked it—what about change of slope?'

So we're off again! However, the interchange is short, and Mr Draycott rises. 'Till 9.40 this morning you didn't know that Nizam had made these admissions?'—'No.'

'In your view, about the Greater London Council document Nizam is telling the truth?'—'Yes.'

'About the note of the Minivan number found in his trouser pocket, Nizam is telling the truth?'—'Yes.'

Then about the ransom letters. 'As one expert,' Mr Draycott says, 'from the expert's standpoint, the suggestion that the handwriting could be Nizam's borders on the ludicrous?'

Mr Fryd (smiling): 'Well, it borders on the ludicrous.'

Mr Draycott sits down. Truthful Nizam! (I am fascinated by the artless way in which counsel try to establish in the eyes of the jury the truthfulness or untruthfulness of a witness, as if either were a 100% thing. Surely a jury can't be so simple as not to know that everyone speaks the truth on some occasions and lies on others?)

The last forensic expert has appeared in the witness-box, a young woman, a Senior Scientific Officer in the Metropolitan Laboratory. She is the expert in identifying paper—so we move from fingerprintery and calligraphics to physics and chemistry, a very different cup of tea. She has examined the paper of which the relevant documents are composed, measuring the weight per unit area, the thickness and the spacing of lines and margins. She has done colormetric tests, identifying the dyes used in variegated Kleenex tissues. And she has compared the staple marks and the profile of torn edges on the letter to the editor of *The News Of The World* with those on the sheet of paper taken by the police from the box in Nizam's bedroom. Within the limits of error in her experiments the results all confirm the Crown case.

Mr Hudson asks his Lordship if Mrs Mohammed may be recalled. He questions her about part of her written statement: *On the 1st January we watched TV in the afternoon and early evening. Nizam had stomach-ache and went out for an hour and a half to get tablets.* He asks: 'Was it early evening as opposed to afternoon?'

M3 telephoned Arthur Road at 7.45 p.m. and 7.49 p.m. The nearest time Mr Hudson can get from Liley is afternoon, between 2 p.m. and 6 p.m.

Attorney General: 'When Nizam came back did he speak of tablets?' Liley: 'I was very upset by his going out.'

The Judge (kindly): 'You were cross with him?'—'Yes.'

Mr Draycott: 'You were furious that he'd gone out and left you alone with Arthur?'—'Yes.'

(Are they satisfied with these answers? I am not.)

The prosecution witnesses really are near the end. We have now only supplementary police evidence. First from Detective Sergeant Parker, who has sat in court with Chief Superintendent Smith and Inspector Minors. He was responsible for collecting the exhibits and has remained in charge of them. A biggish man, likeably open-faced—he is the man around whose neck Nizam, in one of his breakdowns into weeping, flung his arms. He is also the man who should have collected the 2½ in. Elastoplast tin off the radiogram at Rook's Farm; and he, as well as his detective inspector, nobly takes the blame for it.

The Attorney General asks for Inspector Minors to return to the witness-box. Mr Minors confirms that when, on the 22nd April, Arthur and Nizam were charged with the further offences, i.e. Counts 2–7, Arthur said:

'I am innocent of all these charges. All those charges are false.'

Nizam said: 'I know nothing about these charges.'

The Attorney General announces the end of the Crown case.

But all is not finished. Mr Hudson has something more to say. He stands up and tells his Lordship that he wants to make a submission in the absence of the jury.

6

The crunch

Once again the jury are sent out. It is the end of a short day, so they get their usual advice from his Lordship about how to comport themselves outside the court. Then Mr Hudson, with Mr Draycott associated with him, makes a submission:

That on Count 1, murder, in the circumstances of the evidence before the jury the case should not proceed further.

As on the previous occasion when the jury was sent out, the proceedings change into a more committee-like form—acute professional minds at work, governed nonetheless by the Judge but freed from some of the protocol to get the work done more quickly between themselves. The whole discussion takes place in the presence of the accused men: nothing happens behind their backs. And this particular legal issue is the crunch for them: Are they to be up for murder?

Mr Hudson, law-book in hand, cites the main sources on which he bases his claim. The gist of them is that a case may proceed if the existence of a *corpus delicti* can be proved by some circumstantial evidence; or if circumstantial evidence is so cogent and compelling as to convince a jury that no other rational hypothesis than murder can account for it.

Mr Hudson reiterates that what became of Mrs McKay is on the evidence the basis not for rational hypothesis but only for speculation. 'There is a *prima facie* case, I agree, that she is dead. But I submit there is not one scintilla of evidence that she was at Rook's Farm or met her death at Rook's Farm.' From that he branches into two arguments: (i) that there is no evidence to say whether indeed her death was violent or *accidental*, (ii) that the proposition that she did *not* meet her death at Rook's Farm implies that other people are involved.

Over the first argument his Lordship points out that there is *prima facie* evidence that Arthur Hosein was involved in kidnapping and that the kidnappers had written, 'If you don't pay, we execute her', and 'We've got her and will exchange her for £1,000,000' up to the 6th February. Thus on (i) there is evidence for the jury to investigate as to whether they did or did not carry out their threat. On (ii) his Lordship, hypothetically conceding that other people were involved, points out that it is nevertheless a plot to kidnap in which there is evidence of the Hoseins being involved; that is to say there is evidence of its being a joint enterprise which, however many other people may have been involved, still gives cause for the jury to investigate the part played by the Hoseins.

Mr Draycott, who has been whispering to his junior, now joins in, to emphasise that Mrs McKay could not have been at Rook's Farm, but somewhere else; meanwhile Arthur and Nizam, according to the evidence of Liley, were most of the time at Rook's Farm.

The Judge listens. He looks at them.

There is no other rational hypothesis, he tells them, than that those who abducted Mrs McKay are responsible for the fact that she is not on this earth. There is a case for the jury to consider Count 1.

So the Hosein brothers are up for murder. The question that has preoccupied every layman—'How can they be convicted of murder if there's no body?'—has got as far as being answered with, 'They *can*.'

In the dock the two dark-faced men, never, never looking at each other, sit listening, watching, hearing. . . . If I were they I should not like the sound of it.

7

Opening speech for the defence

(*Arthur Hosein*)

22nd September, *morning*

'Members of the jury, there is a great deal more evidence in this case than you have already heard.'

So begins Mr Hudson in the defence of Arthur Hosein. He leans a little forward towards the jury: though he avoids a rhetorical flourish, the opening sentence has a commanding note. The three women and nine men who represent us all look nothing if not attentive: they are commanded.

The effect of hearing the prosecution's case may be to make one think 'They've done it!'; the effect of hearing the defence is certainly to shake one. That is how it should be—that is how the whole thing works.

Mr Hudson issues the usual warning—not without cause, if one has been keeping up with newspaper headlines. 'You decide this case on what you hear in this court and nowhere else.' And the issues, he goes on to tell them, are not whether the crimes have been committed, but has the Crown proved either of the men is involved? '*Proved*,' he says, pausing, 'not by way of speculation; but on proper evidence.

'Arthur Hosein's defence,' he says, 'is that he had nothing to do with this dreadful crime at all!'

Nothing at all! After Nizam's admissions, how on earth can this be made sense of? One feels stunned.

Mr Hudson asserts this is what Arthur has said from the beginning, from the moment when he was taken to the police station without arrest or charge, and held for four days—while the police were trying to find evidence—before the charge was laid. 'Four days,' he says, hitting the small folding desk he uses as lectern and receptacle for papers. (Several counsel on the front row use such desks, which have a slightly gimcrack look, as if they may collapse when hit for emphasis.)

Arthur Hosein denies his guilt. It is not enough to say that. In support of his protestation of innocence, the most important part of the case, *he* will go into the witness-box, though he is not compelled to. Automatically everyone glances up at the dock where Arthur sits, thoughtfully, his hand cupping his chin. He is dressed for this day in a black suit and a white shirt.

Mr Hudson takes off his spectacles and continues. 'He may make errors. What he said to the police officers may not be exactly the same as what he says today.' Mr Hudson asks the jury to consider Arthur's predicament, *if* he is innocent, being rushed to the police station. 'I might ask you,' he says, giving each member of the jury in turn a friendly eagle-like glance, 'What did *you* do on December the 29th?'

Whoever it was who engineered this crime, Mr Hudson says, were obviously acting from before 6 p.m. on the 29th December. They were men with heavy matters on their minds. He pauses. Then he exhorts the jury to keep on asking themselves time after time: 'Is she dead? If she is dead, where did she die? And above all, if she is dead, *how* did she die?'

Mr Hudson develops the argument he put to the Judge, when submitting that the charge of murder should be dropped—the prosecution's fruitless search for forensic evidence of Mrs McKay. 'Not a single piece of evidence, even flimsy, can be brought to this trial after so long and detailed an investigation,' he says. 'During the period of remand, no evidence was produced in court week after week. We know Mrs McKay was alive at 8.50 p.m. on the 30th December—because of the reference to her daughter being heard on television. Less than twenty-four hours later Mrs Mohammed arrives, pressed to come. She stays, is allowed to wander round. . . . Certainly Mrs McKay, whether dead or alive, was not at Rook's Farm when this young woman came to stay.'

He now suggests the necessity of looking at Arthur Hosein's life right up to the moment of his arrest. Lucidly he explains the rôle of the advocate in assisting justice from whichever side he acts. The way a trial works is by *both* sides putting their arguments. So far the jury have heard only *one* side, the prosecution's. Now they are going to hear the other side. When both sides have been thus presented: 'You can go away and say "We've heard everything said by the Crown, and everything said by these two men in their defence." Then you can reach your conclusion.'

He sketches out Arthur's life. A tailor who has lived here for fifteen years—when we come to analysis of the tape-recordings and accents, for example the telephone operator was impressed by an American accent; and the instruction was to go to a *gas*-station, whereas Arthur says *petrol*-station. Arthur has a good house: he is a good tailor. He has out-workers, finishers, etc. He is married to a German lady who will go into the witness-box. There are two children. In the course of business he goes into London and collects articles and pays for work done. (Eight shillings a time!) He has a good job, and to all intents and purposes he is – 'unlike some people on trial' – a man of good character. He has been court-martialled for desertion from the Army and has convictions for speeding; but there is never any indication of dishonesty or violence. No dishonesty, *no violence*.

On the 13th December Mrs Hosein went to Germany with the children. The two brothers were alone at the Farm. The girl nurse was telephoned to come and look after them.

So we come to December 29th. 'Arthur Hosein will tell you that he never went to London, let alone to Wimbledon, at all.' The evidence is that Arthur was ill at the time—he had a cold. In the afternoon he and his brother visited a farmer nearby, at about 3 p.m. If the jury are satisfied he was at that Farm then, it is not an alibi that he was not at Wimbledon at 5 p.m. But Arthur will say that because he was not well he went back home and went to bed. During the course of the evening Liley telephoned on two occasions without getting a reply, but on the third, at 10.30 p.m., the telephone was answered by Arthur.

'The explanation is that he'd gone to bed. Nizam had been using the telephone downstairs and so the bell in the bedroom was switched off.'

An enquiry agent has examined the telephone and will tell us that the bell downstairs cannot be heard in the bedroom.

That night Nizam left the house at 8.30 p.m. and Arthur does not know where he went. At 10.30 Arthur was on the telephone; he will say that on that day he never left the district, never left the Farm except to visit Farmer Pateman at 3 p.m.

Turning to the 1st January, there was an alleged telephone call to Arthur Road ending at 7.45 p.m. and a second call ending at 7.49 p.m. 'You will be satisfied,' Mr Hudson says to the jury, 'those calls were not made by Arthur Hosein. Mrs Mohammed says that on that day Arthur never left the Farm at all.'

There is no evidence of any call from Rook's Farm to Arthur Road. Whoever made them, wherever they were made, those two telephone calls to Arthur Road were not from Rook's Farm —Liley says *Nizam* left the Farm at some time between 2 p.m. and 6 p.m. when he went out to get tablets for his stomach-ache.

Between the 6th January and the 6th February we know Arthur was going about his business, to all intents and purposes going on with his normal life. Mr Hudson reiterates his earlier remark emphatically and with gravity:

'Whoever these evil-doers were, they were men with a great deal on their minds.'

The next important date is the 1st February.

'Now on the 1st February, whoever came to collect the money; whoever telephoned to the police officers, disguised as the chauffeur and Ian McKay, on the way; whoever wrote the instructions on the Piccadilly cigarette packet—saw that a trap had been set. As it happened the number of the vehicle was not taken by the police.' Mr Hudson pauses. 'Whoever was M3 was bold enough, foolhardy enough to fall into another trap!'

(This reminds me of what had crossed my mind when we covered the ground for the first time—the *luck* of the police! They set one trap, if that is what it can be called, and their man side-stepped and they missed him. They set another, almost identical; and he fell into it! Extraordinary hopefulness on one side; crazy greed on the other.)

On the 1st February, Mr Hudson says, Arthur went to London and left Nizam there. Arthur returned to Hertfordshire. Nizam was still out and did not return till about midnight, when he disturbed the household by coming in soaking wet. There was a row and Arthur ticked him off next morning. Arthur never went near Dane End or High Cross.

On the 6th February the independent witnesses for the Crown

are supported by the defence witnesses, over Arthur's movements at the public house. He hands Nizam the car, goes to the pub, and then spends a jolly evening with the television actor and his two girl friends.

'According to the evidence, at 9.0–9.30 p.m. Arthur is in the pub, drinking a good deal, emphasising that he is waiting for Nizam; while Nizam is driving around, looking at two suitcases—Nizam slows down but a motor horn sounds behind him and he drives away.'

Mr Hudson invites the jury to picture one brother tense, so tense that he jumps when a horn is blown; the other brother relaxed, 'with not a worry in the world'. When Nizam came, Arthur will tell us, he himself begged the others to stay and drink. If the Crown is right he was thinking only of a million pounds! The actor refused to stay and Arthur will say he went home with Nizam and never did drive around the area known as Gates Garage as alleged.

'You will listen with care,' says Mr Hudson, 'to what Arthur has to say. There are many other matters of evidence that I'm going to call up in support of his evidence.'

Mr Hudson pauses, and changes tone. 'There is one other matter—with reference to the tactics of m'learned colleague, Mr Draycott. It may be one's unpleasant duty on behalf of one brother to make suggestions and allegations against the other. You may have felt when Mr Draycott rose to his feet, before the Crown said a word, apart from the Attorney General's opening; you may have heard with surprise, from a man who's pleaded Not Guilty, the admissions that (i) Nizam went to the G.L.C. about the car ULO 18F, (ii) he planted paper flowers at Dane End, and (iii) he drove around Gates Garage.... You may think this a strong indication that Nizam was taking part in some of M3's activities—it has been crying out from the moment the admissions were made. But the case against Nizam is in the hands of the Crown. I don't know what Mr Draycott's case is going to be.'

(So Mr Hudson does not know what Mr Draycott's case is going to be? To a non-legal person it gives the defence a very peculiar twist. From the first day it had looked as if something were afoot. Against Arthur the alleged forensic evidence is very damning: he replies by denying everything. Against Nizam there is no forensic evidence, so, as the lawyers put it, 'He's got a run'. That 'run', though goodness knows what it can be, will be Mr Draycott's business.)

Mr Hudson is coming to his peroration, warning the jury that it is early days to make up their minds. If they do not feel there is a possibility of changing their minds it is because of a view that has already set in. Mr Hudson reminds them that evidence of fingerprints and handwriting will have to be debated. Also the writing-paper: 'The mere fact, I submit to you, that you are satisfied that the writing-paper belongs to Arthur Hosein because it is similar to paper kept in Nizam's room, doesn't mean that *he* was the person who posted that letter.' He pauses. 'We, on behalf of this man's defence, do mean to deal fully with the forensic side, the alleged fingerprints and handwriting. They'll *have* to be dealt with.' He stops.

'The point now is to hear that man'—with his spectacles in his hand he points to the dock—'tell his story. I call him!'

8

Arthur Hosein

We all look at the dock, where a warder is opening the side door. Arthur Hosein goes down the steps, walks past the long table in the well of the court, and ascends the steps into the witness-box. He is smaller than I thought, seeing him on high in the dock. And for the occasion he has selected a slightly peculiar garb—at first sight it looks as if he is in a dinner-suit. It is black, single breasted, with a U-shaped waistcoat that displays a bulging white expanse of chest under a black bow-tie. But the collar and cuffs of the white shirt are black with white polka dots. 'Selected' is the correct word: he has appeared in a different suit every day, and is reported to own fifty suits. (How does he keep *that* up, as well as Rook's Farm, the Volvo, and all the rest?) We have already heard of his boastfulness; his appearance makes one suspect that he is vain.

In the witness-box he stands a moment under the shadow of the light oak canopy and against the dreary background of light oak, his hand to his face, touching his moustache. The black and white collar makes it difficult to see which is his neck and which is his shirt. He gives his profession.

'Fashion designer, cutter, etc.'

We hear details about his coming to this country in 1955; buying Rook's Farm on a mortgage. Mr Hudson asks him to take his hand away from his mouth. Details about the German lady to whom he has been married for ten years, having known her for fifteen years; and about his brother coming to stay with them in August 1969.

Mr Hudson asks him about his business. 'Because of S.E.T.,' Arthur says, favouring us straight away with political opinion, 'I closed my shop.'—'That's why you opened the work-room?'

—'Precisely.' Arthur's speech is rapid and fluent, nervous—with a constant hint of the provocative.

Details of his business practices. Mr Hudson asks if trade was slack at Christmas.

'I am well known,' he says haughtily. Then adds: 'But in general I do get slack.'

Details of Mrs Hosein's going away on 13 December, no special date for return apart from the children's schooling. Mr Hudson says: 'How were you feeling at Christmas?'

'Good heavens, under the weather! I had a bad chest. My outlooks don't show the suffering inside.'

'Where did you spend Christmas Day?'—'At home in Hertfordshire.'—'You'd heard of Mrs Mohammed?' Arthur smiles momentarily: 'Yes.'

The details of Monday 29th. 'My usual, awake between 11 and 12' (His usual: is he a 'night person'?) 'I had a terrible cold. There was a 'flu epidemic.' Nizam was up, it was his duty to look after the animals.—'Did you go out?'

Arthur: 'I buy milk by bulk, so I keep calves—to get rid of the milk. Nizam said we had too much milk, could we have more calves? I didn't mind, said the fresh air might do me good. So we went to Pateman's farm, between 2.30 and 3.30.' Later: 'After Nizam and Pateman put the calf in the boot of the car we went back to Rook's Farm.'

'How long does it take from Pateman's to Rook's Farm?'—'Half an hour. But when there's a young calf in the boot it takes longer.'

(A live calf in the boot of the Volvo. . . .)

'What then?' Mr Hudson asks. Arthur: 'I told Nizam to take care of the rest.'

Mr Hudson asks him again if he will take his hand away from his mouth. Arthur: 'Well, I'm a bit nervy.' (By the way, his voice is deepish, but not noticeably so.)

And then? 'Mr Coote telephoned between 5.15 and 5.30. I advised Nizam to take any telephone calls about business. I don't want to take them: Nizam can take them. I take the call from David as a colleague. Nizam came in and told me it's Mr Coote, so I spoke to Mr Coote.'

The Judge verifies this piece of evidence, and Mr Draycott

makes a note of it. 5.30 on the evening of the kidnapping. If it's true this really is an alibi. *If.*

Mr Coote, Arthur's solicitor, a tall bespectacled young man, is sitting in court just below Mr Hudson, at the long table.

Mr Hudson: 'What did you do for the rest of the evening?' Arthur: 'I told him who David Coote was.'—'Did your brother stay?'—'After making me something to eat, coffee and biscuits.'—'Did your brother stay in the house?'—'I bid him goodnight at 7.30. I took up a bottle of scotch and ginger ale to my bedroom, closed the door. There was I.'

There was Arthur. And very grand he sounds, at that. Mr Hudson says:

'Did you go to the toilet?' (After The Raven, everyone in court uses the plebeian word 'toilet'.)—'Yes. At about 9.45.'—'Did you notice from the toilet window what had happened to the car?' Arthur: 'It was not there.'

'When you went to bed, did you do something with the telephone? Someone rang up?' Arthur: 'Yes, yes. I knew who it was, at about eight o'clock. I pressed the bell button to switch off the bell, for Nizam to answer downstairs.'

Mr Hudson (patiently following the procedure): 'Did you later switch on the bell?' Arthur: 'After I'd been to the toilet I tried to telephone my wife in Germany, saying I was not well, to ask her to come home. I spoke to my brother-in-law.'

Mr Hudson: 'At 10.30 Mrs Mohammed telephoned and you answered.' Arthur: 'I thought it was my wife.'

'When did you fall asleep?'—'I don't know.'—'Did you check if the car was there?'—'No.'

That is the end of Arthur's day on the 29th. There was he, so to speak. Mr Hudson moves on to the 30th December.

'Did anyone call at the Farm that day?'

Arthur thinks—he seems disturbed. 'I woke up at about 11.30.' Mr Hudson (persisting): 'Did anyone come to the Farm?' Arthur: 'I can't remember. I've had a very strenuous time, kept in captivity twenty-three hours a day.' His tone conveys both anger and paranoia. 'I *can't* remember!'

Mr Hudson reminds him of the 31st, when they collected Mrs Mahommed in the car to come to the Farm. On the 1st

January, she says he, Arthur, never left the Farm. Can he recall Nizam leaving the Farm? (The stomach-ache incident.)

Arthur: 'I think he mentioned a bit of fresh air. I can't give the precise time.'

The Judge: 'Did he go out of the house?' Arthur (grandly): 'The driveway is 200 yards.'

Mr Hudson: 'We know the Farm has fourteen acres, so there was no need to leave the Farm. Do you know where he went?' Arthur (now high and mightily): 'He could do as he wishes.'

Mr Hudson comes back yet again to telephone calls. 'We know a number of telephone calls were made to Wimbledon in January and February.' (Arthur has heard the transcripts read out by the Attorney General.) 'I have two questions: Did you make any telephone calls to Wimbledon?'

Arthur: 'I made no telephone calls to anyone at any time.'

The Judge: 'Do you mean that? Not even on business?'

Arthur: 'I don't make telephone calls on business. My wife makes them.'

Mr Hudson, with his second question: 'Did you hear anyone in your house telephoning, and using words like that in your house?'

Arthur (from behind his hand and dropping his voice): 'Well, sometimes . . . I might be wrong about these telephone . . .'

The Judge asks him to take his hand down. Arthur: 'I'm a bit edgy at the moment.'

The Judge, repeating the question: 'You said you heard something?'

Arthur (looking down): 'I believe that during the absence of my wife . . . No, I never heard anyone using my telephone, or any voices. Apart from the voices of four men whom I met on those occasions . . .'

It is difficult to catch the whole of what he says, but it is enough to make everyone in court sit up. Mr Hudson presses him.

Arthur: 'I have to be frank. But if I hadn't been so badly treated by Smith'—he sends a glance of pure hatred at the Chief Superintendent sitting below him at the long table—'they'd have found out.'

So we hear the story of an introduction, 'a compulsory introduction', at 2.0 a.m. while his wife was in Germany.

Arthur: 'I heard voices. I was drinking heavily. I sleep in my shorts. I thought it was the TV so I went down to switch it off. When I have been downstairs I saw there four men with my brother. I think one was British, one American, two French'—faint smile—'Maurice Chevalier sort of talk.'

Mr Hudson asks if his brother said who they were.

Arthur: 'My brother said to me these men have influence in the House of Parliament and could use their influence to get him a permanent stay in this country.'

Mr Hudson asks if he had any conversation with them.

Arthur: 'No. I don't make friends very easy. I'm hard to get to know. They offered me a drink of my own whisky. I said goodnight—I was embarrassed, in my shorts.'

The Judge asks if this was before Christmas. 'Yes.'

Mr Hudson: 'Did you ever see those men again?'

'During the early part of the morning on two other occasions. At 1.30 or 2.0 a.m.'

'Soon after the first time?'

'After Christmas I saw these men for the last time once.' He looks distracted again. 'This happened quite a long time ago. . . . This is the first time I've been called upon to recall my movements.'

(When the case began the external circumstances of the crime contained an element of sheer fantasy. Now sheer fantasy has been introduced into the internal circumstances of it. Can anybody in the court, one asks oneself, believe it? Yet is it more fantastic than some of the things we already know we have to believe?)

Mr Hudson refers to the policeman whom Arthur invited to come shooting over the Farm at the time of Mrs McKay's disappearance. 'Anyone interested in shooting and gaming,' Arthur says, 'I am quite enthusiastic.'

Mr Hudson asks about the local Master of Foxhounds hunting over the Farm.

Arthur: 'He did quite a lot of destruction.'

Mr Hudson: 'Did you give him permission to hunt over your land?'

'Yes. After Christmas.' (He smiles.) 'I said: "Do as you like, but don't bring down my buildings!" '

Now we come to Farmer Smith, he of the billhook, or bill—B, I, double L. The visit to the caravan on 27th December, at which Mr Smith said he did not converse with the brothers. Arthur: 'He made a considerable sum of money from me.' And then: 'He came into the caravan and said he'd had 'flu. I was drinking his brandy.'

'He did come in and sit down and talk to you in the caravan?'—'Good heavens, yes.' (One gets the feeling that there is no love lost between Farmer Smith and Arthur—does that bear on the evidence?)

Mr Hudson: 'From the 6th January on, did you carry on your business as usual?' Arthur: 'I see no reason, why shouldn't I?'

End of that. On to 1st February, paper flowers at Dane End. Mr Hudson: 'Did anyone visit the Farm on Sunday 1st February?'

Arthur thinks, clasping his hands together. 'Yes, yes. Gerald Gordon and family. They left at about six o'clock.'—'You've heard Mr Rosenthal give evidence?'—'As Gerry Gordon was about to leave, Rosenthal arrived. Six o'clock.'

'Did you expect him?'—'During the earlier part of the day I'd been in court for a speeding offence. He or my wife telephoned each other about an order.'—'Did you know the reason for his visit?'—'He is a business colleague. My door is open at any time! . . . Some sort of business.'

Almost everything Arthur says displays something about his personality, in its extraordinarily fluid combination of the grandiose and the over-sensitive, the haughty and the uncertain, the boastful and the suspicious. Time after time a question seems to touch him in one place and the response to spring out somewhere else—*not* as an answer to the question. Is it hysteria; is it cunning; is it what? The police, one can guess, will certainly think it is cunning: cunning is what their professional training focuses them on combating. But the intimations of hysteria are strong. We wait.

Back to Mr Rosenthal's visit. Arthur: 'He came to deliver the items this court has seen.' (The big parcel.) Mr Rosenthal said he came on spec to get an order. It is all very puzzling, since it appears not to make any difference in either case. There comes a voluble account from Arthur of what he said to Rosenthal.

Mr Hudson: 'Before you left did Mr Rosenthal give you any cigarettes?' Arthur: 'Rosenthal held up a packet. I took one, and dropped the packet on the bar in the lounge. They were Piccadilly tipped.' (Haughty, not to say cool!)

Mr Hudson studies the detail of the trip to London to the finishers: the schedule is important because of the M3 calls directing the ransom bringer ultimately to Dane End, calls at 9.55 p.m. and 10.45 p.m., and the Volvo was seen at Dane End at 11.45 p.m.

Arthur and Nizam left Rook's Farm soon after six. The Judge asks how long the journey took to the first finisher. Three-quarters of an hour.

Arthur confirms that Nizam borrowed money to telephone. 'My brother suggested on the journey he would like to see his girl friend. I think he borrowed sixpence to telephone his girl friend.'

The last finisher they visited was at Hackney Wick, at 7.50 p.m. After that there was the incident when Arthur sent Nizam into a pub to buy him some cigarettes.

'I gave him a note and asked him to get Stuyvesant.'

'What did he do?'—'I waited for ten minutes, circulated, assumed he'd gone to his girl friend.' Then: 'I know my brother can find his way home, so I went home.'

Arthur says he went down the A11—Dane End is on the A10—getting back at 9.15. His wife said Rosenthal had left at 9.0 and had dropped some material.

Mr Hudson: 'What time did you go to bed? Arthur: 'I sat in the lounge, had a drink, I'm enthusiastic about news—saw the ten o'clock News. Then we both went to bed.'

Mrs Hosein was worried about Nizam. 'I said "He's old enough. He has money." ' (Actually we have so far only heard of Nizam asking for, or being supplied with, money.) Nizam returned at midnight, disturbing the house. 'His clothing was wet. I said "Take off your clothes or you'll get pneumonia!" '

Mr Hudson: 'Did you question him?' Arthur: 'No. I didn't want to provoke him.'

Later Nizam's story comes out: he telephoned Liley, who was not in, so he hitch-hiked home.

'My wife was furious because I didn't give him a stern

warning. He is twelve years my junior, a stranger in a strange land. My duty is to protect him. I didn't want to provoke him. But all the while I had considerable concern about him in this country.'

"A stranger in a strange land." The phrase caught everyone's attention.

We pass on to the 6th February. (M3 calls the telephone kiosk in Church Street, Tottenham, at 4.45 p.m., in Bethnal Green at 6.0 p.m., in Epping at 7.30 p.m. Nizam is at Gates Garage at 9.0 p.m.)

Arthur and Nizam delivered goods to the tailors that afternoon. Arthur interrupts himself to say to the Judge: 'I've said I made no telephone calls. I meant for the ransom. I made calls about business.'

They went to Percy Chaplin at Bethnal Green at about 4.30 p.m. Mr Hudson: 'How long were you there?'

Arthur: 'About half an hour. His Mum made a cup of tea.' (His '*Mum*'—an echo from the transcripts.)

Then they made for home. 'On the A11. The traffic was very congested.' Nizam was in the car on the way to Bishop's Stortford. 'My brother said he would like to see a girl friend in Bishop's Stortford. I said you might as well have the car—let him have a bit of enjoyment! I took a taxi. My brother didn't tell me the name of his girl friend.' (We know it was the mythical 'Susie'.)

They made their arrangements. 'I said I meant to go to the pub. I said to him, "If you finish your enjoyment by closing time, pick me up." Otherwise I would walk home. It is only fifteen minutes' walk.'

Mr Hudson: 'What time did you arrive at The Raven?'

'I shall remember to my dying day! It was very cold. I sat at the front of the taxi. Between seven o'clock and five past seven.'

Mr Hudson asks about going to the toilet. Arthur: 'To be polite I joined the publican in the public bar. I must explain exactly what happened. I ordered a drink, and asked to use the toilet. I observed that there were no lights, and drew the attention of the publican to it. He switched on the lights and waited. When I'd finished, he switched them off.'

'Did you go to the toilet again?'—'I must have. At about 9.30.'—'Any question of going to telephone?'—'Good heavens, no! I had no cause.'

'There is a call-box, 100 yards away.'—'I don't use a call-box. I use the telephone in my home or in private friends'.'

Mr Hudson: 'Are the call-boxes in your area S.T.D., or the old-fashioned Button A and B kind?' Arthur: 'I wouldn't know because I am not an enthusiast.'

'What time did your brother arrive?'—'If the witnesses say ten o'clock, I agree. It was of no importance to me.'

'Did you invite your actor friend to stay?'—'I enjoy his company more than my brother's. So I tried to persuade him and his friends to stay.'

'How much did you have to drink that night?'—'Ten or eleven double scotches.'

'Is that exceptional?'—'No, no . . .'

Mr Hudson: 'Your friends left. You left with Nizam?' Arthur: 'I just mentioned it. My brother is less talkative to me.' The Judge rebukes him for the remark. 'I asked my brother if he had enjoyed himself. I offered him a drink.'—'Did he have one?'—'Yes.'

'After that?'—'I said you might as well drive me home.'

'Did he?'—'Yes.'—'Do you remember what time it was?'—'I have to. I believe it is essential. My life depends on it. He carried me home . . .'

Mr Hudson: 'What time, Mr Hosein, did you leave The Raven?'—'At 10.20.'

'What time did the pub close?'—'Eleven o'clock.'

'Your brother drove you home. What happened then?'—'My brother drove me home. I said goodnight . . .'

The Judge: 'After all that drink, are you able to tell us?'

Arthur: 'Yes.' He goes on. 'My wife was in bed already. I said, Good heavens . . .'

Mr Hudson: 'Do you know what Nizam did?'—'After I bid him goodnight, no.'

There are questions over the landlord's wife having said, in her evidence, that he asked her to give him change, in pennies. 'I don't think it's true,' Arthur says. 'No.'

Mr Hudson comes back to Farmer Smith, his identifying the

billhook which he says he lost at Rook's Farm. Arthur says: 'I think that is his own theory.'

Mr Hudson: 'He told us about when he went to London to sign a paper, saying he was going to employ your brother on his farm. You say you gave him £20.'—'Yes.'—'He says you didn't.'

Arthur: 'No farmers do anything for nothing.'

The Judge says: 'He says you took him to a Chinese restaurant and you borrowed £1 to pay the bill.' Arthur denies it vehemently.

Mr Hudson asks for Arthur to be handed Exhibit 5, a billhook. Arthur handles it possibly with interest, certainly not with revulsion: he touches the blade casually.

Mr Hudson: 'Can you identify it?'

Arthur: 'No, I can't really.'

The Judge: 'You *couldn't*. . . . It's the one taken from St Mary House!'

Mr Hudson now asks for him to be handed the other billhook (taken by the police from the Rook's Farm kitchen on 7th February). Arthur behaves in the same way with it.

'Do you use a billhook?' Arthur begins: 'A calf died through mishandling.'

(Died through mishandling? . . .)

He goes on: 'We were going to bury it. Mr Pateman said: "Skin it and cook it!"—as food for the dogs.'

The Judge: 'Did you chop the calf up?'—'I instructed my brother to.'

The Judge: 'Was it fed to the dogs?' Arthur: 'I believe so.'

Mr Hudson comes to 7th February and the police search of the Farm. 'Did Inspector Harvey identify you as the passenger seen in the car at Gates used-car lot on the preceding evening?' —'No.'

'Or anywhere else? At the police station?'—'No, no!'

Mr Hudson: 'The police say you went round the Farm with them.'—'I was shut up in my room. I couldn't even use my own toilet!'

Mr Hudson goes back to before the events at the police station, and has him handed the album of photographs of Rook's Farm: the lounge, the TV set, the radiogram, the Elastoplast tin . . .

'Do you see on the radiogram what appears to be a tin?'—'Yes.'—'Have you any recollection of having Elastoplast in the house?'—'It's difficult to say. . . .'—'Looking at the picture, you have no recollection of seeing it there?'—'Good heavens, no.'—'You realise the police officers say it was found there?'

Arthur (loudly): 'This was planted after my arrest.'

The Judge: 'If the police say they found one, they brought it?'

Arthur: 'Precisely!'

Mr Hudson goes on to Arthur's conversations with Mr Smith and Mr Minors at Kingston Police Station. 'Chief Superintendent Smith said: "Have you ever been in Wimbledon?". And you said: "Where *is* Wimbledon?"

Arthur: 'I remember he asked the question.' Suddenly going on at a great pace: 'I'm an N.G.R. member! I own greyhounds! I've taken greyhounds to Wimbledon!'

Mr Hudson: 'Mr Smith asked you about reading the newspapers and watching TV. You said: I never watch TV and never read newspapers.'

Arthur makes a sudden movement forwards. 'Those were the police's own words! It is an example of the vindictiveness of the police, indicative of the cruel way they work. . . .' He addresses the Judge. 'I hope my Lord is aware of these things!'

Mr Hudson (trying to calm him): 'Did you say to the police "I want to help you all I can? I realise you have—" '

Arthur: 'I have co-operated in every way with the police and I've been very badly treated by them! Tortured mentally and physically!' He looks down with passionate hatred at Chief Superintendent Smith. 'Smith beat the hell out of me while under the influence of drink! He had a bottle of scotch in front of him. He hit me in the belly and slapped my face. Commander Guiver was not so bad: he held my head when I was about to faint. I had sleepless nights for two nights—I was wakened by the police every ten minutes! That is the truth, the *whole* truth!'

The silence of the court quivers.

His Lordship coolly glances at the clock and nods. The morning session is over. 'Be upstanding!'

22 September, *afternoon*

The court reassembles. We await Arthur again. Hysteria, paranoia? Megalomania, *folie de grandeur*? All four? The fluidity with which he switches from one to another is amazing. Is he mad? One feels the answer is No. Certainly not binnable—there are plenty of people outside the bin who carry on like Arthur; one has met them. All the same, crazy. He is under grotesque strain, of course, whether he is innocent or guilty. The atmosphere is still slightly quivering.

Mr Hudson completes his examination-in-chief. He picks up a few things from earlier on. (Practically all of his examining and cross-examining is done without referring to his notes.)

About the 1st January, the day of Nizam's stomach-ache and of M3 calls. 'Nizam went out for an hour and a half. Did he take your car?'—'No. I was unconcerned.'

On 6th February, the afternoon visit to Percy Chaplin, the tailor in Bethnal Green. 'Did Nizam stay in the car?'—'Yes.'

About Arthur's turn of speech. Mr Hudson: 'M3 kept on using the words "honestly" and "O.K.". Do you use them?'

'They're common words. I may use them. Not frequently.'

'Do you say "man"?'—'To be honest I used it in the West Indies.'

'But you've been here fifteen years. Do you use it now?'—'No.'

Mr Hudson asks about his letter-writing habits, letters to his relations in the West Indies—airmail paper was found at Rook's Farm.

'I don't write on airmail forms.'

'On an ordinary writing-pad?'—'An ordinary-writing pad, and an envelope.'—'You don't use airmal paper?'—'No.'

'Did you write the ransom letters?'

Arthur: 'Good heavens—I'd be stark staring mad!'

The Judge: 'You have not answered the question.'

Arthur: 'No.'

Mr Hudson: 'Did you write the directions on the cigarette packet?'—'No.'

'Have you any knowledge at all about the despatch of these

letters and the calls to this telephone?' Arthur: 'I have absolutely no knowledge of these suggestions.'

Mr Hudson sits down. That is the end of that.

It is now Mr Draycott's turn to cross-examine. Mr Hudson's manner is compelling—often eloquent, often sharply penetrating. Above all, the effect is always of his being on easy, very natural terms with the court—one feels that his manner outside the court and inside must be pretty much the same. Mr Draycott's manner even inside the court changes the moment he rises to his feet. His stylised examining manner is in its way a work of art.

Mr Draycott first questions Arthur about his relationship with his brother. (This relationship clearly lies at the heart of the case—there can have been no doubts about that since the brothers' defence split up, let alone since Nizam made the admissions that have put them both in the cart. Through seeing them in court we have our intimations about what their relationship is now. But what was it *then*?)

Mr Draycott begins with a reminder that Nizam was only in this country for a short stay—"A stranger in a strange land". But for his arrest, Nizam would now be back in Trinidad. (I wonder! . . .) While he was over here Arthur provided him with accommodation? 'When he asked for it,' says Arthur.

Mr Draycott: 'And he did all the work about the Farm?'—'Assisted by my wife.'—'But when she was not there he did it all?'—'Yes.'—'He was fond of animals? The Farm occupied all his time?'—'Yes.'

'As regards money, you gave him a little from time to time?'—'He had only to say what he wanted.'—'Anything he wanted he was given. Is that the position?'—'Yes.' Arthur says Nizam would not really need to ask him. 'My wife held £500–£600 and he had only to ask her.'

Mr Draycott: 'He made certain trips with you in the course of your business. Would it be right to say, as far as the detailed geography of London and its surroundings is concerned, he was a stranger?'—'Yes.'

Mr Draycott is smoothly establishing Nizam's position. 'His concern was to see if he could get into the R.A.F.? But that was denied. Had that not been denied he would have gone back to

Trinidad?' Arthur: 'He asked me to help him to stay *here*. That was his ambition.'

'He got an extension of his visa?'—'At *my* intervention—to see if he could get a permanent stay.'

'And the permanent stay was not granted? Is this when you gave Mr Smith the £20 . . .?'—'Put it this way. I'd do anything for the happiness of my brother, even if it means spending money.'

'I see. And you treat him gently and kindly all the while?' Arthur: 'I don't treat him gently and kindly all the while. I try to make him realise his position as a stranger. I try to be lenient, and semi-lenient.'

'I notice you say "I instructed him", and "I allowed him".' —'Realising I'm twelve years older. And he's a stranger in a strange land.'

Mr Draycott asks Arthur what he means by lenient and semi-lenient. 'Does it mean chastising him?'

'Good heavens, no.'

'There is no reason to say he's afraid of you?'

'No reason at all.'

Mr Draycott turns to the album of photographs of Rook's Farm. The tumbledown building used as a dog kennel, the coal-house with a piece of sacking in place of a door. The work-room, a big room at the front of the house, no curtains to the window so as to give as much light as possible—a window by the front door.

Mr Draycott (as courteously measured as ever): 'Was Mrs McKay ever at the Farm?'

Arthur: 'I haven't met, seen, or heard of such a person.'

'So you don't know what became of her?'—'If I did I shouldn't be in this situation now.' He adds: 'Nor my brother.'

Mr Draycott turns to a different line. 'I'm now going to go through the dates with you, put things to you that you'll probably disagree with. If you disagree, say so!'—'Yes, I will.' Arthur adjusts his cuffs.

'The 29th December, Monday,' Mr Draycott begins. 'You know the day . . .' We learn that Nizam will say that he finished work (presumably after the calf-buying expedition) at 3 p.m., when Arthur left the Farm, saying he was going to see some finishers and 'he'd see you when you saw him'.

Arthur protests. Mr Draycott is aware that Arthur has said he was at the Farm all day, that Nizam told him Mr Coote was on the telephone for him at 5.15—'when somebody in a Volvo was cruising round Wimbledon'. Arthur protests again.

'That night at 8.30 or 9.0 you went to bed. And Nizam sneaked off with the car.' Arthur: 'I didn't say so. My car is at his disposal.'

'He went to visit relatives.' Arthur: 'I didn't know then. I do now. From a letter he showed my brother . . .' (To Adam in Brixton).

The Judge: 'Something somebody told you?' Arthur: 'After I was apprehended and kept in captivity, I found out.'

Mr Draycott refers to Liley's being on the Farm on 1st January and Nizam's going out, complaining of stomach-ache. When he got back relations between Arthur and Mrs Mohammed were strained.

The Judge: 'She was afraid of Arthur, she said.' To Mr Draycott: 'If he wishes to elaborate . . .' Arthur: 'She was not afraid. She had no reason to be.'

And now we come round again to the four strangers in the night. Mr Draycott says: 'In your evidence you described coming downstairs at 2 a.m. and finding Nizam with a group of Mafia types.' Arthur (hotly): '*I* didn't mention Mafia!'

Mr Draycott (as smoothly as if he had never said a naughty thing in his life): 'No, I know you did not. *I* did.' Pause. 'What were they like?'

Arthur: 'I was embarrassed, being in my shorts . . .'

Mr Draycott: 'What were they like?' Arthur: 'I could recognise them if given the chance.'

Mr Draycott: 'They were an international bunch?' Arthur: 'I don't know.'

'Could you recognise one of them?' Arthur: 'I believe I could. . . .'

Mr Draycott (enquiringly): 'Who is that one?'

Arthur becomes agitated. 'I'm not vindictive, and I don't wish to say—I haven't got enough proof. . . . I believe it was Robert Maxwell, Member of Parliament.'

(*Robert Maxwell!* We all know who Robert Maxwell is. Originally a Czech soldier, now British: founder of an enormously successful publishing house: former Labour M.P.: and recently in the public eye with take-over bids. *He* bid for a newspaper, *The Sun*—and was beaten to it by none other than Rupert Murdoch, owner of *The News Of The World*. Thus a connection with the case!)

Mr Draycott expresses interest in 'where this story came from'. He says: 'There was a time, up to committal, when you and your brother were allowed contact. And then you were separated. The reason for the separation is that there was a fight.'

Arthur intervenes incoherently.

Mr Draycott continues: 'You attacked your brother and thereafter you were separated.' Arthur: 'I didn't attack him. There were prison officers there. I wanted to get out of him who these people were!'

'This man you have named—you'd seen his photograph in the newspapers?' Mr Draycott begins; and puts it to Arthur that he suggested to Nizam that he should say this man was one of the four men who approached him. The Judge makes it still more pointed—that Arthur introduced the name of a well-known person to make Nizam agree to tell the story.

Arthur: 'I have seen in a paper one of the persons whom I recognised in my home. My concern is not to implicate anyone. My concern is to prove I did not at any time do this crime!'

(While Mr Draycott is insisting to the contrary, one's mind reels before the ingenious craziness of connecting Robert Maxwell with the affair, if that is what we are supposed to believe Arthur means—the kidnappers' chosen victim was Mrs Murdoch, the wife of Maxwell's business enemy!)

Mr Draycott has come to the 1st February. One of the most characteristic and extraordinary features of a long detailed trial like this is the way the same old events keep coming round and round, as if they were on a roundabout; only each time a different gloss is put on them—somebody says 'That didn't happen', or 'That isn't *how* it happened', or 'The circumstances were quite different'. But the effect of these glosses in a trial is usually the opposite of the effect of literary glosses in scholarship—one is more puzzled rather than more enlightened.

The night of Sunday 1st February, when Arthur and Nizam parted company. 'You dropped him when he went to buy a packet of cigarettes after you'd been to the finishers. He bought two cans of Black Label lager.'

Arthur: 'I don't drink lager. I drink scotch.'

(One may trust that the two lager cans are going to come round again.)

Mr Draycott: 'Let's start on common ground!' (A highly dangerous invitation from him!) 'That night the police say your Volvo was lurking about the café at Dane End and disappeared.'

'What time?'

'Around midnight. And from 7.50 onwards that car was in your possession.'

'My brother was never with me on that day after eight o'clock.'

Mr Draycott persists in dealing with the circumstances in which they parted company. Nizam will say they both drove towards Dane End together. Arthur says he drove home on the A11, alone. (Dane End is on the A10.) Nizam will say Arthur told him to plant the paper flowers. Arthur says he was at home by 9.30. Then there was a quarrel, suggests Mr Draycott. 'No.'

'Because you told Nizam to go back and pick up the suitcase, and he wanted to know what it was *about*?'

(So Nizam did not know what it was *about*? . . . So Nizam was innocent of it all? Light begins to dawn on us.)

'There was a row, a fight.' Mr Draycott goes on with his quiet, formal intimacy. 'Nizam was tipped out of the car and was on his own. *That's* why he arrived home soaking wet, after you?'—'I sent him to buy cigarettes and I didn't see him till midnight.'

Mr Draycott suggests that Mrs Hosein's concern was with why he, Arthur, had got rid of Nizam. 'Nizam got rid of himself!'

Mr Draycott moves on to 6th February, when Nizam was cruising around Gates Garage.

'Using your common sense,' Mr Draycott suggests, 'whoever was in the Volvo that the police saw on the night of 1st February got away by a hair's breadth. . . . He would be reluctant to try again on 6th February?' The Judge stops this line.

Mr Draycott reminds Arthur of being at The Raven—while Nizam sat around at Gates Garage. Nizam will say that Arthur told him to pick up the suitcases.

Arthur: 'I'm not concerned with what he'll say.'

When Nizam joined Arthur at The Raven he gave an excuse for not picking up the suitcases, so then they both went to Gates.

'He drove me home.'—'The police say you and he drove past in the Volvo.'—'I was not implicated in any crime!'

Mr Draycott makes one or two points about the notepaper in Nizam's bedroom, in a box that was 'a family box', and sits down.

The Attorney General takes over. We hear questions about Arthur's having been in Wimbledon, knowing Arthur Road. And Arthur's answers. 'Six or seven years ago.' And, 'I've only been to the Stadium.'

Then about the G.L.C. application. Arthur knew nothing about the application till he saw Nizam's deposition that it was in his handwriting. Arthur did not know why: it came as a surprise.

'You knew only too well that you and he were being charged together with the murder of Mrs McKay!' The Attorney General goes on: 'Do you know Rupert Murdoch?'—'I saw him on TV.'

The Attorney General asks if that is all.

Arthur: 'I had a difference of opinion—over his publishing the Christine Keeler scandal again in *The News Of The World*.'

'You've heard M3 say he wanted the wife of Rupert Murdoch and got Mrs McKay instead?'

(Momentarily one's mind reels again. Surely this can't be hinting that the basis for the choice of victim was a personal grudge of Arthur Hosein's against Rupert Murdoch for publishing something in *The News Of The World*? Who's crazy in this case? I begin to wonder if it's me.)

The Attorney General returns to the visit to County Hall, when Arthur denies being with Nizam. 'You've described him as "a stranger in a strange land". How could he know how to go to the G.L.C.?' Arthur: 'He's quite clever.'

(One glances across at Nizam in the dock; very still, very

quiet, looking straight ahead. So Arthur says he is clever—and not just out of family pride at that.)

The Attorney General has come to the four strange men.

'My brother said he'd met them when trying to enlist in the R.A.F. It was my duty to help him.'

(One notices the references to 'family duty' constantly floating through Arthur's speeches. West Indian families in England are said to have a particular clannish concern.)

'Were you surprised to see them?'—'I'm not surprised to see anybody in my place.' And, 'People come to my place after the pub.' (More vistas of social life in Hertfordshire!) Arthur, now more used to the witness-box, has his hands in his pockets. He says:

'I have reason to believe these four persons knew what was going on and have *used* my brother. He thinks they were going to assist him to stay here permanently.'

The Attorney General tries to discuss when Arthur saw the four men. Before Christmas and after—on the night of the 28th, when Nizam drove him home after an enormous amount of drink. The Attorney General enquires if he was at home on the 28th. There were two visits from the police that day. One from a P.C. we have already heard of—a check following Nizam's running out to get the police in the early hours of the 27th. The other by two detectives enquiring about an entirely different affair, 'when a white man and a coloured man were seen hitting a white man'. (An entirely different affair!)

We come to where Mr Coote, according to Arthur's evidence, telephoned between 5.15 and 5.30 on the afternoon of the 29th. Attorney General: 'Is Mr Coote going to give evidence?'

Arthur: 'No.'

Significant pause; very significant pause. The Judge says: 'What did he ring about?'

'He wanted to bring his girl friend for the weekend of the 4th.'

The Judge: 'When did you remember that call?'—'When I was in my cell, I remembered.' Arthur says Mr Coote was speaking from his office in London, and finally came to Rook's Farm on the 10th.

The Attorney General goes over the written evidence of people seeing the Volvo in Wimbledon on the evening of the 29th.

'Why didn't they take the number?' says Arthur.

Then Farmer Smith and the billhook. The Attorney General asks if Arthur sees any reason why Nizam shook when he was shown it, but the Judge rules that question out. Then the Judge says:

'Are you and Mr Len Smith on good terms?'

Arthur (bitterly): 'Until he was responsible for auctioning my animals!'

The Judge: 'Was that before you gave him the £20 to go to London?'—'After.'

The Attorney General turns to the Elastoplast tin. Why does he say it was planted? Because he would have seen it—and would have had time to tell his wife to take it away. The copy of *The People*; the palmprint is alleged to be his. 'So I've been told,' says Arthur. 'It's not proven, not yet.' Is it his copy? 'I don't know,' says Arthur: 'I'm not H. G. Wells's Invisible Man who turns invisible.' Then: "These people early in the morning of the 29th. It is possible that they may have taken my paper.'

Attorney General: 'Mr McKay says someone had brought a copy of *The People* to his house.'

Arthur (hotly): 'If I were going to commit a crime, would I take my newspaper? Would I take my car without changing the number plates?'

The Judge counsels him not to forget his manners. Arthur: 'It is my way of speaking.'

(One recognises that it is his way of speaking, that he may have forgotten his manners: but one also recognises some questions that everybody in the court must have asked themselves.)

The Judge: 'Assume it is your palmprint. Can you imagine how it could get to St Mary House?'—"That paper could have been taken from my place. My brother has said there were four people at my farm at 2 a.m. on 29th December.'

Attorney General: 'Assume the billhook was the billhook Mr Smith lost at your farm.'—'Another person will say it is another billhook!'

The Attorney General turns to the first M3 telephone call

from Epping at 1.15 a.m. on the 30th. The route from Adam's house would go through Epping. 'Was Nizam home with you at 1.15?' Reply: 'I was ill.'

The night of the 26th and the quarrel. It was when they got back from the pub. Liley wanted to be driven home. The roads were icy. They fought over the car-key. Attorney General: 'You know Nizam went to the police?'—'I knew when the police came on the 28th to see about the other charge.'

Then back to Nizam's visit to Adam, with whom Nizam had been living before he went to Rook's Farm.

The day is wearing on, and Arthur, for all his standing up to the Attorney General's technique, is also showing signs of wear. He answers questions quickly, over-quickly. His fluidity is increasing rather than decreasing. After answering a question from the Attorney General, 'Weren't you *working*?' with, 'I never worked till my wife came back!' he suddenly looks up at the Judge:

'In captivity I lose my sanity. What little I have, I'm trying to control it!'

The Attorney General turns to the letters and fingerprints. On the 30th M3 said he had posted a letter to Mr McKay. 'Were you in London on that day?' Arthur: 'No.'

'The letter arrived. It is said to bear your thumbprint. Did you handle any such letter before it was posted?'

Arthur: 'No.' He argues that it would have to be proved that it was his thumbprint and that it had been taken from his home. 'It is possible that my home was used, unknown to me.'

'This impression appears over the stamp. Look at it.' Arthur looks at it. 'Yes, yes,' he says. Then he tells how he has a lot of envelopes at the Farm, stamped ready for Christmas cards that he did not post because he was too ill. He says:

'If this is factual, not an assumption, and this is my fingerprint or thumbprint, then there is no other way of explaining it than someone has used my home behind my back!'

The Attorney General: 'Would you say your brother had been used?' Arthur: 'People helping him to remain in this country were telling him to do things, take my car . . .'

The Judge: 'Has your brother any reason to say *you* told him to do it?'

Arthur: 'If my brother says I told him to do that . . .' It is too much for him: he rounds on the jury dramatically. 'If you believe I told my brother to do these things, then you can find me guilty on *all* the charges, not just one!'

The Judge stops him addressing the jury. Equably he says: 'Your counsel will do it better.'

It is the end of the day.

23rd September

Arthur still in the witness-box. He is wearing the same near dinner-jacket outfit as yesterday. One hand behind his back again, the other again cups his chin. Napoleon.

Mr Draycott picks up a few omissions from his cross-examination. First about the visit to the G.L.C.

'Is it not right that you went with Nizam in the Volvo on a day when you were going about your ordinary business, and took him to the offices where that application was made?'—'I did not do any such thing.'

'Is it not true that Nizam does not know his way about London?' Arthur: 'If he doesn't know his way about London, how did he find his way from Rook's Farm to Surrey?'

The Judge: 'You must answer questions, not ask them. The question is: Does your brother know his way about London?'

'I wouldn't know, my Lord.'

'Then the answer is no?' (Arthur's answer comes from behind his hand.) The Judge says: 'Are you saying "I don't know"?'

'If you want a direct answer . . .'

Mr Draycott (continuing): 'Nizam will say you asked him to go in and find out the actual person driving the car. Is that new to you?'—'Yes.'

Mr Draycott: 'It is right, what you have said in your evidence, that somebody was making use of Nizam?'—'That's what I said yesterday.'

'Making use of him without his having full knowledge of what it was about?'—'Assisting him in getting a permanent stay.'

Mr Draycott: 'I'm not asking you about a permanent stay.' (*We* know that, now that we have had a preliminary view of Mr Draycott's line of defence.)

Arthur: 'I believe he was used. And because of that, I've given you a name, because I saw a photograph in *The Daily Telegraph*.'

'Don't go into that any more.' Mr Draycott sits down.

The Attorney General returns to his charge. 'You deny you were outside at the G.L.C. office?'—'Very untrue.'

We begin a litany.

'If Nizam says you were in the Volvo with him at Dane End on 1st February, is that true or false?'

'False. I passed Dane End at 4.20 on the way home.'

'If Nizam says you told him to take two paper flowers, etc.'—'Very untrue.'

'If he says you told him to pick up the suitcase? . . .'

'Good heavens, it would be false. The only reason I am implicated is because of the car registration number.' (Which nobody took that night, anyway.)

'If your brother says on Feb. 6th you told him to pick up the suitcases?'—'False.'

'If he says you were in the Volvo with him by Gates Garage, etc.'—'False.'

The Attorney General comes on to the four men he saw 'on on two occasions'.—'*Three* occasions! Two before Christmas and one after.'

The Attorney General asks who is suggesting these men were concerned in the kidnapping of Mrs McKay. 'I'm not making suggestions. I believe. Otherwise there is no other way to implicate my brother. . . .'

Attorney General: 'When did you first think these four men were implicated?'—'When I was charged. I thought it was a fiction. Then . . .'

'Why didn't you tell the police when they asked about the kidnapping? Why didn't you tell the police then?'

'If I'd been treated humanely by the police, you'd have found most likely I wouldn't be facing you here today.'

The Judge reminds him of what Mr Smith and Mr Minors say. Arthur: 'I'm not vindictive, my Lord. If I have some ideas, I want backing, I want grounds.'

Attorney General: 'Why didn't you tell the police then?'—'Crime was not in my mind.'

'You were shown the billhook and the paper flowers. Why *then* didn't you say?'—'My aim was to get the hell out of the police station.'

The Attorney General goes on with more detail about the writing-paper and the envelopes, about where he was on the 30th December, etc., and Arthur replies from a growing hysteria that seems to have been re-created by his recollection of the scenes in the police station.

Did he see Diane Dyer on TV? He cannot recollect—he says he was both 'under the weather' and drunk at the time. Does he recollect now he sees her in court? 'I've been so long in captivity, I can't recollect. I have no enthusiasm in crime whatsoever.'

Liley and the 1st January. '*She* will remember. My brain has been washed off.'

The Attorney General reminds him of her evidence that she did not know of the work-room. 'The key is always kept on the outside,' he says: 'there are no curtains.'

The album of photographs is brought out again. Arthur is handed one. The Attorney General fixes on the work-table. He considers its length and then says: 'There is room for a person to lie or be placed under that table?' (Everyone in court knows what that means.)

The Attorney General considers the tumbledown sheds where the dogs live; sacking over the doorway. 'How do you get into the shed?' The Judge to Arthur: 'Show the jury!' Arthur gets out of the box to hand across the album to the jury. 'It's all right,' he says to them: 'I'm not dangerous!' Everyone laughs, except the jury. Arthur is asked about the height and length of the shed. (We all know why that is, too.) The fierceness of the dogs—'Would they attack anyone?'

Then the cutting up and skinning of the calf. Arthur's wife told him about it. Attorney General: 'Did you witness it?'—'No, Sir Peter, no.' Arthur has seen the carcase 'hanged up' over the concrete surface between the sheds.

More questions from the Attorney General about when was the cutting up? How long did it take? 'Where were the bits, after it was cut up, left?' From Arthur, 'Don't know.'—'Don't know.' He was indoors under the weather, drinking.

(What everyone is thinking about cannot be uttered, because

there is not the faintest trace of forensic evidence to justify it, not the faintest trace.)

The visit of Liley. Arthur alone with her while Nizam went out 'suffering from belly-ache'. The Attorney General presses Arthur for the actual time.

'I just cannot recollect. If I'd known I was going to be involved with murder I'd have equipped myself with a computer.'

The Judge tells him he may just say that it is beyond his memory.

The Attorney General points out that the M3 telephone call to Arthur Road, 'You have gone too far', ended at 7.45 p.m. Did Nizam return at 8 p.m.? 'I can't remember what time. Nizam didn't murder anyone.'

Now we have the ransom letters over again. The Attorney General provides a new gloss—by concentrating on alternatives and spelling mistakes. We begin with the letter to the editor of *The News Of The World*, with the words *OFF* and *SAINT MARYS* inserted, and the indentation on a sheet of paper found in Nizam's bedroom showing the inverted Vs.

'I will be honest,' says Arthur. 'I wouldn't put anything past the police to get a conviction. Anyone can make alterations. I have never corresponded with any unknown persons. There are doubts. If this handwriting is mine, then I have no excuse. Mr Hudson says there is a slight probability.'

'Will you look at the fourth line,' says the Attorney General inexorably. He directs him to a particular word. Arthur reads the word *DISCRETELY*, and says: 'I'd spell it . . .' and spells it correctly. He does not see anything wrong with 'existence' spelt 'existance', but he spells 'occasion'—spelt in the letter with two s's—correctly.

Finally we come to *DISPOSED OFF*. It seems all right to Arthur. The Attorney General asks him if he remembers Chief Superintendent Smith asking him to write. 'Good heavens, yes! I shall never forget it.' He is shown his writings. 'Did I write these words? I was undergoing a strenuous time.'

The Judge asks if he wrote them at Superintendent Smith's dictation. Attorney General: 'The spelling is your spelling?'

'This man showed me the ransom note, and said spell it exactly like that.'

The Attorney General presses further about whose spelling is which. 'Tell my Lord and the jury which words Mr Smith spelt out!' Arthur goes over the details of the letters—he comments to the jury: 'I know it is not good English, but it is what I was told to write.'

For a while it is difficult to see, now, where all this is leading to. We have *OCCASSIONALLY* and *EXISTANCE* all over again. 'I have written fifty pages of ransom letters,' says Arthur. 'After I was beaten, I was told "I want you to write it this way".'

The Judge asks if he is telling us this is part of a police conspiracy. Arthur: 'I was shown a letter and Mr Smith told me to spell it the same way. I wanted to avoid a beating.'

Attorney General: 'Go on to . . .' and we are back again at *DISPOSED OFF*. Arthur misses it. The Attorney General says: 'You've written at the *dictation* of a police officer. You were told to write "disposed of" and you wrote "disposed off".' Arthur: 'This is not unusual. I'm not an English Tutor.' He is addressing the jury. 'The spelling is irrelevant.'

The Judge comes in. ' "Disposed off" is quite common. "Discretely" and "occassionally" are a different matter.'

The Attorney General now produces another album—meanwhile Arthur is enjoining the jury: 'My profession is designer and cutter, not language expert.'

The Judge says to the Attorney General: 'Is there much more?'

From the expression on the Attorney General's handsome face one gathers there is. His Lordship offers Arthur a short rest if the pressure is too great. More letters and fingerprints. We hear again about Arthur not being H. G. Wells's Invisible Man.

The Attorney General confronts Arthur with the pieces cut from Mrs McKay's clothing. 'You're a designer and tailor,' he says. 'How have they been cut?'

'To me, any person can cut off a piece of cloth. Any person can cut it clean.' The exchange goes on till the Attorney General says: 'Could they have been cut by tailor's shears?'

Arthur: 'Yes. Or a knife. Or one of those choppers there.' And he coolly points to the billhooks.

The Attorney General turns to Mr Rosenthal and the Piccadilly tipped cigarette packet. Arthur becomes more agitated again as he is asked what he did with his packet, about his drive to London, and finally about the thumbprint found on the packet. Paranoia bursts out.

'Persons who were using my brother absorbed it [the packet] from my brother. Why didn't you find Mr Rosenthal's fingerprints on it, etc. etc.? Only *mine*!' His voice is raised. 'I am the scapegoat of this affair! As Attorney General, Sir Peter, you should have taken more care!'

The Judge rebukes him, and he apologises for being carried away. The Attorney General resumes. The night of 1st February. 'Did you notice anything wrong with the lights of the car, one night in January?'

It turns out that Arthur was stopped by the police, who wanted to know if he had pinched the car—he had no front lights. Arthur said to them that he *had* lights—Come and look! And found there was no light.

The Judge: 'Which light was it?' Arthur: 'The nearside light.'

On to 6th February. The Attorney General asks: 'Did you know Nizam was waiting at Gates Garage for two suitcases?'

Arthur: 'If Nizam had said he was doing it for murder I'd have blown his head off!'

Attorney General: 'Did you ask Nizam when he came back?'

'I asked him if he'd enjoyed himself. I had no other interest. I had nothing in common with him except getting him permission to stay. . . . I don't want to see him again.'

(The last sentence is patently true—but the earlier ones? Clan loyalty has bound them together. Their personalities are widely different—could they have had anything in common? Could they have had a plan to kidnap for a million pounds in common? *'I don't want to see him again.'*)

The Attorney General has come to where he was first asked about Mrs McKay. 'On the Saturday or Sunday.'—'Did you ask permission to contact your solicitor, Mr Coote?'—'When?'—'On Sunday.' (This was at the time of the alleged beating.) Arthur claims he was denied the permission—Mr Coote was in Yorkshire. He says:

'Mr Smith said: "What is he doing in Yorkshire? Burying the body?" '

The Attorney General asks if he had swollen lips—important as Mr Coote saw him on the following Monday, when Mr Coote said: 'If you know where Mrs McKay is, you must tell.' The Attorney General suggests that Arthur did not complain of the beating to Mr Coote, that it is an invention.

Arthur: 'I'm not vindictive. I'm not a person to invent. A policeman has never yet been found who admits to having beaten up a person!'

At that expression of the truth the Attorney General sits down.

Mr Hudson rises for a final moment of re-examination. First, detail about the work-room. It has fluorescent lighting, bright lighting. Mr Hudson: 'If anyone went in and switched it on, they would see everything clearly? Another light bulb was taken away because there was too much illumination?'—'Yes, yes.'

Then about recognising one of the four men. Arthur did not recognise him at the time. Mr Hudson straightens it out finally. 'Your recollection is similar to a photograph you saw later?' Arthur assents.

Mr Hudson sits down, and Arthur realises this is his last moment in the witness-box. Dramatically he addresses the court:

'Believe me, I have great sympathy for the McKay family. I have a mother myself. I am no murderer even if I am found guilty. These hands'—he holds them out—'are artistic, not destructive. I believe in the preservation of Man. That is what I am living for!'

(The speech produces a momentary dramatic hush. It is astonishing, even if he is innocent. If he is guilty it is simply . . . I was going to say 'chilling', and yet I cannot bring myself to. Because it was certainly spoken out of deep emotion, not calculation and coldness. There is such a multiplicity of strands welded so fluidly together in Arthur's nature that any one of them, at any moment, can be the one along which his emotion flows. *If* he is guilty of murder, one feels he could do the murder and feel sympathy for the family afterwards. *If* he is guilty the speech is dreadful; yet it has not got the chilling, horrifying note of M3 deliberately tormenting Ian McKay with: 'I'm getting fond of your Mum. She's a lovely person. She reminds me of my Mum.'

But who, so far, is to say if Arthur *is* guilty of murdering Mrs

McKay? The only thing one can say on this show of his personality is that one feels he could do anything. He is wily and cunning. Yes. He can tell the truth as easily as he can tell a lie. In fact, when he is telling a lie, does it seem as true to him as the truth? When he is telling a story, for example the story of the four strange men, it obviously seems as real to him as reality. It seems as real to him as the story that a novelist is living when he is writing a realistic novel. 'Feeling embarrassed because he was in his shorts' and 'being offered a drink out of his own whisky'—just the sort of touches that in a realistic novel mark the writer as a good writer, that show he is 'living inside the character'. I cannot believe they do not, while he is saying them, seem as real to Arthur as anything in reality. Or *are* they reality? . . .)

Arthur is settling back in the dock. Leading counsel are sorting out their papers and notes in their little folding desks. The stream of other witnesses for the defence is about to begin.

(Where do we stand now? To me it looks as if, giving them every benefit of presumed innocence, Arthur and Nizam probably kidnapped Mrs McKay. If they did, then it looks as if Arthur did the letter-writing and Nizam did most of the telephoning—it is Nizam who is most often not accounted for when M3 calls are made. To this I could add, as I am only thinking my own thoughts, that the calculated, tormenting note in M3's calls sounds to me more like what I should expect from Nizam if I am on the right lines about his temperament. The note of someone who is standing back, coolly detached from the victim. . . .

Among the joint army of crime-reporters and policemen the term 'schiz' is frequently bandied about, often applied to Arthur. But by my definition of the term, if either of those two—the one volubly, extravertedly fluid and restless; the other incessantly quiet, remote and still—is schizoid, it is more likely to be the one who is incessantly quiet, remote and still. And it is the schizoid, I have to tell myself, who has been known to kill without a tremor. . . .

Nizam's admissions now make it certain, everyone thinks, that he will have to go into the witness-box. So we shall see.)

The proceedings roll on again.

9

Other defence witnesses

The tiny panorama of English society in the dormitory belt resumes its unfolding. First we see Farmer Pateman, from whom Arthur and Nizam are said to have bought a calf on the afternoon of the 29th—after which Arthur says he went to bed with 'flu and a bottle of scotch.

Mr Pateman is examined by Mr Hudson's junior, Mr Hubert Dunn. Like Mr Brian Leary, the Attorney General's junior, Mr Dunn has a clear resonant voice and a vigorous demeanour, both intellectually and physically. Most of these junior barristers, I note, are the sort of active-looking strongly built young men whom one would expect to play a good game of squash. And let me say that anyone who has to stand up to their life in the courts simply has to have sheer physical stamina and vigour.

Mr Pateman is small and bald, small-voiced. He lives with his mother, in partnership with his brother. He has sold calves to the Hoseins since October 1969. He thinks the Hoseins bought a calf on the afternoon of the 29th or 30th.

Mr Dunn questions him about records of sales: Mr Pateman's mother keeps them. On the afternoon of the sale Mr Pateman's mother was 'queer', so she booked it later. Mr Dunn finds the entry in the record book: *30.12.69*. There is something written under the *3*. He wants the jury to see it. The Judge wants to see the record book. His Lordship, it is soon apparent, finds that the system, if any, of farm record-keeping leaves something to be desired by the legal mind.

Mr Draycott cross-examines, taking Mr Pateman back in memory to the period of Christmas Day and New Year's Day. 'Perhaps,' Mr Draycott says, with an invitingly sympathetic smile, 'you had a drink on New Year's Day?'—'I don't drink.'

'I see. Then what makes you remember New Year's Day?'

'Had to work!' (One is reminded of Farmer Smith's telling the policeman who wanted his statement, to come round later, he was too busy with his cows.)

The record is examined again. *29* or *30*? Is the *2* altered to a *3*?

The Judge intervenes. He recalls that Mr Hudson said that whether it was the 29th or 30th was not significant. Anybody looking at that record couldn't decide the date.

The Attorney General duly asks questions about the calf being put in the boot of the Volvo; its weight, 80/90 lb. The Judge interpolates: 'Six stone.' And the Attorney General asks, of course: 'Have you ever cut up and skinned a calf?'—'No.'

We now see the private investigator—a very little man, sharp-eyed, with twenty-four years experience—to whom Mr Hudson referred. Mr Dunn follows the procedure.

'And were you asked to discover the time taken to drive from Rook's Farm to St Mary House?'—'On Monday 10th August it took from 4.30 p.m. to 6.35 p.m.' He outlines his route, through Bishop's Stortford, Epping, London Bridge.

Then to the telephone bells. His tests were acceptably set-up. They confirm what Arthur says, that the downstairs bell is inaudible in the bedroom when the door is closed.

The Attorney General and his Lordship engage him in motoring argument about whether the route he chose was the quickest. So the morning ends.

22 September, *afternoon*

We begin with a succession of Arthur's business colleagues. The first is Gerald Gordon, very short and stocky, the oval shape of his face being enhanced by sideboards and retreating hair. He speaks intelligently and alertly. Mr Dunn examines him, and brings to light an extraordinary piece of evidence straight away. Mr Gordon wanted two pairs of trousers for a customer by the 31st. He telephoned and Arthur had 'flu, so Mr Gordon went and collected them himself, on the 31st.

Mr Dunn: 'What time did you arrive?' Mr Gordon: 'About 7.30 a.m.' He describes the scene. 'I arrived at 7.30. It was dark and cold and the two dogs barked. I flashed my lights and hooted. Nizam came out and invited me in to get the trousers.'

'Where?'—'I went through the front door, into the workroom, sorted out the trousers and went away.'

(At 7.30 on the morning of the 31st! And Mrs McKay saw Diane on television at 8.50 p.m. on the 30th. We recall the Attorney General's questions about the length of the worktable. . . .)

The Judge asks: 'Did you see Arthur on the 31st December?' Mr Gordon: 'Only Nizam. I understood Arthur was in bed, ill.'

Mr Dunn: 'What did you say to Arthur next time you saw him?' Mr Gordon: 'I ticked him off for not delivering the trousers. He said: "Man, I was very ill. I was in no condition" . . .'

The Judge pounces. Arthur said 'Man'. The Judge gets Mr Gordon to repeat Arthur's remark. Mr Gordon smiles modestly, not knowing the court's interpretation of his performance: 'You could call me a mimic.'

We move on to Mr Gordon's visit with all his family on Sunday afternoon, the 1st February. 'Did you take anything with you?'—'Yes, some whisky and some Piccadilly tips.' He left at about 5.30 p.m. 'Was anyone else going to call?'—'Yes, Mr Rosenthal.' (So Rosenthal was expected: he didn't just come on spec.) Mr Gordon saw Arthur next on the following Friday, the 6th February, when Arthur called at his shop—in Stoke Newington, N.16. The Judge asks him about the proximity of N.16 and N.17. (N.17 is where a letter was posted from.)

The Attorney General cross-examines, with even more startling results. Mr Gordon telephoned Rook's Farm on the 30th. 'Nizam said Arthur was ill. I wanted the trousers. Nizam said he'd try and see what he could do about it. I thought I'd pick them up myself.'

'Arthur was too ill to speak on the telephone?' Mr Gordon: 'I phoned up again that night, at about 9 p.m., and Arthur said O.K.' (The telephone in the bedroom.) 'I said I'd come next morning.'

(So Arthur took the call in the bedroom while, according to the Crown case as I understand it, Mrs McKay was watching television in the lounge below! And Arthur agreed to Gordon coming out to the Farm early next morning. Incredible.) Mr Hudson re-examines to rub in the point.

Next Mr Gordon's younger brother vouches for Arthur's work not having deteriorated and having been delivered on time. A buttonhole maker and his wife, also from N.16, give similar testimony—Arthur seemed throughout the relevant period as obliging, helpful, jolly as usual, inviting people to come down to Rook's Farm. A couple from a cottage up the road from the Farm noticed nothing unusual going on.

Then we see a thin, sharp-featured young woman with thick dark hair who turns out to be Liley's sister—and the mother, before her present marriage, of a child by Arthur Hosein. The child is in Trinidad.

At about 9 p.m. on the evening of 2nd January, Arthur came to see her in Edmonton. He asked, not for the first time, for the child, to take to his house. Her husband said no. In the dock Arthur looks thoughtful and anxious. The young woman leaves the witness-box, and Arthur's wife is called.

Mrs Hosein—Arthur is her second husband, the first being an English soldier stationed in Germany who brought her back home to England with him—makes her way through the court. She is a good-looking woman, bigger than her husband; blonde and blue-eyed. She is well made-up and her yellow hair is thick and wavy and newly done. (She was a hairdresser by profession.) His Lordship chivalrously asks her if she would like to sit down in the witness-box, and she smiles at him and says 'No, thank you'. Her voice is pleasing and she has very little German accent.

Mr Dunn opens her examination-in-chief on a simple friendly note. About holidays in Germany, etc. And then: she remembers Nizam coming to live with them?

'Yes,' she says simply, 'when he was thrown out by Adam.'

(Nizam was 'thrown out'? It sounds odd. What did Nizam do?) About the relationship of Arthur and Nizam. 'Brotherly,' she says. 'Quite good.'

Mr Dunn asks her about Farmer Smith, the visit with him to London, the auction sale and his delivery of the 'bits and pieces' from the auction. Mrs Hosein does not remember the spare wheel being left behind, or the billhook. The only billhook she has seen is the one borrowed from George Curwen to cut up the calf.

When she returned from Germany on 3rd January did she see

anything unusual about the Farm? 'No.' She telephoned Arthur from Germany and he tried to telephone her. When she came back 'he didn't look so good'. Between then and his arrest he worked hard at his business? 'Yes. He is a very hard worker.'

Coming to 1st February and the visitors, Gerry Gordon and family. Then Mr Rosenthal. On the previous Sunday Mr Rosenthal asked if he could come—he always enquired if they wanted anything delivered. (The big parcel of pocketing and wax appears again.) Shortly after Rosenthal had gone at about 8.45 p.m. Arthur came home, Mrs Hosein thinks, with Nizam.

Mr Dunn's questioning about what happened after she and Arthur had gone to bed reminds her that it was the night when Nizam did not come back with Arthur: it was the night when he appeared at midnight, soaking wet. She is a little upset by getting it wrong. The Judge asks, to make sure: 'Can you tell us what night it was?'

She says it was a Friday. The police came on the 7th. Was it the Friday before or the Friday before that?

'I'm getting confused.' She is getting very upset.

From the dock Arthur interrupts: 'My wife wants a glass of water!'

'Silence in court!'

Arthur (furiously): 'My wife wants a glass of water!'

The Judge rebukes him. Mrs Hosein is given some water and she now sits down.

Mr Dunn goes on to 6th February, the night of Arthur's coming home from The Raven. 'He'd had a few. As usual he was very hungry. And then we went to bed.'

Next to the 7th February and the police visit. Fifteen to twenty police officers. Mrs Hosein murmurs something about its being an unfortunate time, the house had broken pipes. 'The police were not very nice,' she says.

The Judge: 'Well, it was hardly a social visit. . . .'

Arthur (shouting): 'I refuse to sit here before that Judge! I would like him changed. He is partial!' The warders leap to their feet. 'Take me down!' he shouts, and turns to the stairs—down which the warders hustle him into the depths out of sight.

The proceedings are brought to a remarkable standstill. His Lordship decides on an interval. Mr Hudson and Mr Dunn go down below. They return and Mr Hudson says his instructions are that Arthur apologises—the doctor is with him. On two occasions wild emotion has sparked across the court from Arthur like a high-voltage discharge. On the first it was hatred for Chief Superintendent Smith; on the other, concern for his wife—and hatred for the Judge.

Arthur is brought back and the proceedings go on. The next part of Mr Dunn's examination elicits more details of the fruitless search. On the night of the 8th, 100 policemen arrived. And so on with searches up to the 10th August. Mr Dunn then asks:

'Did you speak on the telephone to Mr and Mrs Smith about the sale of some pigs?' Mrs Hosein: 'I can't remember.'—'Was there some trouble?'—'There was an auction and Mr Smith should have been there, and was not.'

(This may be to illuminate Farmer Smith's attitude to Arthur, but it reminds me of something quite different. According to the joint army—and they should know—Arthur Hosein, for reasons they are prepared to suggest, sold up most of his pigs in the middle of January.)

It is Mr Draycott's turn. 'When Nizam came from the relatives in Surrey because of trouble, he had nowhere else to go?' he says sweetly. 'Yes.'—'Yours was the only place he had to live?'—'Yes.'—'Do you know the trouble was about his joining the R.A.F.?'—'He tried. He was refused.'

'Now, Mrs Hosein,' Mr Draycott goes on to a fresh line. 'People talk about dates and days, and they're hard to remember, especially when one's in the witness-box.' Mrs Hosein: 'Not really. . . .'

'That's splendid!' Pause. 'Was there a calf that died?'

It died while Mrs Hosein was on a short visit to London—it had not been given enough coarse feeding. The Judge: 'It died of malnutrition?' (How did Mrs McKay die?)

Mrs Hosein: '*I* chopped it up. I cooked it and gave it to the dogs. Nizam skinned it.' With the chopper borrowed from George Curwen.

Mr Draycott now asks her about the cardboard box containing family papers in Nizam's bedroom. (The box found by the police to contain the incriminating writing-paper.) Mrs Hosein does not remember it. 'I can't even see a cardboard box in the photograph.'

'The police say they took out a cardboard box. You say you've never seen a cardboard box containing papers, yours and your husband's?' Mrs Hosein is thinking of cardboard boxes in the work-room, when suddenly the exhibit is produced.

The Judge: 'Come, come, Mr Draycott, I thought it was some substantial box.' Mrs Hosein: 'That's a *lid*.' Mr Draycott: 'You may call it a lid.'

Mrs Hosein: 'I've never seen that before! Anybody could have put it into the house. The police have been all over. They have taken anything at any time.'

The Judge asks Mr Draycott: 'What is the document said to come out of that box?'—'A piece of paper similar to the ransom note paper.' He turns to Mrs Hosein: 'You've never seen this in that bedroom?'

'I have not! And how could my telephone bills appear in Nizam's bedroom?'

'I'm only saying what the police say. There is something here about blood transfusion. Is that your handwriting? I'm only suggesting that it's a box into which members of the family drop things.'

Mrs Hosein: 'This is a document offering blood for transfusion. It was in my handbag. The police took it from *my handbag*!'

The Judge to Mr Draycott: 'It is just possible the police thought it a convenient box, and put things in it.'

(So much for the famous cardboard box in Nizam's bedroom—but of course the writing-paper came from somewhere in the house and may have been in the lid to start with.)

Mr Draycott turns to the night Nizam came home at midnight, soaking wet. 'You were suspicious about why your husband had left Nizam? You suggested your husband had been out with some other woman?'—'I did not.'

'You gave Nizam a towel?'—'I think he's big enough to get himself a towel. He asked me to give him something to eat.' Mr Draycott, as smoothly as ever: 'Your attitude to Nizam was ordinary? When you asked your husband to be stern with him, your husband said: "You can beat him so many times, he may resent it." Do you think Nizam had come to fear your husband?' —'Certainly not.'

'And on the following morning there were two Black Label beer cans in the garden. You spoke to Nizam about those, asking him if Arthur had been out with a woman?'—'I asked if they'd had a good time.'—'But you weren't pleased?'—'Certainly not.'

Mrs Hosein has displayed her spirit. And those two Black Label beer cans have turned up at Rook's Farm. Mr Draycott sits down.

Mrs Hosein now has to face the Attorney General, who begins with Nizam's attempt to get into the R.A.F.; Farmer Smith's promise to employ him; and Nizam's being thrown out by Adam. And then he comes to calf-chopping.

The Attorney General wants to know whether a calf had died while she was in Germany: the one she herself chopped up, and Nizam skinned, died while she was in London between the 10th and 17th January. Had a calf died while she was in Germany? 'No.' Any more when she got back? One more.

The Judge: 'When Mrs Mohammed was there?'—'Yes.'

At that the clock spares us the slaughtering details again. It is the end of the day.

24th September

Both Hosein brothers have had hair-cuts, and look sleeker and glossier.

The benches for distinguished visitors have become markedly more populated in this second week of the trial. The Old Bailey is run mainly by the City of London, which means that the privilege of having tickets for the distinguished visitors' benches goes to City dignitaries, Aldermen and the like, who, it seems, hand the tickets to their wives. A large proportion of the distinguished visitors are very nicely dressed middle-aged ladies wearing good jewellery and hats—the sort of ladies who might well be seen at royal garden parties.

The Attorney General continues his cross-examination of Mrs Hosein. She is shown the Elastoplast tin. She thinks she did not buy it. Attorney General: 'Did you see it after you came back from Germany?'

Mrs Hosein: 'My son used a tin like that as a money-box.'

The Attorney General does not pause, but everybody takes the point: the police could not have planted it.

The Attorney General mentions her absence in London from 10th to 17th January, when the letter was written to the editor of *The News Of The World* and M3 calls were made to Arthur Road, and when her young sister-in-law was at the Farm and Liley taught her how to make paper flowers. Mrs Hosein never saw any flowers in the Volvo.

Then follows a sharper interchange about *when* Mrs Hosein first realised the police had come to Rook's Farm on 7th February to look for Mrs McKay, not just for the jewellery for which they presented the search warrant. The police did *not* tell her, she says. When she heard that Arthur had been taken to Wimbledon Police Station, she remembered Mrs McKay and 'put two and two together'. But this was after she had telephoned Mr Coote, in Yorkshire, later that evening.

Attorney General: 'During the course of that afternoon, the police made a thorough search. Didn't you think they were looking for *somebody*?'—'I couldn't understand it. If they were looking for jewellery, why were they looking at papers? . . . I asked the police what was going on and they told me to shut up.'

'Did you see them in the bedroom?'—'I couldn't watch everywhere.'—'Did you see them with the paper flowers?'—'No, I did not.' The Attorney General asks her if she was not curious about the dogs sniffing round outside. Mrs Hosein: 'If you had that many police descend into your house, you would not look outside. You would worry about inside.'

Attorney General: 'I suggest the name of Mrs McKay was used right at the beginning!' Mrs Hosein: 'Never once! *Not* at the beginning!'

The Attorney General goes on to Mrs Hosein's attitude to Liley. 'I didn't like the association of Nizam with Liley.'

Mrs Hosein says she objected to Nizam and Liley sharing a bedroom—it was a bad thing, when there were young children about the house. The Attorney General changes to the night of the 6th February, when Arthur came home from The Raven. (The time is very important—10.47 p.m. at Gates Garage.)

'10.15 to 10.30,' says Mrs Hosein. She did not look at the clock.

The Attorney General introduces the subject of driving home from The Raven via Bishop's Stortford—it would be going out of one's way. The jury all study the map. Mrs Hosein smiles across the court at Arthur, comfortingly. More discussion about how long the different routes take.

The Judge: 'On that night Arthur came back at 10.30 with Nizam?' Mrs Hosein: 'Yes.' Attorney General: 'I suggest that it was at eleven o'clock.' Mrs Hosein: 'No. Earlier.'

'You asked him where he had been?' Mrs Hosein: 'I never do.' (One can understand that, with a man like Arthur.)

The Attorney General sits down.

The next witness is a young man who helps behind the bar in a nearby village public house. He has got a job in Tesco by day, his half day off being on Mondays. The evidence for the defence takes a more startling turn again—as does the panorama of social life in the region.

The bar-help has a moustache and a small beard and bobbed hair. He is wearing a high double-breasted suit with eight buttons. He is called to give evidence because on the night of the 28th Arthur invited him to call over socially at Rook's Farm. His manner combines geographical vagueness with ineffable self-regard.

Mr Dunn: 'When Arthur asked you to call over, on Sunday night, did you say when you might go?'—'I said I might on Monday afternoon.' In fact on the following Monday afternoon, the afternoon of the 29th, he was driving his car round Stocking Pelham, looking for Rook's Farm.

He failed to find the Farm. His Lordship ascertains that Arthur's invitation did not specify his telephoning first.

There is no cross-examination, and the bar-help is followed, in delightfully striking social contrast, by the local Master of Foxhounds, a tall, vigorous, middle-aged man with a resonant upper-class voice, who resides at Pelham Hall. He is acquainted with Arthur through getting permission to hunt across Arthur's land. (We gathered earlier that Arthur had begun by objecting. The temptation is irresistible to visualise scenes up at the Hall—the classy M.F.H. blandishing the little West Indian tailor into comporting himself like an English country gentleman.)

On Boxing Day he asked Arthur if it was all right, and Arthur agreed. 'Absolutely no objection.'

Back to the Hosein family. At last we see Adam. He is short, stronger and heavier than Arthur, and he has a deep strong voice. He is a business man, an insurance broker, living in Thornton Heath. (He strikes me as the ablest and most powerful of the brothers.) Mr Hudson elicits that Nizam turned up at 11.30 p.m. on the night of the 29th December in Arthur's Volvo, delivering some trousers and collecting some shirts. His behaviour was normal. He mentioned that some people were helping him to get a permanent visa, but did not say who. He said Arthur was in bed ill.

Mr Hudson: 'Has Nizam complained of Arthur striking him ever?'—'No.'

Mr Draycott is on his feet now, getting the picture of his client straight. 'Would it be right to say Nizam's a person who, if anything unusual happens, gets excited?'—'No.'

'It would be right to say that under stress he keeps calm?'—'I only knew Nizam a short while, since he's grown up.'—'And after that, did you see him?' Adam: 'He phoned a couple of times after the 1st January. He mentioned some people helping him to get a visa.'

'He was his ordinary self that night?'—'It seemed so to me.'

The Attorney General asks the things I should have thought everybody wants to know most of all. Even so the facts come through mutedly. The first thing is why Adam 'threw Nizam out'.

Nizam, when he arrived in England, came to stay with Adam in May, and left in September. The Attorney General suggests there was some sort of 'tiff'. Adam: 'He wanted to join the R.A.F. I thought it was best not.'

Attorney General: 'He left the house. When you came back he was gone?'—'Yes.'—'Arthur had collected him?'—'I subsequently heard that.' And that is all.

(That is not what I call 'throwing out', nor is the argument so described good reason for 'throwing out' by most people's definition. On the other hand, if this really is all there was to it, Nizam must be peculiarly wilful.)

The Attorney General asks the next thing. 'Did you expect

Nizam on the night of the 29th? Were you surprised?' (Adam had last seen Nizam in September.) Adam: 'Not really. He knew I had these things for him.'

Attorney General: 'You were not surprised he came, but were you surprised he came at that time of night?' Adam: 'Yes.'

We hear from Adam that Nizam had come from the finishers at Tottenham and Hackney Wick—no mention of the friends at Norbury Crescent. He left Adam at midnight.

'Were you surprised he could find his way about?'—'Not really.'

Locations and routes are checked. Thornton Heath is twenty minutes' drive from Wimbledon. Attorney General (suddenly): 'Have you ever driven from Thornton Heath to Epping? How long does it take?'—'I have no idea.'—'Longer than an hour?' —'Possibly.' (M3 called from Epping at 1.15 a.m.)

Finally Nizam's note for him in Brixton Prison is produced. 'Did you read it?'—'Not really.'—'Did you realise he was asking you not to tell anyone he had been to your home on Monday evening?'—'At the time I didn't understand.'

(Not much change out of Adam. West Indian family rows—I wonder if the jury feel we have got to the bottom of them? And West Indian family loyalties . . . leading, it seems to me, to very odd results. I should like to have heard a lot more from Adam.)

The next two witnesses are tradespeople who called regularly at Rook's Farm and noticed nothing unusual. Then one of the two detectives who called twice, 'about a matter unconnected with the case', at Rook's Farm on the 28th: he said he might call again.

Mr Draycott: 'From the morning of the 28th December onwards, both brothers must have known you could come back *at any time* to make enquiries?'—'Yes.'

Then the young policeman whom Arthur met in the hairdresser's shop on the 5th January and invited to come shooting over the Farm—a general invitation, mentioning that weekend.

Now we come to the defence forensic expert and prepare ourselves for an accumulation of minute detail over an inordinate length of time. The defence expert is Dr Julius Grant, Vice-President of the Forensic Society. The newspapers say he is aged seventy, but he looks to be about sixty, smallish, rather slight in physique, grey-haired. His speech is noticeably cultivated and precise.

Mr Hudson examines him first about writing-paper, in particular *The News Of The World* letter sheet, torn out of an exercise book, and the similar sheet found in Nizam's bedroom. The expert has measured the weight per unit area. The trade tolerance, he says, is 5%: here there are differences of 4.3% which is getting near the borderline. Furthermore he has been to Woolworth's and bought at random an exercise book of the same kind and measured up lines, margins, colour, position of the staples, etc. He agrees that in the prosecution's exhibit the staple marks are in corresponding places, but so they are in his Woolworth's purchase.

The Judge plays an active part in the discussion. 'If you observe a similarity in something fortuitous does it strengthen or weaken your opinion that it came from the same place?' he asks. And: 'If there is correspondence along a whole serrated edge, does it strengthen the view that it came from the same page, not the same book?'

They go over the fingerprints. Like the prosecution expert, Dr Grant takes a figure of sixteen points of characterisation as a safe number for a court of law, and disputes the sixteen on many of the prosecution's exhibits. From time to time he examines original prints with a pocket magnifying glass, the sort with a light in it that a watchmaker holds in his eye socket. He is methodical and precise—which leads to trouble when a succession of documents is handed up to him that has not been methodically sorted out already.

We go over to handwriting, and whether it is Arthur's.

'I find a number of similarities in the writing,' says Dr Grant, 'and I reached the conclusion that there is reasonable doubt that Arthur Hosein wrote the letters. But I cannot exclude the possibility that he did.'

The Judge asks: 'Have there been occasions when you have been asked to compare handwriting and you were *sure* they were *not* written by the same person?'

Dr Grant: 'Yes, but not very often.' He considers it. 'About one-third of them.'

Mr Hudson introduces Nizam as a possible writer, and Dr Grant's opinion is on the lines of the prosecution expert's, with more qualifications. Point by point we go, dots and loops and crossbars. The Judge, who is writing everything down in his big book, in longhand (just as, if I may say so without disrespect, I am), runs out of ink. His wraith-like clerk brings some.

Mr Hudson soldiers on, and so do the rest of us. The documents steadily pile up round Dr Grant on the shelf of the witness-box, and at one moment he finds himself comparing the handwriting on one of the questioned documents with the handwriting on a copy of it—handed up to him by mistake—made by Mr Minors! Many of the documents appear to be numbered twice over, and then on any one document the various points of interest are numbered. Confusion multiplies as a consequence. At one point his Lordship says to Dr Grant: 'We'll take your word for that.'

He comes to the end. Having compared the handwriting of Arthur with the questioned documents, and the handwriting of Nizam with the questioned documents, Dr Grant considers the more similar is Arthur's.

(If only, I think again, these techniques could be more roughly quantified, similarities be expressed even in terms of odds! And then it occurs to me they might then fall into the hands of numerate woodenheads who think numbers are everything. *They* might well make matters worse instead of better.)

'But,' says Dr Grant, with unremitting honesty, 'I cannot exclude the possibility that Arthur wrote the questioned documents or Nizam wrote the questioned documents.'

Mr Draycott rises, and begins with a slighting reference to the mix-up over Mr Minors's handwriting.

The Judge: 'That shows there were common features!'

Mr Draycott: 'Am I right in thinking, Dr Grant, that you cannot say the questioned documents were written by Nizam?' Dr Grant: 'I cannot exclude the possibility that they were written by Nizam.' Mr Draycott asks the same question again. Dr Grant gives the same answer again. Mr Draycott points out that the jury is concerned with what can or can not be proved; and puts the question again. The Judge intervenes.

Mr Draycott: 'Let us put it another way! You would say that

the probability is that the questioned documents were written by Arthur?' Dr Grant: 'No.'

The Judge intervenes finally, saying to Dr Grant: 'What *you* say is: I cannot say either, but if it's one of the two, I'd plump for Arthur?' Dr Grant: 'Yes.'

It is the Attorney General's turn. He begins by pointing out that the Crown have called three forensic experts, one for paper, one for fingerprints, one for handwriting. Each is an expert in an individual branch: Dr Grant is an expert in all three?

Dr Grant says yes.

(One can imagine the wiseacres: "Jack-of-all-trades, etc".) Dr Grant says, unprovoked:

'There are several aspects of forensic science I don't cover. I have a laboratory with forty-five assistants. If you wish I'll explain why I'm in a position to give expert evidence in this case.'

The Attorney General concedes his expertness in dealing with paper. Dr Grant was once in the paper industry. But what experience has he in a Fingerprint Bureau? Dr Grant says none with a bureau, though he has had experience elsewhere that he thinks acceptable. (*We* know who has experience of a Fingerprint Bureau.)

Attorney General: 'Have you ever visited a Fingerprint Bureau?'—'Many years ago.'—'What training have you in comparison?'—'I have attended lectures, read widely.' (Clearly nothing to be compared with twenty-two years in one.)

Attorney General: 'Do you admit the importance of the reputation of a Fingerprint Bureau?' Dr Grant: 'Comparison of fingerprints is a small part of it. One needs the expertise beforehand.'

Attorney General: 'Chief Inspector Brine does thousands of comparisons a month!'

Dr Grant: 'I don't think he could, or he wouldn't have time to give evidence in court.'

Attorney General: 'Can you tell us what part of the left palm was said by Chief Inspector Brine to be on the copy of *The People*, on the ransom-note, and on the letter from Mrs McKay beginning *Alick Darling*?' Dr Grant: 'Here and now, no.'

Attorney General: 'You've examined the photographs. What

part of the palm was it? Before you gave an expert opinion, wasn't it necessary to determine that?' Dr Grant says he would have to look at the originals again.

Attorney General: 'Let's get it clear. There are five separate exhibits that Chief Inspector Brine says show prints of Arthur Hosein. They are . . .'

(The enumeration gives one time to reflect on the plethora of Crown forensic experts and the shortage of free-lance forensic experts available to the defence. May it not be that, as in some other walks of life, no sooner does someone appear on the scene and show useful talent than he is promptly bid for by the Establishment?)

'You're not denying the marks are made by the same palm or finger?' the Attorney General is saying. 'No.'

His Lordship suggests that it could be put that the marks appear to come from the *same source*, at first sight. Dr Grant agrees.

The Attorney General turns to the fingerprints and ridge-formation. 'An expert makes a judgement based on that.' He calls for Exhibit 116 and begins himself—presumably without years of experience in a Fingerprint Bureau—to identify ridge-endings by number.

Dr Grant: 'Brine may be right, but I can't see it. My view is: If it's acceptable it should be seen by the likes of me.' The jury, attentive and stolid as ever, are poring over the fingerprint photographs again. By 'the likes of me' he means *them*.

The Attorney General goes through a succession of ridges. 'Look!' he says. 'I *am* looking,' says Dr Grant, a bit plaintively. Ridge after ridge. These things are very important for the accused men.

'Wouldn't you agree,' says the Attorney General, 'this is where a practised eye counts?' Dr Grant says he thinks what counts is whether it can be demonstrated to a jury. He adds that it is only in 10% of cases that he disagrees with the police.

Attorney General: 'You're not suggesting your evidence is always acceptable?'

'No,' says Dr Grant, with patient preciseness. 'I'm not saying it's always rejected either.'

More ridge-endings. More junctions. The Attorney General is now thoroughly enmeshed. Dr Grant begins to categorise the points as 'less controversial' or 'more controversial'.

The Judge enquires if the curvature of a ridge is important. Dr Grant tells him it is not greatly diagnostic.

The Attorney General plunges into 'lakes' and 'islands'. We come to the familiar sequences 1, 2, 3, 4, 5, 9, 10, 14, 15, 16, and suchlike. The Attorney General and Dr Grant try to agree on various marks here and there.

The Attorney General gets out a magnifying glass.

Dr Grant shakes his head. 'A magnifying glass doesn't help.'

So it goes on, till twenty minutes after the usual ending-time, when the Judge decides the proceedings must stop for the day. 'Be upstanding!' We stagger out into the lobby and over to the café for a cup of tea.

25th September

The Attorney General's examination of Dr Julius Grant continues for an hour or more. It ends with totting up the number of points of identification noted by the prosecution expert which Dr Grant finds acceptable. The Attorney General takes six objects, and Dr Grant accepts a number of points on each—which includes one envelope on which the score for two marks together is 11, and another where for two marks together it is 13. The Judge makes sure that Dr Grant does not deny that the marks might have been made by the same man.

The Attorney General produces his addition sum for the six objects. 'A total of 62 points.'

Dr Grant: 'I accept the arithmetic.'

(Unable to resist arithmetic myself, I calculate that, taking 16 points as being the safe number for a court to accept for a print, $6 \times 16 = 96$.)

The Attorney General reinforces his count with two impressive sequences. Do they, together with the 62 points agreed, he wants to know, point to Arthur Hosein?

Incidentally the Judge puts a question to Dr Grant that answers my own difficulties about accepting the validity of taking for one document the score on two fingerprints added together.

Dr Grant: 'If one were an academic one couldn't accept

adding them up. But by common sense, if they point to the same person . . .'

It is a very fair answer. (Yet I cannot help feeling, and in so doing may be merely sticking my neck out to have it promptly chopped off, that the attentions of half a dozen really first-rate young scientists now, including a young theoretician or two, might put the subject on a different footing.)

The evidence ends with Dr Grant still somewhat troubled by not finding 16 points a time. (One wonders how the jury are feeling about it. Without the faintest evidence to go on—their combination of attentiveness and stolidity is extraordinarily successful in preventing one from seeing their feelings—I should guess they feel more or less as they did before, that things point pretty seriously to Arthur Hosein.)

The court momentarily lapses into a short busy spell of re-sorting papers and documents. And then it becomes 100% attentive. Mr Draycott is going to call his client to the witness-box, Nizamodeen Hosein.

10

Nizamodeen Hosein

In a short introduction Mr Draycott points out to the jury, as did Mr Hudson, that his client is under no obligation to go into the witness-box. He is choosing to do so. (Actually one would have thought that after making his admissions Nizam was bound to.)

The warder opens the door of the dock, and Nizam does not glance at his brother as he passes him to go out.

(One recalls Arthur's 'I don't want to see him again.' Clan-loyalty here is at an end. Having heard Adam in the witness-box, one is struck by the fact that he and Arthur have taken Nizam into their household, yet neither of them seems to have liked him or wanted him. There is an undercurrent of something, some feeling that runs counter to family obligation. There seems to be something mysterious about Nizam. On the other hand it is fair to say that Arthur and Adam have taken no steps to see each other, though they do not live far apart, for months on end. Adam says he *heard* that Arthur had collected Nizam after he, Adam, threw Nizam out. The powerfulness of family feeling for loyalty seems to be equalled by powerfulness of mutual feeling of an opposite kind. Do the brothers all hate each other, one wonders, as well as feeling bound together? Like West Indian Karamazovs?)

Nizam is in the witness-box. He stands, looking nervous, shy, slightly lost. One is struck over again by the Chinesey cast of features which none of his brothers nor his father shares. Mr Draycott rises for his examination-in-chief. One waits to hear, at last, Nizam's voice. Is it going to be 'deep and soft'?

Mr Draycott addresses Nizam, and Nizam replies—completely inaudibly. Nizam's voice appears to be non-existent.

I suppose it might be called soft, so soft that it vanishes before it is halfway across the court. Mr Draycott asks him to speak up. No difference. The Judge asks him to speak up. No difference.

Nizam's posture is one of softly shrinking away: he is asked to speak into the microphone on the edge of the box. Nothing seems to come out. An usher taps the microphone to see if it is live.

'Speak up!' says Mr Draycott. 'Or you'll find me getting irritated.' His Lordship nods his head.

Scarcely any recognisable speech emerges. Finally the Judge suggests one of those small microphones you wear round your neck and Nizam agrees. It is produced from somewhere and he stands submissively while it is hung round his neck. For the rest of his time in the witness-box, which is going to last over two days, he wears it continuously. And even this device is far from effective. Time after time he will be asked by counsel, and even by the Judge, if he is *trying* to be inaudible.

Mr Draycott stands waiting, with sturdy, terrier-like energy shining from his face—and his contrasting elegant, stylised court manner no doubt in store. Arthur sits in the dock, his head on one side and his hand cupping his chin, looking observant and neutral.

(There must be few laymen in the court who are not tense with curiosity to know how Nizam's admissions are to be reconciled with his still pleading Not Guilty to all the charges. For Arthur to say he knows nothing whatsoever about the whole affair *is* reconcilable. But to go to the G.L.C., to plant the paper flowers, to circle around the suitcases . . . How on earth can that be reconcilable?)

Mr Draycott begins with establishing the relationship between the two brothers. Fear . . . 'I was afraid of him,' Nizam whispers. Mr Draycott probes further. Nizam says in a soft, nearly non-existent voice:

'Whenever I don't do something he tells me to do he has a go at me.'

'In what way does he have a go at you?'—'He punches me in the chest.' Nizam, shrinking gently back in the witness-box, seems to be illustrating his state. Between September and

December, he says, Arthur had beaten him on several occasions. At this moment no one could look more beaten.

So, on 19th December, Arthur drove him to County Hall. Nizam had no idea where he was going, and Arthur told him it was 'the Tax Office'. Arthur told him the story he had to tell to get the name of the Rolls-Royce's user and told him to give a false name. Mr Draycott: 'Did he say why you should not give *your* name as the person making the enquiries?'—'No, sir. I didn't ask him because I didn't want any more trouble.'

Nizam says, in giving the false name and address on the G.L.C. enquiry form he wrote his cousins' address in Norbury Crescent because it was the only one he knew.

And after that? Mr Draycott persists. Nizam (looking distant and lost): 'I just put the incident out of my mind. . . .'

Mr Draycott moves on to late on Boxing Night, when there was the row between Arthur and Nizam over Liley Mohammed. Liley wanted to go home and Arthur insisted she should stay. When Nizam was telephoning for a taxi Arthur jumped on him and punched him, and he ran away. He brought a police officer back with him, and they climbed together through the lounge window, where they found Liley so terrified that Nizam spent the night downstairs with her in the lounge.

Next the 28th December and the visits of the police officers. Two different lots, one about Nizam's complaint, the other about 'another matter'. 'Did they come regularly?' Mr Draycott asks. 'Yes, to check if everything is all right.' (All right, indeed! The way *policemen* were in and out of Rook's Farm when, if the brothers are guilty, they must have been on the very edge of a dangerous and frightful crime, sounds fantastic all over again.)

Then the 29th. Mr Draycott: 'As far as you can say, the day began in the ordinary way?'—'Yes, sir.' Nizam is not certain whether they sent to Farmer Pateman's that day or the next, i.e. the afternoon when Mrs McKay was kidnapped, or the afternoon when the Crown alleges she was held captive at Rook's Farm. On the 29th Arthur left in the Volvo—whose lights Nizam knew to be defective—at about 3 p.m. for the finishers. Nizam fed the animals, as usual, at 4 p.m. He next saw Arthur at about 8.15, when Arthur complained of 'flu and went to bed.

When he thought Arthur was alseep, Nizam went to look and saw him under the feather quilt. He then borrowed the Volvo, to go and see first his relatives at Norbury Crescent, and then his brother Adam at Thornton Heath.

Mr Draycott: 'Why did you decide to visit Adam?' Nizam (stammering in a whisper); 'It was New Year's Eve. . . .' (No mention of delivering trousers or collecting shirts.) Mr Draycott: 'How did you find your way through London?' Nizam: 'I asked. . . .'

From Adam's Nizam drove back through Epping. The call at 1.15 a.m.—Nizam denies making it. 'Could it have been that you were in that area at that time? Physically you could have made the call, couldn't you?'—'Yes, but I did not.'

In the morning Nizam did not tell Arthur he had been out in the Volvo. Arthur, the late riser, got up at the usual time. The Judge: 'When did you next see Arthur?'—'At mid-day.'

Mr Draycott now interpolates two questions on what he calls 'general matters'. The first is: 'Was Mrs McKay ever at the Farm, to your knowledge?'—'No, sir.' The second: 'Could she have been at the Farm without your knowing?'—'I was all round the Farm.'

The Judge: 'If a strange woman had been brought to the Farm, could she have been kept there without your knowing?'—'I would have known.'

Mr Draycott turns to the billhook left by the kidnappers at 20 Arthur Road, to Farmer Smith's giving evidence, and to its being suggested by Arthur that he, Farmer Smith, did not enquire about losing it, with the spare wheel, at Rook's Farm. 'Was he asking also for a billhook?' Nizam: 'Yes.'—'And all you found was a wheel?'—'Yes, sir.'

Now Liley's visit on the 31st, and Nizam going out on the next day to get something for stomach-ache. 'What time?'—'Evening, about 3 p.m.'—'How long were you away?'—'About twenty-five minutes.'—'And what was the first thing you did when you came back?'—'I went straight to the animals. I put water into the troughs. . . .'—'And when you finished feeding the animals, where did you go?'—'Into the house.'

Mr Draycott: 'And how did Liley look?' Nizam: 'She wouldn't speak to me.'

The next point is the death of the calf while Mrs Hosein was in London, and the decision about what to do with it. Mr Draycott: 'Were you affected by the calf's death?' Nizam (almost soundlessly): 'I was very upset.' Mr Draycott: 'To do the skinning did you use some implement?'—'Yes, sir. A kitchen knife. A chopper.' Mr Draycott: 'This?' A billhook is produced. Nizam: 'One borrowed from George.'

Sunday 1st February. Nizam did not see Mr Rosenthal give Arthur the packet of Piccadilly cigarettes. He and Arthur went to London to deliver trousers. Mr Draycott checks the visits to the finishers, and checks Nizam's asking for a sixpence with which to telephone Liley—at about 8 p.m., the time she usually called him at home.

Mr Draycott: 'Did you get out of the car to buy something?'—'Yes, sir. Three packets of Stuyvesant cigarettes.'—'While buying those did you buy something else?'—'Yes, sir. Two cans of Black Label lager beer.'

Mr Draycott: 'Arthur says you never went back.' Nizam (in a firm whisper): 'I went back.'—'What did you take with you?'—'Three packets of cigarettes and two cans of lager.'—'On the following morning did you discuss the cans of lager with Arthur's wife?'—'Yes, sir.'

Mr Draycott: 'Having got back to the car was there trouble?'—'Arthur was upset because I'd been so long in the pub. He was in a hurry.'—'He was not prepared to let you stop and telephone?'—'No, sir.'

Mr Draycott: 'Did you drive to Dane End?'—'Yes, sir.'—'What did Arthur say?'—'There were two paper flowers on the dashboard. He said I was to stick them in the ground on the corner of the road.'—'Did you ask about it?'—'Not at that stage.'—'Why not?'—'I do as I'm told.'—'Did you do it?'—'Yes, sir.'

The Judge: 'What passed through your mind?' Nizam is inaudible. The Judge: 'Anything at all?' Nizam: 'No, sir.'

Instead of driving home Arthur told him to drive back to London. 'Did he make a further request?' says Mr Draycott. 'Yes. He said he would leave the car with me and I would be going back to pick up a black suitcase where I had put the flowers. And I asked him why.'—'Did he make any reply?'—'He asked me if I was going to do as I was told.'

Mr Draycott asks Nizam what he said then. Nizam: 'I asked him again what it was all about. As a result we had a punch-up.'

Mr Draycott: 'Did it make any sense?'—'No, sir.'—'Did he say what you were to do with the suitcase?'—'Put it in the boot and drive home.'—'Were you prepared to pick it up?'—'No, sir.'

Mr Draycott: 'As a result of the punch-up what did you do?' Nizam: 'I jumped out of the car and started walking home.'

It was a very cold night: he got a lift: he arrived home soaking wet. Mrs Hosein wanted to know what it was all about. Arthur told him to shut his mouth. Mrs Hosein thought they had been out with other women—next morning she found the two Black Label beer cans.

Mr Draycott: 'Did Arthur ever give you an explanation?' Nizam: 'I never asked him any questions.'—'But didn't you have any thoughts?'—'I thought it was something to do with a woman.'

The Judge: 'You thought some young woman was *eloping*? That was the reason for the suitcase?' Nizam: 'Yes, sir.'

Mr Draycott goes through the events of the 6th February. Nizam had been in London with Arthur, and at Bishop's Stortford Arthur stopped the car and told Nizam to go back to Gates Garage used-car lot, where he would see two black suitcases opposite a Minivan. He was to pick them up, not to open them, and come to The Raven.

Mr Draycott: 'Did he emphasise the colour?' Nizam: 'Two black.' (*Black!*) 'Did you grasp the number of the Mini?'—'He said to write it down.'—'And that was the note you made that was subsequently found in your pocket?'—'Yes.'

Mr Draycott: 'Did you drive on to the forecourt of Gates Garage and hang around?—'Yes, sir.' We hear again about the forecourt being brightly lit, and Nizam's being asked to move on. He circled round, and then the suitcases were there. We hear about his bringing the Volvo to a standstill beside the suitcases, the car hooting behind, and his moving on.

Mr Draycott (artlessly following the procedure): 'Had you noticed something about the suitcases?' Nizam: 'Not at that time.' He came back again, and sat looking at the suitcases.

'Next time did you sit looking at them?'—'Yes, sir.'—'Did

you want to pick them up?' Nizam (with soft but firm pathos): 'I never wanted to pick them up. . . .'

Nizam noticed they were *white*. Mr Draycott: 'Did you try and think of an excuse for *not* picking them up?'—'Yes. I could tell him they were white, not black.'—'Could you have picked them up?'—'Yes, sir.'—'But you didn't.'—'No, sir.' Mr Draycott: 'And what were you thinking about them?' Nizam: 'That they were stolen property.'—'And you didn't want to be mixed up in it?'—'No, sir.'

So Nizam went to The Raven, and told Arthur he had not picked up the suitcases because they were white, not black. Mr Draycott: 'Was Arthur pleased?' Nizam: 'He'd had a lot of drink. He made no comment.' He and Arthur had a drink. 'And what did Arthur say?' Nizam: ' "Drive me back and we'll go and have a look!" And I did.'

(So we now have the gloss of innocence! But supposing the contrary—could Nizam have been watching at Gates Garage, artfully having made sure of getting there first, to see if a second police-trap was being set up? And pausing beside the suitcases to see if there were any sign of police about to pounce?)

Mr Draycott gets Nizam's agreement that the police evidence of their both returning at 10.47 p.m. is correct. (The police got this time as far as taking the Volvo's number, but did not yet know who *they* were).

The suitcases were left there, and Nizam never got an explanation from Arthur of what it was all about. The next day the police came with the search warrant for some stolen jewellery. Mr Draycott: 'Had Arthur told you what to do?' Nizam: 'Keep my mouth shut.'

We go on to the police station. Nizam did not realise the situation till Chief Superintendent Smith showed him the paper flowers and the billhook from Arthur Road: then he was very frightened. He thought it was the calf-skinning billhook. Mr Draycott: 'You realised your position was perilous?' Nizam (in a whisper): 'Yes, sir.'

'Later on you were on the brink of telling the police something, yet you didn't. Why didn't you?' Nizam: 'I was frightened, scared. . . .'

'One police officer says that on the 19th June you said: "I

could get out of 90% of this if I just put my cards on the table." Why didn't you?'—'I was scared.' (The police evidence was that he said he wanted to *think* more about it, which is a very different matter.)

'You realised you had relevant information?'—'Yes, sir.'—'What did you think would be the consequence of telling the police what you've told us?'—'I didn't know what would happen. I was *scared*. . . .'

The Judge: 'Of what or of whom?' Nizam: 'I was scared of Arthur.'

Mr Draycott: 'What did it seem to you would happen if you opened your mouth? Did you think anything might happen to Arthur?' Nizam: 'I thought he is my brother'—voice almost extinguished—'and it was very hard for me to say.'

The Judge: 'What did you think Arthur had done?' Nizam: 'I thought he had some part in . . .' (He fades out.)

The Judge: 'In what?' Nizam: 'In the affair.'

The Judge: 'What affair?' Nizam (just managing to say it): 'The Mrs McKay affair.'

Mr Draycott takes up the story again. The incident in prison in June when Nizam and Arthur were separated. Nizam was beginning to realise he had got to talk. At first he and Arthur had the same solicitor: then a separate solicitor and separate legal representatives.

Mr Draycott: 'Even after you had separate representation, was it easy or difficult to talk?' Nizam (faintly): 'Difficult.' Mr Draycott reminds him of his request to see the police by himself, in an attempt to tell, and yet he did not. 'Why not?'

Nizam (as if about to give up): 'I just ran dry. . . .'

Next the note held up in Brixton Prison for Adam to read. In the exercising yard Arthur had told him to say it: he was worried because he had been out all that night.

The Judge: 'You decided to tell the same story as Arthur?' Nizam: 'Yes, sir.' Mr Draycott asks him if the suggestion made in the note that Arthur was with two farmers was true or false. Nizam: 'I didn't know.'

Finally Mr Draycott turns to Arthur's evidence. 'Arthur told the members of the jury that you were being made use of by a group of international figures; that he came down in the middle of the night and found you. Is there any truth in that?' Nizam: 'No truth. That's the story he was telling me to tell!'

The Judge: 'You might as well mention names, as one has been mentioned already.'

Mr Draycott questions Nizam about Mr Robert Maxwell. Nizam has never seen him: Arthur showed him a photograph from *The Daily Telegraph* and asked him to say Mr Maxwell was one of the men he could recognise—someone who was giving him help to get into the Royal Air Force.

The Judge: 'Is there any truth in the story that on the 29th December four men came to the Farm?' Nizam: 'No truth.'

The Judge: 'Was there any occasion when you had four men at your house?' Nizam: 'No, sir. Only Liley . . . .'

Mr Draycott sits down. It is getting near to the end of the day. Mr Hudson is standing up, but so is the Attorney General. Something unusual? Yes: Mr Hudson is telling His Lordship that he would like to make some submissions in the absence of the jury.

The Judge asks the jury to leave, and they duly file out.

Mr Hudson says he proposes to introduce two previous matters, in the criminal Courts in Trinidad, relating to 'this man'—he glances at Nizam, standing still in the witness-box.

'It depends what it is,' says the Judge.

Now that the jury is absent the Judge and leading counsel revert in their discussion to the speedy, informal committee-like atmosphere in which the question of Count 1's going forward was settled. Mr Hudson says the evidence comes within the principle laid down—he cites his sources—where a defendant gives evidence against a co-defendant. Mr Draycott joins in. He knows the matter of previous conviction of his client, another of suspended sentence.

(So the Napoleonic Arthur hasn't any previous convictions, but the cowering Nizam *has!*)

Mr Draycott goes on with an air of combined aggrievedness and menace: 'I have endeavoured *not* to bring in the character of Arthur.' He has confined his case, he says, very carefully—he has *not* called evidence of the relationship between Arthur and his wife. . . . They discuss it rapidly between themselves; the question is of Mr Hudson's widening the issue, to show that Mr Draycott's client is a violent person.

His Lordship decides to leave it to Mr Hudson's discretion.

Mr Hudson glances at the clock. Because of this new turn, he will not be able to finish his cross-examination of this man tonight.

His Lordship: 'You'd rather not *begin* tonight?' Mr Hudson: 'Yes.'

His Lordship: 'Well, say so!'

End of another day. Revelations to come.

28th September, *half-day only*

Both Hoseins are in different suits. Arthur is in fawn, Nizam, still in the witness-box, is in navy, with a white shirt. An usher hangs the microphone round his neck. Mr Hudson stands up.

'I have a number of questions to put to you about your brother in respect of what you've said about *him*.'

Nizam holds on to the sides of the witness-box. Mr Hudson is leaning forward, his eagle nose jutting without his spectacles. He says:

'First of all the general background. Do you get on well with your brother Adam?' Nizam replies soundlessly. Finally he makes 'Yes, sir' audible.

Mr Hudson (suddenly): 'Are you anxious to disguise your voice?'

'No, sir.'—'Do you swear it?'—'Yes, sir.'

Mr Hudson: 'Why didn't you agree to speak on the telephone at the police station, as your brother did?' (Mr Hudson must have heard the tapes: is he another of those people who are convinced that M3's voice sounds more like Nizam's?)

Nizam: 'I didn't know what was happening. I was frightened. . . .'

'Why were you frightened?'—'I thought it was a trick.'—'What sort of trick?'

The Judge: 'Suppose you'd said into the telephone "I don't know what all this is about". That would have done you no harm.' Nizam gets out an inaudible reply.

Mr Hudson puts a series of questions. 'Are you on good terms with Adam?' 'Do you respect your brother?' 'Would you say your relationship with him is normal?'

The Judge: 'Not frightened of him? Only respect?' Nizam: 'Only respect.'

Mr Hudson: 'You've seen Mrs Hosein. Do you get on all right with her? Has she always been kind to you?'—'Yes, sir.'

The Judge: 'When you said I have only respect for my brother, which brother did you mean?'—'Adam.'

Mr Hudson: 'Mrs Hosein was kindness itself?'—'Yes, sir.'

'As I understand it, you've told the court you did these incredible things, picking up suitcases . . .'

The Judge pounces again: 'You're not entitled to say "incredible", Mr Hudson.' He warns the jury.

Another series of questions from Mr Hudson. 'You say you were frightened of your brother? Were you frightened when you went to Gates Garage?' And then: 'Did you go to your brother's wife and say so?' Nizam: 'He told me to keep my mouth shut!'

Mr Hudson suggests he never was frightened. The Judge intervenes: 'Was Adam scared of Arthur?'

Nizam: 'They never speak to each other.'

(Again one asks: Are they all powerfully bound together as a family and do they all hate each other as men?)

Mr Hudson: 'I suggest what you've been telling us about fear is an invention. You've told us that when you were with the police under interrogation, you were afraid to tell them what you've been telling the court now.' Pause. 'You were brave enough to call in the police on the 28th December, when you made a complaint?'—'Yes, because Arthur was doing something wrong. . . .'

Mr Hudson now pounces: 'What bigger incentive to tell the police than when you were held on a graver charge—why didn't you?' Nizam (cowering): 'I couldn't get myself together. . . .'

'You had weeks to "get yourself together"!' Right at the beginning, in February, Nizam had his own solicitor, his own counsel, who had nothing whatsoever to do with Arthur, and so on—reiterating, 'You were brave enough on the 28th December.' Nizam, nearly inaudibly, seems to be saying something about Liley.

'When you were in a perilous situation?' Mr Hudson goes on, recalling Mr Draycott's description of it. Nizam: 'I was scared.'

The Judge: 'Scared of what? Nizam: 'Of what Arthur would do.' He adds, again nearly inaudibly, that he wanted to help Liley out of it.

The Judge: 'You were charged with murder. Was that more or less important than keeping Liley out of it?' Nizam: 'I didn't know what it was all *about*. . . .'

Mr Hudson returns to the charge. What fear could he have had in July or June when he saw his solicitor? 'I just couldn't tell. I just couldn't speak the words.'

Mr Hudson says he cannot follow it: after weeks and weeks in custody Nizam had nothing to fear from Arthur. Nizam asked to see Mr Smith and Mr Minors, and then was unable to come out with the story. Nizam: 'He was my own brother. . . .'

Mr Hudson: 'Or is there an alternative—that you hadn't got your story straight, that it was an invention?' Nizam: 'I had the story in my mind. . . .'

'And you weren't sure it was the right story in your own interests? What about that?' Nizam: 'I didn't know *how* to tell the police. . . .'

Mr Hudson suddenly switches to the 29th December. Nizam has told the court, Mr Hudson says, that Arthur left the Farm in the afternoon and came back at 8.50 p.m. Nizam (correcting him): '8.15'. Mr Hudson: 'And you left at 8.50 p.m.?' Nizam's reply is soundless again.

The Judge: 'You must give evidence so that you're audible. You don't look incapable. The jury may think you don't want to be heard.'

Mr Hudson's point is that Nizam says he did not leave the Farm till 8.50; so why didn't he answer Liley's call at 8 p.m.? Nizam has the answer: 'At that time I was out on the Farm, walking the dogs.'

Then Mr Hudson goes on to Nizam's trip to London: 'You visited Adam and others. You told him your brother was in bed and that you'd been to the finishers?'—'I told him Arthur went to the finishers and then went to bed.'

'Why did you go to London at all if you hadn't seen Adam

for months?' Nizam has the answer again. 'It was the Christmas season in Trinidad. . . ."

'Adam gave us your reason as that you were going to the finishers. You didn't go to the finishers?' Nizam shakes his head: 'No, sir.'—'You were capable of finding your way?'—'It was not easy. I asked the way. . . .'

Mr Hudson: 'You never conveyed to Adam that you were unhappy at Rook's Farm. Why didn't you?' Nizam: 'It was no use. Adam and Arthur didn't speak to each other.'

Mr Hudson suggests he might have gone back to Trinidad. Nizam has come on a charter flight and the return date has passed. He wants to stay in England for his education.

Mr Hudson: 'Adam has told us he spoke on the telephone to you after Christmas: you said certain persons were assisting you to obtain permanent residence in this country. Did you say that?'—'No, sir.'—'Has anyone after Christmas given you assistance?'—'Only Arthur and Farmer Smith.'

Mr Hudson now uses the difference between Arthur's story and Nizam's story to open up the relationship between all the brothers. Over the four men assisting him to get a visa, Nizam swears that he did not discuss it with Adam in January. But later he did, and 'Adam said, "If you don't stick to Arthur's story . . ." he'd never see me again in his life!'

Mr Hudson: 'So Adam is against you?' Nizam: 'Yes, sir, *now*. . . .'

(The out-of-court gossip has been that Nizam is now deserted entirely by the rest of the family: it sounds as if it may be true.)

Mr Hudson switches again to the 1st January. 'Arthur says you had tummy pains, and went out in the Volvo.' (*Did* Arthur say he went in the Volvo? He did not.) Nizam says he walked to a local pub and had some bitter beer.

Mr Hudson: 'You were away at least an hour. You were enjoying the bitter beer?'—'There were no chemists open.' Mr Hudson (sarcasm making its appearance): 'Did you think bitter beer would help?' Nizam: 'I'd try anything.'

The question: What time? The Judge puts in: 'Some time before the pub closed. You mean in the afternoon?' (The M3 calls were made at 7.45 p.m.) 'Yes, sir.'

Mr Hudson (frankly sarcastic): 'And did bitter beer cure it?'

Nizam: 'I still had it.' He returned to the Farm, Liley was furious, etc.

And then Mr Hudson launches into the final gambit. 'I suggest that you are quite capable of dealing with a situation involving violence.' Nizam shakes his head.

'And that you are not afraid of people?' Nizam is soundless.

'You were brave enough to use a knife in Trinidad?'

Nizam: 'My brother told the magistrate . . .' He tails off into incoherence.

Mr Hudson: 'You did *stab* your brother?'

'It was an accident.'

'Your oldest brother? You say a knife found its way accidentally into your brother when it was in your hand?

'I was in the kitchen.'

'It was not a kitchen knife. It was a straight knife—what might be called an offensive weapon?'

Nizam: 'It was a knife in the kitchen. . . .'

Mr Hudson goes on inexorably. 'In the following year, when you were only twenty, you were charged with assaulting somebody on 14th May 1969. Your mother was ordered to enter into a recognisance of 150 dollars for you, and you were put in the hands of a Probation Officer?'

'I came into my father's house drunk. . . . He's against it. I broke some glasses.'

Mr Hudson: 'What did you do?' He reads out the charges.

The Judge: 'Is that correct?' Nizam (faintly): I can't remember the wording. . . .'

Mr Hudson leans forward over his desk, as if to get nearer to Nizam: 'What *I'm* concerned about is why you were placed in the hands of a Probation Officer!' Nizam: 'I drank too much.'

Mr Hudson: 'And *hit* people.' Nizam: 'I never hit anybody.'

Mr Hudson: 'You were charged with assaulting and beating!' Nizam: 'I never assaulted and beat . . .'

'Then why were you charged?'

'My father was against drink . . .'

'*I* suggest'—Mr Hudson's eagle-eyes flash devastatingly—'you're *perfectly capable of defending yourself*!'

Mr Hudson sits down.

So Nizam may shrink and cower in the witness-box, his voice

may be so soft and gentle that no-one can hear it; but is it all a performance, a performance which can be so convincing as to be touching—he really does look as if he may be about to break down—and yet may also be 100% artful? Arthur said he is quite clever. He *is* quite clever. (Incidentally his English is better than Arthur's: it has none of Arthur's pidgin eccentricities.) When he is audible he can come up with the perfect, evasive, side-stepping, self-preserving answer. Even the whispered 'I was *scared* . . .' produces its effect, reiterated. *Scared, scared* . . . making one think, inexcusably, of voodoo.

Mr Hudson sits down. Has he done his own client any good? It is difficult to say. He has uncovered the truth, anyway. And he has prevented Nizam escaping at Arthur's expense. If the two are innocent, then, never wanting to see each other again, that is that: if they are guilty, they will go down together.

A glance at Arthur in the dock—is there the faintest glint of sarcasm in that sallow brooding face with large eyes? It is interesting how the picture of them has changed. Vain and voluble, Arthur's character, beside Nizam's with its resources in the labyrinthine and the astute, begins to look shallower, emptier.

Now the final cross-examination by the Attorney General. Lamb-like Nizam waits, the microphone hanging round his neck. The Attorney General starts with the 19th December and the visit to the 'Taxation Office'. Nizam is back on the same ground as before. 'I was told to. I would have got into trouble. I have to do as I'm told.' Arthur wanted the information.

'When did you first hear the name of Rupert Murdoch?' Nizam: 'When I was in custody.'—'Not before? Your brother says you look at TV.'—'I only sometimes watched TV.'

Nizam failed to get the information. The Judge: 'Did you think Arthur wanted it for a dishonest purpose?'—'I didn't give it a thought at the time.'

The Attorney General makes him repeat the remark. Then asks: 'When did you next give it a thought?' Nizam: 'At the police station.'

Nizam denies following the Rolls, and agrees that he heard on TV Mrs McKay had been taken or had disappeared. The Attorney General insists: 'The wife of the acting chairman of

The News Of The World had disappeared. Did you not cast your mind back to the enquiry you made about the owner of the car on 19th December?' Nizam (quietly as ever): 'Not at all. I was working on the Farm.'

'You never spoke to your brother about it?'—'Never.'

The Judge: 'Did you speak about it to yourself?' Nizam: 'That's all it was.'

The Attorney General still insists—the statement of the clerk at County Hall is read out. 'Ten days after—did you think back?'—'I never thought about it.'—'Did it not occur to you ...?' Nizam: 'It never occurred to me in my mind.'

The Attorney General tries the 29th December, and the drive in the Volvo after Arthur had brought it back. A cold, dark night. 'You set out to drive to Norbury Crescent to see relatives. Did you very much want to see them?' Nizam: 'At Christmas, back home ...'

'This was four days *after* Christmas.' Nizam explains something inaudibly. At Norbury Crescent they were not expecting him? This was not unusual, 'back home'. He stayed about ten minutes—the man in the house had gone to bed: Nizam saw his wife, asked her for a drink.

Attorney General: 'Did you feel in *need* of a drink?' Nizam: 'No. It was just the Christmas season.'

'Was the purpose to get some witness who'd say where you were?'—'I never thought of that. I wanted to see them. ... I hadn't seen them since May.'

Then to Adam. *He* was not expecting him, either. 'Suddenly, after all those months,' says the Attorney General, 'between half past eleven and midnight, without warning.' Nizam: 'Yes, sir.'

'Did you get what you came for?' Nizam: 'I never got a drink. He had some things from Trinidad, upstairs.'—'Where his wife was asleep?' Then: 'So you didn't get what you came for?' Nizam: 'It was just a social visit. Just Christmas. ...'

The Attorney General refers to the journey back, through Epping; the call at 1.15 a.m. Nizam: 'I could have been in the area, but I didn't make the call.' The Attorney General has the transcript of the M3 call handed to Nizam. 'Will you read it? "This is Mafia Group 3" and so on.'

Nizam reads, just audibly, hesitating occasionally. "We have your wife. It will cost you a million to get her back. . . . You had better get it. You have friends. . . . This is M3, Mafia in England. We tried to get Rupert Murdoch's wife, but we couldn't get her. So we took your wife instead."

'When did you first hear of Rupert Murdoch?' Nizam: 'Sometime in January.'

'Are you sure you weren't speaking from the telephone box?' —'I was in the area, but I didn't make the call.'

Attorney General: 'You say you got back at 3 a.m. You left at 9, spent ten minutes at Norbury Crescent, ten minutes at Adam's. *Where* were you for the rest of the time?' Nizam: 'I had to enquire my way. . . .' (Very neat!)

Attorney General: 'Now look at Exhibit 7!' A billhook. 'When shown that at Kingston Police Station you shook your head and closed your eyes.'—'I thought it was the same one I used to chop up the calf.'

'Why should that make you close your eyes?'—'I didn't want to chop up the calf.'

Attorney General: 'That chopper is not the one from George Curwen. But Mr Len Smith says it was his, lost at an auction or at Rook's Farm.' Then: 'And that billhook was discovered in Mrs McKay's house!' Nizam: 'I don't know how it got to Mrs McKay's house.'

'When did you last see it?'—'I saw something like this in the police station.'

The Judge: 'When you were asked if you'd ever seen it before, you wouldn't answer.' Nizam repeats almost inaudibly something about chopping up the calf.

Attorney General: 'Why should you close your eyes?'—'I was scared stiff. . . .'

Attorney General: 'All the more reason why you should tell the police all you knew!'

Nizam is shown the copy of *The People*. The Attorney General says: '*The People* used to be delivered at Rook's Farm.' Nizam: 'I never read it.' Attorney General: 'But it was delivered.' Nizam admits he saw it delivered.

Now the strip of adhesive plaster. The Attorney General: 'Do you remember being shown this at Kingston Police Station?' Nizam (faintly): 'I don't remember.' Attorney General: 'At 9.30

on 9th February it was shown to you. You said "Let me die! Let me die!" Why did you say that?'

Nizam: 'I was saying "Let me die!" when I was shown the paper flowers.'

'Why were you begging to die?'—'Mr Smith said they were all connected. . . .'

'You might be scared, but why should you want to die?'

The Judge: 'Mr Smith said "Have you seen this before?" Then you started trembling and said "Let me die!" '

Nizam: 'I was trembling from the beginning, since seeing the flowers.' (The flowers—he has admitted to them, of course.)

Attorney General: 'You didn't tremble and say "Let me die!" when you were asked to speak on the telephone. You said no!'

'I was scared all the while.'

'Had you good reason to tremble?'—'Yes.'

'Had you good reason to say "Let me die!" when you saw the adhesive tape?' Nizam: 'I never wanted to be in trouble!'

'Were you involved in the fact that someone was missing?' Nizam: 'Mr Smith said . . .'

'Were you involved in the fact that *Mrs McKay* was missing?' Nizam: 'I was involved with the paper flowers.'

Attorney General: 'Then why should you say "Let me die!"?'

Nizam (on the edge of breaking down): 'Mr Smith said I'd murdered her. Mr Smith said it was not a calf I chopped up, *it was a woman! . . .*'

(The words are out! The words that have never, so far, been uttered in the court. The prosecution has gone round and round the chopping up of the calf, and we all knew the implication. It is, of course, *one* of the two bizarre public rumours that have been circulating for weeks. . . . The words were never uttered by counsel, because there is no trace whatsoever that Mrs McKay was ever even at the Farm. Now the words have been uttered—albeit in quotation of somebody else—by one of the defendants!)

The Attorney General says instantly; 'Look at these pieces of material.' Nizam is handed the cellophane packet of cuttings: the green jersey material, the black and brown reversible cashmere, the cream coloured leather.

'Tell me where those pieces of material come from!' Nizam (trembling): 'They just came from the police.'

'From whose clothing are they?'—'I was told they were from Mrs McKay's.'

'When you were shown them on the 9th February, you trembled and said "Let me die, let me die! Why don't I die?" '—'I was trembling because I was scared stiff. . . .'

'Why were you scared stiff if you knew nothing?'—'Because Mr Smith told me something, and I said "I don't know . . ." ' And again: 'I was scared.'

The Judge: 'But why did you want to die?'

Nizam: 'I'd rather die than be interrogated like this!'

The Judge interpolates: 'You told him you knew nothing about the paper flowers.'

Attorney General: 'Why did you tell him you knew nothing about *them*?'—'I was scared stiff.'

'Had you any reason to be scared stiff?'—'They were holding me.'

'Did the pieces of material remind you of anything?'—'Mr Smith told me they . . .'

The Attorney General hammers on with his questions, about why he did not tell.

'I was scared . . . I was scared stiff . . . I didn't know what I was doing, what to say . . .'

The Attorney General moves to Tuesday, the 30th December. After six hours' driving in the early hours about Surrey and Hertfordshire, what else was he doing? Nizam says he didn't feel good. Was he watching TV? He doesn't remember. Did he see Mrs Dyer? 'No.' Does he know her Christian name? 'Diane.' The Attorney General produces transcripts of the next M3 calls at 4.30 p.m. and makes Nizam read them aloud. "Your wife just posted a letter. . . . Don't call the police! You have been followed. . . . Did you get the money? . . ."

Nizam says he was at the Farm at 4.30 p.m. He went to the pub at mid-day. What about the evening? 'I don't go to pubs at night, not by myself.' Did he go out with Arthur that night in the Volvo? 'No, sir.' Not to N.17 at 6 p.m. where the letter was posted? 'No, sir.' Nizam remembers the day quite well.

On the 31st he telephoned Liley, saying he was homesick.

'It was my first Christmas away from home.' Attorney General: 'Living with someone you were terrified of.'—'Yes, sir.'—'You didn't telephone her on the 30th, but you did on the 31st. You had to persuade her to come and visit you—after the incident of the night of the 26th?'—'Yes, sir.'—'Why were you more homesick on the 31st than on the 26th?'

Nizam (tearfully): 'Back home the boys and girls get together on the 31st . . .'

The Judge glances at the clock. It is a half day only. Time to stop. *In media res* we disband till next morning.

29th September

Nizam still in the witness-box. The Attorney General cross-examining.

Thursday the 1st January, Liley was at the Farm. Liley had wanted to go to a party, but Nizam had to look after the animals. She was scared of Arthur, but Arthur 'had promised not to interfere with her again'. It was important, Nizam agrees, not to leave her with Arthur. Yet he did.

'You remember she was frightened. What made you leave Rook's Farm and leave her alone with Arthur?'—'I had tummy-ache.'—'She is a nurse. Wasn't she just the person to help?'—'Yes.'

'Why didn't you take her?'—'She didn't want to. . . .' (He has said he asked her.) 'She preferred to stay with Arthur?'—'She knew I wouldn't be long.'—'There was no chemist around. The Volvo was at your disposal. You took it?'—'No, sir, I walked. To the pub.'—'What did you expect to find at the pub that would help your tummy-ache?'—'Some bitter beer.'

The Attorney General wants to know why he did not persuade Liley to walk up the lane with him, why he did not borrow the Volvo to go to a chemist's shop in Bishop's Stortford. He asks: 'What was so important that you wanted to go on your own, without Liley?'—'I asked Liley.'

The Attorney General tries to make him fix the time. There were two M3 calls before 8 p.m. Nizam said evening, 3 p.m. 'You call that evening?'—'In Trinidad we call it evening.' When he left Arthur and Liley were watching television. 'In the *afternoon*?' (TV does not begin till later. But if it were what we in England call evening, television would have begun.)

'Was there a telephone box near the pub?' says the Attorney General. 'Yes, sir.'

'How did you feel after the bitter beer, better?'—'No, sir.'—'Did you tell Liley?'—'No.'—'What happened when you went into the house?'—'Liley was mad with me.'—'Why?'—'Because of Arthur having a go at her.'

Back again to the time it took to walk to and fro, the time spent drinking. Liley said he was away an hour and a half. Nizam says he went straight to the barn to feed the animals, which takes two hours. The Judge points out that he must have been away from the house for over two hours.

The Attorney General makes Nizam read telephone call No. 3 aloud.

(He did not make Arthur read the telephone calls aloud. Does the prosecution, too, belong to what now appears to be an extensive school of thought which identifies the caller M3, mainly with Nizam?)

Nizam reads haltingly, successfully passing the pronunciation tests of 'Diane'. The call: "You've gone too far, now." Attorney General: 'Was it your voice that spoke those words?'

Nizam reads the next call. "Look it's concerning your Mum. . . . Now you tell them they've gone too far. Tell them they've gone to the police. . . . They've got to get a million pounds in fivers and tenners, etc." Attorney General: 'Is that the important business that kept you out?' And: 'Did anything happen at Rook's Farm that could be called going too far?' Nizam: 'Nothing happened that could be called going too far. . . .'

Nizam reads a later call in which M3 speaks to Mr McKay: "Hello Alex. . . ." Attorney General: 'Have you heard of Alick?'—'Yes.'—'Have you heard of Alex?'—'I've heard of Alick.'

Then the calls in which M3 describes what Mrs McKay is wearing, and in which he says they traced the car ULO 18F.

Attorney General: 'You recollect trying to trace down a car ULO 18F?'—'I didn't trace the car.'

(While the interchange is going on there is time to reflect that the discovery of the G.L.C. enquiry came to light when *The News Of The World*, trying to avoid any further publicity for

Mr McKay, sent an application to the G.L.C. for the registration number to be changed. It was the result not of police detection but of Civil Service record-keeping!)

The Judge: 'So far as the evidence goes there was only one enquiry about the user of ULO 18F. Only one. That was you. M3 says 'I told the boys to trace the car.' How would you describe what you did at the G.L.C. office?' Nizam: 'I was finding out the car owner.'

More M3 transcript reading. 'I've got to leave tonight for Malta. I got to go around to Malta to see about this job, and then go back to America . . .'

Attorney General: 'Have you ever been to Malta?'—'No, sir.'—'Do you know anybody who's been to Malta?'—'Yes, sir. Adam.'—'Were you at his home when he returned from Malta?' —'Yes, sir.'—'Was that your voice, talking about Malta?' Nizam: 'I never made any calls.'

Now the dreadful call to Ian about his mother being very worried, offering herself to the doctor.

Attorney General: 'Do you realise what a terrible thing it was for a son to hear those words?'—'Yes, sir.'—'Did you speak them?'—'I never did.'

A change from the telephone calls to the ransom letter, with instructions: then M3's telephone calls guiding the ransom-bringers to Dane End. First Nizam's asking one of the finishers for 6*d*. for a telephone call. Later the row when Arthur punched him for staying so long in the pub. After that the paper flowers in the dashboard and Arthur's instructions, the wet and cold night at Dane End. 'I'd been punched before. If I asked him any questions I'd be punched again. . . .' Nizam cowers in the witness-box.

Attorney General: 'You said you thought some woman was eloping. That was the reason for picking up the suitcases?'—'On Saturday I thought that. On the first night I didn't think anything.' And: 'On the first night I was thinking of some stolen property.'

'I'm asking you about the time you were asked to plant the paper flowers and pick up a suitcase. You told the jury you thought it was some woman eloping.'—'All types of things were going through my mind. . . .'

'You know that M3 had told the McKay family to put money in a suitcase. I suggest you knew at the time what was in the suitcases. That was the plan?'—'I never knew about the McKay money. . . .'

The Judge says to Nizam: 'Didn't it strike you that your brother must have been potty—you know what I mean by potty? Your brother must have been out of his mind, to ask you to plant paper flowers by the side of the road?' Nizam: 'No, my Lord.'

The Attorney General has marshalled his next notes: he begins the final assault.

The second ransom attempt. That evening Nizam was delivering trousers with Arthur: they went to Percy Chaplin's at Bethnal Green. 'Mr McKay' (i.e. Inspector Minors) was directed by M3 from a first kiosk to a second in Bethnal Green. The Attorney General says: 'Do you remember being in Bethnal Green that evening?'—'Yes, sir.'—'Were you watching?'—'Yes, sir.'—'Did you see anyone?'—'There were lots of persons. . . .'—'Were you watching the call-box for some purpose?'

The Judge: 'Are you accepting that you were in Bethnal Green, near to the telephone box?' Nizam: 'I could see the box.'

A startling admission. The Attorney General asks: 'Were you watching the call-box to see if Mr Alick McKay went into it?'—'No, sir.'

The Attorney General points out that the instructions to Mr Alick McKay to go next to Epping gave the Hoseins the chance to get to Bishop's Stortford ahead of him. Did Nizam get to Gates Garage by about 8 p.m.?—'Yes.'

Nizam had been told to pick up the suitcases. The Attorney General wants to know what he thought this time. More suitcases. Nizam says he was more suspicious, but too frightened to ask. Attorney General: 'Did you think Arthur was doing something criminal?' Nizam: 'Yes.'—'So you did what you were told?' Nizam: 'I never picked up the suitcases.'

The Attorney General points out that he, Nizam, wrote the name and number of the Minivan on the piece of paper which was subsequently found in his pocket. Nizam says he wrote it down while he was on the Bishop's Stortford road—and this raises a new point which both the Attorney General and the

Judge seize on. Attorney General: 'Did *you* decide where the suitcases were to be left?'

The Judge: 'If you passed Gates Garage and saw the Mini-van, why should you have to write it down?'

Isn't it more believable that he noted down the number much earlier in order to give it over the telephone to Mr Alick McKay? The Attorney General hammers it in with one accusing question after another. Nizam looks more frightened. He says that when he wrote it down, at Arthur's instruction, he was not at Gates Garage.

'You wrote that when you made the plan, etc?'—'I never made a plan.'—'You were at that garage. You circled round. It was well lit. You knew when you made your admissions that the police had identified you as the driver and had found that piece of paper?' Nizam: 'I admitted what I did.'

The Judge: 'Did Arthur say "Be careful nobody is watching"?' Nizam: 'He said "Pick up the suitcases, put them in the boot, and drive to The Raven".'

The Judge: 'Did he say anything about not telling anybody?' Nizam: 'No, sir.'

The Attorney General now goes over the detail of Nizam's actions after the suitcases made their appearance. Why didn't he pick *them* up? 'There was a car behind. . . .' Why didn't he wave him on? 'The traffic was heavy.'

Attorney General: 'You suspected people might be watching you? You remembered the previous occasion?' His tone is becoming increasingly formidable.

'I never knew if anyone was watching!' And: 'I never wanted to pick up the suitcases. I was just looking for excuses.'

'Why not go back and tell your brother they were the wrong suitcases?' Nizam: 'I went, after . . .'

Attorney General: 'After going round them three times!' He goes on. 'You drove back from The Raven with Arthur, and pointed out the suitcases. What did he say?'—'He said "Drive on!" '

'Why didn't you ask him then what it was all about?' Nizam: 'I wanted to be out of it.'

'Didn't you think it strange that he didn't think they were the right suitcases?'—'I didn't think about it. . . .' Nizam is showing signs again of breaking down, as he reiterates his same replies—replies which, nevertheless, have the knack of giving nothing further away.

The Attorney General moves on to the police arrival at Rook's Farm on the following day, saying first that they were looking for stolen jewellery, then for a missing woman, then for Mrs McKay. Nizam: 'It was not till later on, they said Mrs McKay . . .'

Attorney General: 'You remember being shown the paper flowers by the police. Did you realise then that the suitcases and the paper flowers had something to do with the kidnapping?' Nizam: 'Yes, sir.'

'Why didn't you tell the police?'—'I was scared. . . .'

'You were scared of the truth?'—'Arthur told me to keep my mouth shut. . . .'

'Did you ask Arthur why he told you to keep your mouth shut?'—'I was too scared. . . .'

'When you were shown the paper flowers, was it the truth that made you tremble?'

'I never knew why I was involved. . . .'

'Was it the truth that made you say "Let me die! Let me die?"?'—'No, sir.'

'Was it because on 29th December you did go with your brother to that front door, that night?'

'I didn't go with him. . . .'

The questions pound on Nizam. That front door. Breaking in.

'Did you have the billhook with you?'—'No, sir.'

'When you were shown the adhesive tape why did you say "Let me die! Let me die! Why don't I die?"?'

'Mr Smith was insisting that I knew where Mrs McKay was.'

'Were you speaking the truth when you said "Let me die! Let me die!"?'—'Yes.'

The Attorney General seems to lean nearer and nearer to him, as he goes on:

'Did you at that moment *want* to die?'

Nizam, nearly inaudibly: 'Yes, sir. . . . Because I was speaking the truth and they never accepted it. . . .'

'Why, if you were speaking the truth, did you say "Let me die! Let me die!"?'

'I never knew what trouble I was in.' Tears are in Nizam's eyes.

'You said to Detective Sergeant Parker, "Oh my God, what have I done? Arthur always gets me into trouble." '

'I didn't know what I'd done! . . .' He is breaking down.

'Was it your desire to die because you knew you'd done something *dreadful*? . . .'

Nizam: 'I'd rather *die* than be charged with *murder*! . . .'

He is unable to speak for weeping. The Attorney General sits down. Nizam gets out his handkerchief, standing there helplessly. He has broken into tears. He has broken down. But what in the last resort has he broken down into *admitting*? That he has done the murder? . . . Not on your life! That he would rather die than be *charged* with murder. Even in the moment of breakdown he has preserved himself. There is still not the faintest admission from him that he is guilty—only that he is innocent.

Mr Draycott asks if Nizam may sit down to regain his composure: it is no good going on asking him questions while he is weeping. Mr Draycott wants to re-examine him. His Lordship adjourns the court for ten minutes.

After the ten minutes the Judge asks Nizam if he would like to remain sitting down. Mr Draycott (to the Judge): 'I should prefer him to stand.' (To Nizam): 'I want to ask you about certain matters that Mr Hudson mentioned about your having no reason to be afraid of Arthur because you could have gone to Mrs Hosein.'—'Yes, sir.'

'From your knowledge, was Mrs Hosein afraid of her husband?' Nizam: 'She was afraid.'

Mr Draycott then refers him to an incident he will remember at Rook's Farm, on the weekend in January when certain friends were staying there—there was some trouble later between Arthur and his wife.

The Judge questions the relevance of this evidence.

Mr Draycott says it becomes admissible because it has been suggested that Nizam had no reason to fear Arthur, and that the atmosphere was such that Mrs Hosein could help.

The Judge: 'Arthur may be a wife-beater, but it doesn't follow that he's knocked his brother about.' However he allows Mr Draycott to go on.

We hear about the incident. Nizam describes in detail a drunken scene after the party came back from the pub at midnight—Mrs Hosein shouting for Nizam from the kitchen, where Arthur had punched her in the stomach.

Mr Draycott (courteously): 'That will be sufficient for my purpose. Was that the only incident?'

Nizam: 'There were other incidents. Yes, sir.'

'You told us Arthur struck you. Also that Arthur struck his wife. Would you say that on these occasions he was in control of himself?'

'Yes, sir. He's a ruler.'

The Judge: 'What do you mean by that?'

Nizam: 'A master.' And he adds that over Arthur's attitude to the local hunt crossing his land the M.F.H. had once called Arthur 'King Hosein'.

A succession of minor points follows. On his second appearance before the magistrates in Trinidad there is reference to 'his age and previous good record'. (After stabbing his brother?) Shariff Mustapha is the name of a Trinidadian school friend. In Trinidad, mid-day to 3 p.m. is 'afternoon': 3 p.m. to 6 or 7 p.m. is 'evening': after that, 'night'. (He has said that he went to the pub on the 1st January at '3 p.m. evening'. M3 calls were made to Arthur Road at 7.45 p.m.)

At last Nizam faces repeated questions about his presence at Dane End and at Gates Garage. At Dane End, in the early hours of the morning, he had no idea what it was all about. That it might be an 'elopement' was put into his mind when Mrs Hosein asked 'Where's the woman?'—after he had walked home in the rain. Before that he had no idea of the reason for picking up the suitcase at Dane End.

The Judge asks: 'I wonder if in an hour's trudge you thought about it.' Nizam: 'It was very cold, sir.'

Mr Draycott: 'But it just didn't make any sense, did it?' Nizam: 'I never made any conclusions. I was just suspicious of it.'

Mr Draycott again stresses Nizam's absence of concealment at Gates Garage. 'Did you take *any steps at all*,' he asks, 'to hide yourself?'—'No, sir.' About the suitcases: 'If you'd wanted to pick them up, was there anything to stop you?'—'No, sir.'

The Judge: 'The Crown are saying you were testing if the coast was clear, that you wanted to see if there were any police cars around.'—'I never paid attention to anyone.'

The Judge brings Nizam's evidence to a close: 'You did say that at some stage after the police came to Rook's Farm, you thought your brother had something to do with the disappearance of Mrs McKay.' Nizam: 'At the police station I was told . . .'

The Judge: 'When did you think about it? There were the paper flowers, the suitcases at Dane End.' Nizam: 'I thought about it at the police station.'

The Judge: 'In February or March?'—'At the police station.'—'At Kingston?'—'Yes, sir.'

The Judge: 'Until June, until the punch-up happened, you saw Arthur every day?'—'Yes, my Lord.'

'Did you ask Arthur about Mrs McKay?'

'No, my Lord.'

The evidence of Nizam is over. He returns from the witness-box to the dock. His counsel calls no further witnesses. The whole case for the defence of both brothers is over. We are now to have the closing speeches from counsel, and the summing up from the Judge.

And then the verdict from the jury.

Nizam has gone up the steps into the dock and has sat down in his place between the warders—without a glance at Arthur. Nor has Arthur glanced at him, though his facial expression shows an awareness of Nizam's presence.

Nizam has ratted on Arthur. Nizam has tried to say that Arthur is to blame for anything he, Nizam, is accused of; and beyond that Nizam has said there is no truth in the story Arthur tells in his own defence.

On the other hand, one reflects, Arthur has not really ratted, certainly not to anything like the same extent, on Nizam. Arthur has told a story which accounts for what Nizam *has admitted* and which incidentally gets him, Arthur, out of the jam completely; but that, to my mind, is very different from ratting on Nizam. If it really is true that the rest of the family have now deserted Nizam but not Arthur, one can see, after a fashion, why.

I ponder still further over ratting. Suppose the brothers did take part in the kidnapping, even in the murder; if somebody else was involved, why has neither of them ratted on *him*? Nizam, at least, does not appear to be specially inhibited from so doing. Either ratting on him would not help either of their cases; or he is someone whom neither of them could bring himself to rat on. Or—back to Square 1—he does not exist.

11

Closing speech for the prosecution

The Attorney General's closing speech, like his opening speech, is relatively short. Standing up straight and tall, he tells the jury, in his untheatrical, man-to-man tone, that he will not be repeating what he has said before. (For any absence of repetition they may well by now be truly thankful!) He first of all warns the jury (in case, I suppose, they should have read a headline in one of the superior Sunday newspapers) that the trial is 'not a game'. People are tried on the *evidence*; in an atmosphere of reason not emotion: the accused must be protected from matter that is irrelevant (this being, I suppose, the bizarre rumours); and it is the duty of the Crown to *prove* its case. The jury will accept what the Judge says is the law: *they* will decide what is fact.

The Attorney General reads through the charges: murder, kidnap, demands of £1,000,000 ransom, threats to kill. He says: 'Once you're satisfied of the identity of M3, the motive for murder is clear, and the verdict is inexorable.'

Of the brothers he says that each is trying to saddle the other with some or all of the guilt. 'The crime,' he says, 'was committed by both.' The more they said, the more they revealed:—

Arthur by denying everything: the evidence of the car, where it was; the palmprints and fingerprints; the paper flowers. The invention of the international gang only made it the more unreal, the more false. His aim was to put the blame on his brother . . .

Nizam, more sophisticated, by admitting what he knew must be admitted—the paper flowers, the note to Adam, the false application at the G.L.C. Whether, in so doing, he told the whole truth is for the jury to decide.

The Attorney General points to the two men, each saying: 'Not I, not I. *He* did it!' which may satisfy the jury, he suggests, about the guilt of both.

What is suggested by the Crown, he says, is that those two, calling themselves M3, kidnapped that woman: seeking Mrs Murdoch, they found Mrs McKay. Left behind were the adhesive tape, the billhook, the copy of *The People*. Who *left* them?

The farmer lost the billhook at Rook's Farm and never saw it again. Who took it from Rook's Farm to 20 Arthur Road?

Does the jury think the adhesive tape came from Rook's Farm? After Mrs Hosein returned, the tin was used by her child as a money-box.

Does the jury doubt Chief Inspector Brine, with twenty-two years' concentrated experience in the greatest Fingerprint Bureau in the world, when he says the palmprint on *The People* is that of Arthur Hosein?

From the written statements of people seeing a Volvo or a dark saloon car in Wimbledon, on the afternoon and evening of the 29th, does the jury doubt it was the Hoseins' Volvo? (If I were a juror I should not be too happy about that sort of evidence, derived from 'Did you see XYZ?' type of questions.)

The Attorney General suggests that, leaving aside these pieces of evidence, they consider Nizam's going to County Hall on the 19th December, to trace the user of the Rolls-Royce ULO 18F. Nizam claims that he was told to do it, and did it solely out of fear. Yet his determination to get the information shows that he knew full well what he was doing. His fear was an invention, the Attorney General says, 'just as much as the four men invented by Arthur'.

(Well, was it? one asks oneself. I find myself stirred into a mood of counter-suggestibility. Mr Hudson has shown that Nizam can defend himself, can assault and beat, can stab. . . . Beyond that I am willing to hear of Nizam being capable of killing, more capable, in the long run, than the shallow, bombastic Arthur. If one of the two were the hatchet man, I should find myself saying it was the still, withdrawn one and I should not find myself without plenty of members of the joint army who agreed with me.

Nevertheless I am far from sure that Nizam, in his quiet

introverted shell, is *not* afraid of Arthur, not genuinely frightened when confronted with Arthur's wild, incomprehensibly uncontrolled moods. The two aspects of Nizam do not seem to me to be irreconcilable—apparently dominated in the externals of their complex brotherly relationship, but intrinsically capable, when faced with the necessity of murdering, or of disposing of a corpse. As the Attorney General seems to me now to be concentrating on Nizam, perhaps the Crown as well think he, of the two, is more likely the hatchet man? But I just doubt his argument that Nizam's fear is total invention.)

The Attorney General goes through some of the crucial stages in the story. The night of the 29th, when Nizam went to see Adam, and later tried to get Adam to deny it. Six hours' driving, two visits of ten minutes and fifteen minutes only, and the Epping telephone box on the route. There is good reason, says the Attorney General, why Nizam, when shown the billhook, was troubled, when shown the adhesive tape said 'Let me die!'

'Is such behaviour natural?' asks the Attorney General, 'if Nizam hasn't done something dreadful? Is it only out of fear of his brother? Or is it in a moment of truth that he says "Let me die!", a moment of conscience?'

The Attorney General pictures Mrs McKay, on the night of the 29th December, trussed and gagged, laid on the seat of the car, or forced into the boot. 'Was there ever any thought of releasing her?' he asks the jury with quiet penetrating force. 'If she was released, could she not have identified those taking her?' He pauses. 'Was not her own death warrant signed when she was taken away? . . .'

On 30th December Mrs McKay was in the possession of those two men. A letter from her was posted in Tottenham, a vicinity where those men were on that day. And on the letter was the palmprint identified by Chief Inspector Brine as Arthur Hosein's. He rapidly goes through the fingerprint evidence—62 points on six objects—quoting some of the letter's heart-rending sentences: *Can you do something? . . . What have I done to deserve this?* Those prints, the Crown says, show that she was in the possession of the Hoseins.

The Attorney General emphasises the jury's rôle in considering the situation. It is not a matter of law: the Judge will direct them on that. 'No,' he says; 'if you are satisfied there are such circumstances as render the committing of the crime certain, that there is no rational hypothesis except that the crime was committed, then you are entitled to conclude that she was murdered.' He pauses, and then exhorts them to think of:—

the threats to execute,
the pieces cut from the clothing,
the total silence after the brothers were arrested.

There is no rational hypothesis but that she met her death at their hands.

The 30th December was 'an empty day in the life of the Hoseins'. But it included posting the letter from Tottenham which arrived at 20 Arthur Road next morning. Diane Dyer appeared on TV—referred to in a letter received three weeks later. 'You may think that by 21st January Mrs McKay was long since dead.'

On the 31st December, Liley was at Rook's Farm. Was it *only* homesickness that was disturbing Nizam? And Nizam left Liley alone with Arthur for an hour and a half. He puts it at 'evening' in Trinidad language—2.30 p.m. to 3 p.m. 'You may know when TV programmes are on. You may think he wants to put his absence in the afternoon, not evening, because of the telephone calls to Arthur Road.' (M3: 'You've gone too far.') 'You may think something more important than stomach-ache made Nizam leave his girl friend that evening for an hour and a half.'

The Attorney General deals with the letter to *The News Of The World*, and the forensic evidence of handwriting and spelling mistakes—pointing to Arthur Hosein. The letter received on the 22nd January, the ransom note, probably written in the handwriting of Arthur Hosein, in which M3 gives instructions about the money and where it is to be left.

'Who would you expect to be waiting to collect the money?' he asks. 'M3?' He pauses. 'And who do you find? A Volvo car. . . .' And Nizam admits to planting the paper flowers. He touches on the most poignant pieces of evidence, the cuttings of cloth and leather; on seeing which Nizam cried: 'Let me die! Let me die!'

At the end of that trail, the Attorney General suggests, there can be nobody but Nizam.

Next he comes to the two ransom-collecting attempts. The absurdity of Nizam's excuse at the first one that, when he thought about it afterwards, he thought it must be some woman eloping! (Actually it was the Judge who first used the Victorian word 'elope'.) On this occasion the two brothers' stories are different. One or the other must be not telling the truth. Arthur says he has never seen the paper flowers: if that is a lie, it is the lie direct. Nizam says he put them in the car. So it goes on, evidence piling on evidence, lie on lie.

At the second attempt the kiosks were being watched. M3 had criticised Ian McKay because police cars were swarming round at the first attempt. So 'Alick' and 'Diane' are moved from kiosk to kiosk. *Who* happens to be there, near the kiosk in Bethnal Green? Nizam. And when it all ends, who is at the end of the trail? The Hoseins in the Volvo.

The Attorney General refers again to the piece of paper found in Nizam's trouser pocket giving the number of the Minivan. Nizam says he went to Gates Garage and it was there and then that he wrote down the number: if he didn't say that, it would show he played a part in the plan. The Attorney General shows the absurdity of Nizam's statement, and reaches the conclusion—the rôle of Nizam was not that of someone who acted out of terror, but of someone who planned.

'Turn it around,' the Attorney General suggests, for a change. 'If the Hoseins were not M3, what were they doing at Gates Garage? Or at Dane End, with the paper flowers?'

(One asks oneself: what, indeed! There have been times during this closing speech when, as during the corresponding opening speech, it has seemed to me that there is an odd *thinness* about the Crown's case. I find it difficult to put the reason why into words. At the root of it must be, I suppose, the absence of *corpus delicti*; which, if a grisly pun may be permitted in the cause of seriously trying to express the truth, tends to take the body out of the case so far as my instinctive response to it is concerned. But another cause, more definite in the sense of explaining the apparent thinness in texture, is that there are so *many* gaps which have to be bridged by inference rather than evidence—again, purely to my own way of thinking, and I may, in so thinking, be trying to wrestle, single-handed and inexperienced, with the very complex problem of how trials and the law connect. On the other hand, at moments such as this: 'If the Hoseins were not M3, what were they doing at Gates Garage?', the case is at its most cogent. What, indeed?)

The Attorney General comes to the later stages. 'From Arthur,' he says, 'we get the constant lie. Over claiming not to know what the search was about. Over claiming that he had been beaten at the police station—if Arthur bore marks of beating, why didn't his solicitor, Mr Coote, come into the witness-box and say so?'

The Attorney General reminds the jury that Arthur said Mr Coote telephoned him at 5 p.m. on the 29th December. 'Mr Coote could say if it was true,' the Attorney General says. 'But he has not given evidence. There is only one inference to be drawn. That Mr Coote does not agree with the story.'

The Attorney General drives on to his final arguments. Arthur's invention of the four men, who Nizam himself has told the jury never existed. The name of a public figure was dragged into the case—and dragged in vain. But could Nizam have been as innocent as he told the jury from the witness-box that he was? Was Nizam the one who made the telephone calls? Why was he the one who refused to speak into the telephone for the test?

'And who said "Oh, my God, what have I done?"' The Attorney General's voice resounds with emotion and emphasis: 'The one *honest* cry that *either* of them has uttered!'

He calls for a verdict of Guilty on all counts for both brothers.

12

Closing speech for the defence

(*Arthur Hosein*)

'This is the last time that I, who am charged with defending this man, Arthur Hosein, shall have the chance to speak to you on his behalf.'

Mr Hudson has folded up his spectacles and put away his notes. He is beginning a speech that will last for many hours, over this day and the next, made extempore throughout. He leans forward a little, eagle-nose and chin jutting, to rest his left fore-arm for support on his little portable desk—will it collapse under him or won't it?—thus leaving his right arm free for gesture.

'You'll have come to the conclusion,' he says, reminding the jury of what he explained at the start, 'that everything has been said that could be said *from either side*. . . .' (Obviously it has, though one suspects he still may have a thing or two up his sleeve.)

He points out that the Crown is represented by the senior Law Officer of the Crown: this is not because of any desire to exert extra pressure, but because it is such a grave case. It is important that such a case should be put by the highest authority.

'But it puts *no* implication on whether either man is guilty.'

He goes on. 'The first count charges my client with murder. You may have to ask yourselves questions that you will find the gravest difficulty in answering. I make no admissions, but assuming the lady is dead, you must still ask yourselves:

'If she is dead, *how* did she die? . . . *when* did she die? . . . *where* did she die?

'I say this with the greatest possible respect'—he acknowledges the jury's great attentiveness to the proceedings—'that when you look at every possible nook and cranny, When, How, and Where, have not been indicated by inference. I'd go so far as to say it's impossible to speculate on the answers. And you've been warned: Don't speculate!' He pauses. 'Yet if you don't speculate, those questions can *not* be answered!'

He deals first with When? Mrs McKay was alive to hear TV at 8.50 p.m. on the 30th December. He refers to M3's call to Ian McKay on the 1st February, when he asks Ian's 'solemn word' that Mrs McKay will not be interrogated by the police. This may be some indication that on the 1st February Mrs McKay was still alive. Such emphasis was put on it; the undertaking on Ian McKay's part was asked for, and pressed home. . . . It might be *some* indication.

Mr Hudson then says: 'If she *was* alive then, she was not at Rook's Farm.' He pauses. 'When you examine the evidence—people were inundated throughout the period with invitations to hunt, shoot, walk over the Farm, come to stay, sleep the night . . . every invitation was given.' Is this consistent, he asks, with what the Crown is saying?

Mr Hudson invites the jury to look at the evidence, beginning with the visits of Mrs Mohammed, who was first invited for Christmas Day. She was reluctant and it was Arthur who persuaded her—to come till New Year's Day or beyond: he wanted her to cook for them. The crime, he says, has the hallmarks of being carefully planned: the men who were going to do it must have had much on their minds. 'When they were planning that foul deed, would they be pressing somebody to come down?'

There is Arthur's giving permission for hunting, *with hounds*, over his land; his inviting, on the 28th, the barman to come over on his first half day, the following Monday afternoon—when in fact the barman actually was driving around Stocking Pelham. At 9 p.m. on the evening of the 30th, almost at the same time that Diane Dyer was appearing on TV, Gerry Gordon rang up about his trousers and asked if he could collect them. The following morning, at 7.30 a.m., Mr Gordon arrived at the Farm, knocked on the brilliantly lit work-room window by the front door, was let in by Nizam, and went into the work-room to pick up the trousers.

Mr Hudson reminds the jury of Arthur's visit on 2nd January, to Liley's sister, the mother of his child—is that consistent with having the crime on his mind? Of Arthur's invitation to the policeman in the barber's shop to come and shoot. 'Psychologically you'd run a mile from a policeman!' Of Mr Rosenthal's visit. And of the visits to Rook's Farm about 'another irrelevant matter', of policemen whose parting words were that they might be coming back.

Mr Hudson submits that the invitations were going on constantly, with nothing sinister about them. 'They are *completely* inconsistent with anything evil going on at Rook's Farm, or anything evil going on that was being done by this man, Arthur Hosein.' There is not a single trace or clue to show that Mrs McKay was ever at Rook's Farm at all. A search was made by one of the most efficient police forces in the world.

'I go further!' Mr Hudson bangs his fist on the folding desk. 'When you consider what sort of life this man was leading, there is positive evidence that he was not involved in these matters.' And he cites Arthur's normal pattern of work throughout the period. There is evidence that Arthur was ill at Christmas, had 'flu and felt rotten: but that does not indicate he was involved in the crime.

'If you are not satisfied Mrs McKay was at Rook's Farm,' he says to the jury, 'then everything that happened about her death, relating to Count 1, the charge of murder, is speculation. You may say to yourselves: "I didn't think a man could be convicted of murder without a body being found." He can. His Lordship will direct you. There are indeed rare instances of such things happening in the courts. But if no body is found, and nobody sees the person meeting his or her death, *you are speculating*! You're taking—and I urge this upon you with all the force in my power—an *enormous* speculation. And that is one thing we must guard against in a criminal trial in this country.' He pauses. 'If the unfortunate woman met her death, I repeat, it is impossible to know how she met her death. I must join issue with m'learned friend. Nobody can tell how she met her death except her murderers. If it could be proved that she met her death at the time of kidnapping, one could say she met her death by violence at the hands of the men who kidnapped her. We know she didn't! She refers to seeing her daughter on television on the 30th December.' He pauses again. 'And if she met her death at Rook's Farm it can only be after TV at 9 p.m. that night and before the arrival of Mr Gordon at 7.30 a.m. next morning. She couldn't have met her death at Rook's Farm outside that narrow period of time. But there is no clothing, no jewellery, nothing to show she'd been at the house at all. If you ask How, When and Where? and those questions can not be answered, how can the charge of murder go ahead?'

The light in the court is going down and a glance at the clock shows it is nearly time for the day to end. Tomorrow the greater part of his address, Mr Hudson tells the jury, is going to be concern ed with the evidence for Arthur Hosein's not being involved in the kidnapping, neither committing the crime nor being party to it. But for the present:

'I submit that it is not good enough for the Crown to put the case as it's being put now.' He pauses. 'There is far too much speculation, in any case, on Count 1.'

So the day ends, for once on a note of more drama—and for me, as I join the crowd filing out, on a note of more doubt again. . . . From Mr Hudson's emphasis on the extraordinarily narrow period of time within which, according to the prosecution, Mrs McKay met her death at Rook's Farm, I go back to his earlier emphasis on there being *some* indication, from M3's telephone call on the 1st February, that she was still alive then. M3 did sound absolutely serious about it—only somebody absolutely serious about it could have made such a stupefyingly unrealistic demand, asking Ian McKay's 'solemn word' meanwhile. And to have gone to the lengths of making it when the victim had already been dead for five weeks—that makes it even more stupefying.

And in the same mood I return to another point I have never been quite happy about, swayed as I am by the prosecution's case plus the supposedly accurate American statistics that 70% of victims kidnapped for ransom are murdered within twenty-four hours, and at most forty-eight hours. Mrs McKay's letter, *I am deteriorating in health and spirit*, received on the 22nd January, over three weeks after the kidnapping, is alleged by the prosecution to have been written much earlier. Yet it does not sound like the sort of letter she would either have written herself, or the kidnappers would have thought of making her write, within twenty-four hours; 'deteriorating' is normally used for things a bit slower than that. On the other hand the letter goes on to exhort co-operation with the gang: *"Use the code number M3"*—hardly necessary advice, weeks later. Nothing, nothing in this case seems to me to add up properly.

30th September

Mr Hudson resumes. 'It's not easy to keep all the essential details in mind, even for us!' Yesterday he dealt with the cogent factors of what was happening at Rook's Farm during the cogent time. Countless invitations; countless callers *without* invitation, including members of the police force who said they may return. Cogent, positive, provocative evidence that Arthur Hosein is innocent. He, Mr Hudson, now purposes a detailed analysis of Arthur's account of his own life at the time.

First, Arthur's pressing Liley to come and stay at Christmas, to cook for him and his brother in his wife's absence. Then on the 29th Arthur recollects he went with Nizam to see Farmer Pateman. Mr Pateman doesn't know if it was the 29th or 30th, but is certain that it was one of those two days. If it was the 29th, such a visit, to say the least, was far removed from criminal activity—according to the Crown the brothers were just about to set out for Wimbledon. If it was the 30th, the conclusions are even more incredible: while they were at Pateman's the brothers had left Mrs McKay at Rook's Farm, alive.

Mr Hudson deals with Liley's telephone calls on the 29th, the third of which was answered by Arthur at 10.30 p.m. The enquiry agent's evidence explains it perfectly. Arthur went to bed early with his bottle of whisky and, thinking Nizam was downstairs, switched off the upstairs telephone bell. Going to the lavatory at about 10 p.m. Arthur noticed through the window that the Volvo was gone, taken by Nizam; so he switched the upstairs bell on again.

Turning to M3 telephone calls, Mr Hudson points out that even at this stage there are two calls which the jury can be assured, without a shadow of doubt, that Arthur did *not* make.

The first was on the 1st January, at 7.45 p.m. when Arthur was at home all day, confirmed by Liley's evidence. In parenthesis he observes that he is not here to put up a case for the prosecution against Nizam; but it is a peculiar thing that Nizam, with tummy pains, went out and drank a pint of bitter.

The second was on the 6th February at 7.30 p.m. to the box at Epping when 'Mr McKay' was given his instructions to deposit the suitcases by the Minivan at Gates Garage. Arthur was at The Raven and went to the toilet at about that time. But the call lasted *six minutes*—quite a long time. The evidence of the licensee and his wife is not consistent with his having been out long enough to go to the local box 150 yards away, and they would have seen him if he had gone to their private telephone in the living-quarters.

Going on with Arthur's life at the time, there is masses of evidence between 28th December and 1st February. It is on the latter date that there comes the first clear conflict of evidence between the two brothers. The trip to London and Arthur's return to the Farm without Nizam, who came in after midnight soaking wet. Mr Hudson turns to the evidence of Mrs Hosein, and the impression she made—granted that as a wife, fond of her husband, she'd do her best for him. It was a good impression. She was disapproving of Nizam's association with Liley: but she detected in Nizam nothing of the fear and domination that he speaks of.

Again there is conflict on the night of the 6th. Mr Hudson re-creates the scene in The Raven, when Nizam comes in at 10 p.m., as the prosecution would have it, Arthur asking if he's got the money, was he spotted, what happened? Instead Arthur turns to the actor and his girls and proposes more drinks! The question of Arthur asking for change from the licensee's wife has no importance, because *no* telephone calls from M3 were made after 7.30 p.m. On the night of 6th February, Mr Hudson says, Arthur was acting as if he were not concerned in these matters. He went home and went to bed, as his wife confirms.

Mr Hudson deals next with Arthur's identification by the police as the passenger in the Volvo at 10.47 p.m. The policemen were not in a first-class position to identify anybody, crouched on their knees behind palings. One officer in the witness-box identified Arthur; but the other only gave a description which could fit Arthur—but to settle it the police had never asked Arthur to go into an identity parade. The Crown couldn't produce *two* police officers identifying the passenger as Arthur Hosein.

Mr Hudson turns to Nizam's evidence. The jury may think that Nizam's defence is to put anything that might implicate him on to Arthur. He suddenly rounds on the jury:

'Do you think Nizam is a timid, unintelligent, frightened man?' And he instances Nizam's catching two newspaper headlines the previous evening with 'King Hosein'. Doesn't that show imagination, glibness, quickness to adapt himself to circumstances? Then gravely, he goes on stage by stage to question Nizam's case that he did what he did out of fear. He recalls Nizam's being adjured by his solicitor Mr Coote: 'If you know anything about Mrs McKay, if she is alive, you must tell the police what you know.' Not a word from Nizam. Mr Hudson quotes his Lordship asking Nizam whether, while they were in prison, he did not ask his brother what he knew about Mrs McKay. And Nizam said he had never asked.

'I suggest that he has invented this story,' says Mr Hudson, 'in order to escape the possibility of conviction at this trial. You may think he has perhaps an ingenious mind, a quick mind. He's prepared to see any way out!' He pauses. 'He made certain admissions at the beginning of this trial. I suggest that, facing the evidence, he saw that the only way to get out'—Mr Hudson raises his voice fractionally—'was on the back of my client!'

Mr Hudson waits a moment, and then says: 'Nizam refused to have his voice-test taken. You may think he has kept his voice down in the witness-box. He was the one who refused the test, not Arthur!'

We hear again about Nizam being brave enough to go for the police on the night of the 28th, to 'pinch' his brother's car on the 29th to go and see Adam; and about the incidents in Trinidad.

'One thing I can say. There has never been any suggestion against Arthur, in the sixteen years he has been in this country, of violence or dishonesty. Arthur stands before you as a man against whom there has never been any such suggestion, no conviction of any kind in the context of the sort of dreadful things that have happened in this case.' Mr Hudson makes a gesture with the open palm of his right hand. 'I'm the first to appreciate that when I have to make these comments against the co-defendant, it doesn't do my client's case any good. But what else am I to do?'

There is a moment's silence before he goes on, next, to treat a matter which has been, he says, the subject of a lot of comment. The four strange men.

'Arthur has never said one of them was Robert Maxwell. He merely mentioned that man because he looked like a man whose profile appeared in the newspaper that day. He hasn't named him as the man he saw in his house, nor has he said it in the witness-box. He *has* said he found his brother in conversation with four men, and there was discussion going on about Nizam being allowed to stay on in this country.' Mr Hudson reminds us that Adam says Nizam referred to such discussions later, on the telephone, but Nizam denies it. The jury may think Adam is reliable. Beyond that Arthur's case is 'I don't know what happened'—Nizam's case that Arthur forced him to plant the paper flowers is untrue.

Mr Hudson now comes to the forensic evidence. He gets out the photographs of fingerprints and handwriting, and puts on his spectacles. He compares what Chief Inspector Brine says and what Dr Grant says about individual prints, what one says he can see and what the other says may be there but he can't see. We come round again to the 62 points of characterisation between six objects. From a commonsense point of view they point to Arthur Hosein; but they are not enough to enable one to say *with certainty* that it is he.

'And even if they did, where does it take you?' Mr Hudson demands. 'To Rook's Farm, not to Mrs McKay!' The Attorney General has said Arthur's palmprint on *The People*, found at 20 Arthur Road, means that he went to 20 Arthur Road. 'Of course it doesn't! It means the newspaper was at Rook's Farm. It doesn't mean Arthur took it to Wimbledon.' Mr Hudson looks at the jury over the top of his spectacles. 'At this moment somebody is reading the newspaper I should have read at breakfast: someone has left it at Southwark. That doesn't mean *I* went to Southwark!'

He goes back to the palmprint; first to remark on the divergence of opinion, and then to emphasize that if the print is conceded to come from a particular source it doesn't mean that that person is involved in the crime. The same goes for the writing-paper.

'If, contrary to my submission, you feel justified in accepting the other expert opinion without hesitation, you still have to get over other problems. You get to Rook's Farm.' He pauses. 'That doesn't mean anybody who lives at Rook's Farm is guilty.'

Continuing parenthetically: 'I might as well say here and now —quite possibly somebody at Rook's Farm was involved, despite the fact that Mrs McKay never came to Rook's Farm. But it doesn't follow, because somebody at Rook's Farm was involved, that everybody at Rook's Farm was involved, let alone Arthur Hosein.'

He completes the forensic evidence with the handwriting and the spelling. Again a divergence of opinion among the experts shows the true case may not be as strong as that presented by the Crown. Over the Piccadilly cigarette packet he frankly attacks Mr Rosenthal as unreliable, as he does Farmer Smith over the billhook. In the case of the latter, with divergent stories about the trip to London, and later about a meeting in a caravan, Mr Hudson suggests the old farmer's memory may be playing tricks. 'I defy anybody to say that's not my billhook!' Even if it was, Mr Hudson points out, it only indicates that whoever went to Wimbledon was connected with Rook's Farm. As for Mr Rosenthal, Mr Hudson recalls his 'extraordinary demeanour', and the discrepancies in his story. 'I wasn't suggesting he was doing anything he shouldn't be doing,' says Mr Hudson; 'but he got into—I submit—a terrible tizz over it.' Nevertheless Mr Rosenthal's unreliability is important, because the Crown say Arthur took the cigarette packet to the telephone box on the road to Dane End.

Mr Hudson takes off his spectacles and relaxes again.

'I have tried to put myself in your position, by not speaking to you in a prepared form.'

(True. One recalls that Marshall Hall, even when he had prepared a form, never used it.)

Once again he explains that he has put to them Arthur's case as he sees it—it is not his function to say what Arthur wants him to say: the arguments he has put are his responsibility and his duty. 'And I have to be a realist,' he adds. 'We are not living in a world of fantasy.'

(Having listened to the whole of this case, the last thing I'd say is that I'm sure about that! Especially so far as his client, Arthur Hosein, goes.)

'The Crown are saying Arthur Hosein was involved in the kidnapping. I've been saying the evidence doesn't justify you in coming to that conclusion, that there's a reasonable doubt—that he *may* have had nothing to do with the kidnapping.'

If, however, the jury do disagree with him, if they find Arthur Hosein was involved in the kidnapping, he would say, as he said last night, that when they consider Count 1, they are speculating to a degree beyond which they must not go. They have still to ask themselves:

What *happened*? How did she die? When did she die? Where did she die?

'You can't answer it,' he says. 'If the only thing you've got is "These two people were involved in the kidnapping", that doesn't mean they murdered her. They have lied. Either or both of them has lied, to save themselves being found guilty of kidnapping.' He pauses. 'This is where I submit that absence of a body means that How, When and Where must be the subject of speculation.'

Mr Hudson asks the jury to consider the possibility that she may have died not as a result of brutal murder but of criminal irresponsibility. That would not involve the Hoseins in the charge of murder. It doesn't follow, even if the jury are against him about the brothers' participation in the events at Wimbledon, that the brothers are involved in the charge of murder. 'You mustn't speculate!' he says yet again.

And on the edge of his peroration he glances critically in the direction of a crucial argument in the Crown's case. (Although Mr Hudson does not quote it as such, the argument was concentrated into a single sentence by the Attorney General in his opening speech: 'We may infer that those who threatened to kill, *did* kill.' Also it seems to me to have been an element in the Judge's argument for rejecting Mr Hudson's submission that the case should not proceed under Count 1.) He invites the jury to consider threats to kill and what the Crown has said about them. He makes these points:

There were threats to execute in circumstances when she *wasn't* executed: therefore they weren't real threats.

For threats to kill to be *real* threats, in order to conform to the Crown's charges under Counts 5 and 7, Mrs McKay had to be alive at the time, i.e. up to the 6th February.

The threats to kill, if they were real, exclude the possibility of Mrs McKay being kept at Rook's Farm—because she was not alive at Rook's Farm.

There is a hint, on the part of the Crown, that if she was taken to Rook's Farm, Mrs McKay died between 8.50 p.m. on the 30th December and 7.30 a.m. next morning. (Actually the Attorney General said so.)

The points do not add up. 'The Crown can't have it both ways!' Mr Hudson says. And then goes on: 'It is complete speculation. . . . It is very, very wrong to say the Crown have proved their case on Count 1. You may say with some safety that she's dead. But you can not say How, When and Where. . . . Even if you're against me on other counts, the Crown can't bring that charge home!'

He waits for a moment, as if for the echo to die away. 'One last word, that may be of importance in the jury-room.' His tone is quieter as he comes to ground where there can be no possibility of anyone being against him. 'All human beings are vulnerable. Don't allow your anger at an ordinary woman being brutally kidnapped, at the anguish of those near and dear to her . . . don't let it affect your reason! Because it has taken place, we all want the people responsible to be brought to justice. But only if you are *sure*. . . . It must be something of which you are sure. Even if you think he's probably guilty'—he glances at Arthur in the dock—'that is different from being sure.'

Finally: 'On all the charges, I submit, there is reasonable doubt. Arthur Hosein has never given any indication, he has emphatically denied, knowing anything about the crime. If there's just a *possiblity* that what he's said so often may be true —you must find him Not Guilty.'

So Mr Hudson sits down, for the last time in his defence of Arthur Hosein. The court adjourns for lunch.

13

Closing speech for the defence

(Nizamodeen Hosein)

Mr Draycott is on his feet, looking small and sturdy, strong-nosed and bright-eyed, ready as ever with lively terrier-like energy to address the jury in his own, special, examining-manner. I have already suggested his manner is in its way a work of art. Only art could put across his opening sentence:

'Members of the jury, I've waited for this.'

He goes on: 'I'm going to deal with the evidence'—rather as if this differentiates his activities very sharply from those of certain other persons he could name. 'Nizam's defence requires me to do so. There is no conflict between him and the evidence. Throughout the whole of the week that the prosecution evidence was adduced, I was not saying it was wrong. You may have noticed that every point I put to the prosecution witnesses was either accepted or reinforced by the prosecution, and in particular by the police officers. That is very, very unusual in a criminal case. . . . Conflict on fact has come with the co-accused.' He keeps his eye fixed on the jury, not glancing at Arthur. 'Wherever Nizam's evidence agrees with the prosecution he has been accused of lying.' He asks the members of the jury *not* to accept this . . .

There is an interruption. Visiting barristers on this climactic day have been to-ing and fro-ing noisily. His Lordship calls for quiet.

Mr Draycott is saying he thinks the case for the prosecution has been presented with proper retraint, in circumstances that could be inflammatory. 'I propose to follow the same line.'

He reminds the jury of the provision by Act of Parliament for an accused person, if he wants to put his cards on the table, to make admissions—it assists the prosecution so that they may know what witnesses they need not call, what crimes the jury must turn its mind to. The jury may think it right for Nizam to admit the handwriting and the signature on the G.L.C. form. But that is not important. The most important admission was No. 2, the planting of the paper flowers at Dane End. Apart from that admission, neither before the trial, at the outset, or now, was there any evidence that he placed them. 'You may recall the gasp,' says Mr Draycott, 'that went through the court—that anyone should admit it.' It couldn't be proved now: there was no one else there to see. 'The only evidence about it is his, that he planted the flowers.'

Having, as it were, complimented Nizam, Mr Draycott compliments the prosecution, and then the police. 'I make, and Nizam in the witness-box made, no complaint against the police. He has not said they ill-treated him.' And in *fact*, as opposed to *inference*, there is the unique situation of common ground between prosecution and defence. The inference to be drawn is a matter for the jury: and they will be directed by his Lordship. He exhorts the jury to be careful to consider each man separately, and each count against each one. 'You may find they could for certain counts be lumped together. But you must consider *Nizam* separately on each count. Don't approach it as "the Hoseins", "the brothers", unless the evidence compels you to it. It is a very, very easy mistake to make.'

He begins with the written statements about the Volvo in Wimbledon. 'What I am concerned with is not whether *that* Volvo was there, but whether it was Nizam driving it. In this day and age perorations to the jury are irrelevant. You want evidence as it relates to Nizamodeen Hosein. That's what I'm going to do.' Like Mr Hudson he warns the jury about being satisfied so that they are *sure* before finding either Guilty. If there is a reasonable doubt, then the verdict must be Not Guilty—'criminal trials are concerned with people and reality, not with fairy stories'.

Reality, not fairy stories—it is only a few moments before Mr Draycott has his finger on the essential fantasy of the case, the demand for a million pounds; and he is fixing it directly on Arthur. Grandiose ideas, lack of grasp of reality. . . . (Who can grumble at that?) Mr Draycott quotes Arthur: 'I am very sorry for you, Mr Smith. You have a very difficult case to solve.' Then: 'Contrast that with the brother who puts his arms round a policeman's shoulders and weeps!' (Touching, but pretty fantastic, too—even granted that Detective Sergeant Parker seems to be a particularly amiable, fatherly sort of policeman.)

'The whole thing,' says Mr Draycott, 'is the plan of a mind that has no understanding or grasp of reality.' Having established Arthur's being thus off his rocker, Mr Draycott goes on: 'So that when Nizam gives you to understand, and the police give you grounds to understand, that the relationship between these two was not a normal one, there was no affection but only fear, that point has been established time and time again.' He touches on the scenes in the police station. 'Arthur will kill me. He beats me!' Even in prison there was the attack which led to their separation.

Mr Draycott says he is going to the best of his ability to face the difficulties Nizam is in. At the end of the day the jury will regard the totality of the evidence. They must consider Nizam's situation. If he is guilty he deserves no pity. Mr Draycott does not know whether any members of the jury have sat on a jury before: they have only got to sit there, and the facts unfold.

'Guilt stands out like a palm tree in a desert.' (Does it indeed? How come, then, that we have all been sitting here for three weeks? . . .)

But in the case of Nizam they have suspicion, association. That is not enough. Proof of intent to kill, of intent to do grievous bodily harm, is necessary before they can conclude that he is guilty. 'I'm going to deal with the charge of murder,' he says boldly. 'The Crown put their case in this way, and rightly so.'

Mrs McKay disappeared, and has not been heard of for a very long time. 'Probably she is dead, poor soul.' The next step is to consider that she died while in the captivity of whoever kidnapped her. The trouble is, he submits, that Mrs McKay may well have died, as opposed to being killed. She was a nervous woman, subjected to treatment that put her under great strain. How she met her death, we don't know. A telephone call threatening to kill *is* evidence; but the jury must bear in mind that sort of demand is common form and it doesn't necessarily follow that the intent is going to be carried out. 'Are we satisfied,' he asks, 'that she was deliberately done away with?'

We have come round again to the absence of *corpus delicti.* Mr Draycott refers the jury to two cases within recent times of murder where no body was found. He is obviously going to describe them. The court—where all the judiciary, the police and the Press will know what those cases are—is suddenly hushed.

The first case, he tells the jury, involved a woman called Gay Gibson, who disappeared from a boat at sea: there was irrefutable evidence that she was pushed through a porthole.

The second case was that of a Pole in Glamorgan, where there was no body: the local rumour, Mr Draycott methodically explains, was that the body was fed to the pigs. There is such a rumour in this case. . . .

(The words are out! The second of the dreadful rumours has been uttered in court—in this case the prosecution not even having circled round it, as they did over the first rumour about chopping up. Being myself irrevocably persuaded that the way, the only way, to kill a rumour is never to mention it, I can scarcely believe my ears. Public denial of a rumour only puts it into people's heads if it wasn't there before; and if it was there before only makes them think there must be something in it.)

'The point here,' Mr Draycott is saying with great emphasis, his obvious intention being to kill the rumour by showing irrefutable grounds for its denial, 'is that there is no evidence at all, *forensic or otherwise*, about this vanished woman.'

(So there it is. My astonishment, right or wrong, stays with me for the rest of the day. *Both* rumours brought into court, and by the defence side, of all people. I can't get over it.)

'I won't quarrel with you,' Mr Draycott is saying courteously to the jury, 'if you come to the verdict that somebody murdered Mrs McKay, if you satisfy yourselves that that woman could not have met her death in any other way. She was a woman from a comfortable background, in a nervous state—she wouldn't open her door to her husband without a code on the doorbell, and she had a chain on the door. I don't want to quibble with the evidence. I do accept the evidence you've got to start with. But you are dealing with a bizarre relationship. . . .

Much of what happened would not happen between you and I, but could happen in bizarre circumstances.'

He considers steps taken to involve Nizam. 'Don't forget that whenever anyone is to go "over the top" there is someone else down below.' And he reminds the jury: 'One of the characteristics of the criminal mind is self-preservation.' (For myself I have to say that if anyone in that dock has shown a fantastic knack for self-preservation it's *his* client! Nizam in the witness-box broke down completely—and never admitted a thing.)

Mr Draycott now reiterates some of the most cogent of the defence arguments, linking them with the idea that somebody else must be concerned in the case. There is no evidence whatsoever that Mrs McKay was ever at Rook's Farm—suggestions that she was kept in the dog's kennel or under the work-table are sheer speculation. If she was not there, she was somewhere else: therefore there must be more people in this than the Hoseins. (I agree with that: it could have been in somebody else's house that she heard the television and then wrote the letters, more than twenty-four hours after the kidnapping.)

Mr Draycott begins with Mrs McKay's actions on the 29th, with 'the suggestion that Mrs McKay would open the door to two black faces asking for Mrs Murdoch!' He follows this by asking the jury if they think *anybody* on the 29th December would take Mrs McKay to Rook's Farm, when, on the previous day, *three* policemen had been there? It is for the jury to say; but if Nizam were in the plot, would he have gone out and brought a policeman back to the Farm in the early hours of the 27th? Furthermore, witnesses for Arthur's defence, brought to show that ordinary life was going on at the Farm, were even more assistance to Nizam—Gerald Gordon at 7.30 a.m. on the 31st December. In order to hold Mrs McKay, as Mr Hudson worked out, she would have to be there. The Crown allege she was taken somewhere and murdered.

'Human bodies,' says Mr Draycott, 'are not easy to dispose of, and forensic science not easy to fool.'

He considers the matter in more detail. (Mr Draycott, whose manner combines the most quietly sensible with the most coolly distanced, is the one who finally comes out with the most grisly and chilling details.) The time to chop up a body and dispose of the pieces—hair, fingerprints, clothing. He points out that there were no fingerprints, and a witness had been called back to say Mrs McKay did not perspire as much as ordinary people and so rarely left fingerprints. 'If one thing makes a person sweat,' he says, 'it is fear!'

Mr Draycott rubs in the fact that no forensic evidence whatsoever was found, by a police force which is unbeatable. 'Rook's Farm has come out,' he says, 'with a clean bill of health.' (By a Freudian slip he interpolates 'not'.) No trace of Mrs McKay was found. That is why somebody else must be involved. From the absence of forensic evidence connecting Mrs McKay with Rook's Farm, he passes to the absence of forensic evidence connecting Nizam with 20 Arthur Road—no evidence at all.

Of Nizam's reactions in the police station to being shown the paper flowers and the billhook, he points out that at the former Nizam must have thought: 'I'm in it up to the neck', and then at the latter he thought the billhook found at Arthur Road was the one with which he had chopped up the calf. He nearly died of fright. 'What has Arthur done to me?'

'What looks suspicious in a criminal case,' says Mr Draycott to the jury, calmly and slowly, 'if you take your time thinking it over, may turn out not to be suspicious.' He pauses, and adds tellingly: 'You may notice that Nizam made no bones about recognising that billhook. It was Arthur who wouldn't have it at all!'

As for the telephone call at 1.15 a.m. from Epping, Nizam had the opportunity to make it, but did he? The telephone operator says the voice was very deep and had an American accent: Gerald Gordon, when mimicking Arthur, said 'Man'—the operator says also that the caller kept saying 'Man'. And, although Nizam was often inaudible in the witness-box, whatever else can be said, he read transcripts of the calls with competence, in a voice that was clear—no huskiness, no inaudibility—so that his voice could be judged.

From the way the light in the court is changing it is apparent that the day is ending. Mr Draycott is only part way through his closing speech; however he moves into a sort of day's peroration. It is about Nizam's truth-telling.

'It is true Nizam behaved when in custody wrongly, stupidly,' he concedes. 'If he'd coughed up, he might well not have been in the dock now.' (One thinks, 'Good God!') 'He's twenty-two. He has a brother whose behaviour is not rational.' And so on. 'The police say, time after time he was on the brink of telling what he knew.' And then: 'In this case, when police officers are accused by Arthur of brutal conduct, Nizam asks to see them alone. He comes to the brink, and back he goes.'

Mr Draycott invites the jury to imagine Nizam's appalling situation: it is obvious to *him* that Arthur is involved: once he opens his mouth Arthur is finished. The story is against his brother and he cannot tell it.

'He'd got his family to think of,' Mr Draycott reminds the jury. 'Indians are not white people with brown faces: they have a different culture.' (As the brothers are *West* Indian and Hosein is a Pakistani name, the Government of India could well protest on two, if not three, counts.) The pressure on Nizam, Mr Draycott continues, was appalling, to support Arthur's story. 'Either he goes into the witness-box and tells the story about being made use of by the Mafia; or he admits to evidence involving him, and involving Arthur, his *brother*.'

' "What has Arthur done to me?" I submit the involvement of Nizam began at an early stage, and it has taken a long time to get to the end of the line.' Mr Draycott leans forward and emphasises his point by greater quietness, greater tension. 'Nizam has told you a great deal of the truth. You've got to give him credit for it!'

Mr Draycott sits down. The Judge nods his head. 'Be upstanding!' Another day is over. We are left with our thoughts as we disperse. Incidentally I notice that I have kept referring to 'we'. Somehow the regular attenders at the trial have become 'we'. The court is so small that everyone attending regularly now recognises each other by sight. I am now on passing-the-time-of-day terms with all sorts of people, outside the joint army who acquiesced to my company in the pub and the café across the road. A trial appears to turn into what our American cousins call 'a group activity'.

As I walk in the autumnal sunshine to Blackfriars Underground Station, I meditate on some of Mr Draycott's earlier points. Mrs McKay could simply not have opened the door to 'two black faces' asking for Mrs Murdoch. Yet, accepting the theory that when she got back from driving Mrs Nightingale home, the instruders were already in the house, how were they to know that she was not bringing back a couple of friends with her for a drink, or that Mr McKay was not going to come home early for once? The riskiness of the venture is incredible.

And going back a stage further, to what Mr Draycott has called the absence of preparation on the part of the Hoseins, if they were the kicnappers. If they watched the movements of people in and out of 20 Arthur Road, they could only have started on the 20th December. (If they had followed the Rolls-Royce before the 19th December it would have led them not to Mrs McKay's but to Mrs Murdoch's house.) And if they watched 20 Arthur Road between the 20th and the 29th, there was Christmas in between, when, one imagines, the McKays' domestic routine must have been affected by entertaining. Mrs McKay and her husband had lots of friends and were very hospitable, as we know from the number of people who rang up or came to the house as soon as they heard on the night of her disappearance. . . .

The riskiness of the venture, if it was carried out by the two Hoseins unaided, seems only the more incredible the more one thinks of it. And equally, if it was carried out by the two Hoseins unaided, what fantastic luck they had! If they got into 20 Arthur Road at about 5.30 that evening, any of goodness knows how many things might have been in store for them. Was Arthur full of double scotches, Nizam of beer? Even so . . .

And come to that, were they, after all, doing it entirely unaided? Out of the blue I recall that Mrs McKay's jewellery, six hundred pounds' worth of it, has never been found. *Somebody* else must know something about that, for instance. Were they indeed doing it entirely unaided?

Or—one must still, even now, ask the question—were they doing it at all?

2nd October

Mr Draycott continues his closing speech for Nizam's defence. From events on the day of the kidnapping and events before, he moves on to the days after, in particular to the two M3 calls to

20 Arthur Road ending at 7.45 p.m. and 7.49 p.m. on the 1st January, when Nizam went out with stomach-ache. Mr Draycott first establishes the reliability of Liley as a witness, because her testifying that she made the paper flowers and put them in the Volvo indicates that she is not assisting Nizam and Arthur. So when she says it was afternoon when Nizam went out, neither Arthur nor Nizam could have made the calls: somebody else must be involved.

'If Liley was being assaulted,' Mr Draycott says, meaning by Arthur in Nizam's absence, 'you might think she'd remember whether it was afternoon or night.'

He then produces the revelation that the calls were S.T.D., while the telephone box near the pub where Nizam drank his 'pint of bitter beer' as cure for stomach-ache is an old-fashioned 4*d.* box.

(I listen to this with some neutrality, being inclined by now to the joint army's theory that Nizam drove the Volvo into Bishop's Stortford much later, telling Liley that he was going to see Susie—that is why she was so furious with him when he got back. The Bishop's Stortford boxes would be S.T.D. But it is interesting to see Mr Draycott at work.)

Mr Draycott's next revelation is that the M3 call at 7.45 p.m.—'give me your solemn word'—on the 1st February from Tottenham, to make which Nizam is alleged to have borrowed 6*d.* from a finisher, was not made from an S.T.D. box requiring the sixpence, but from one requiring four pennies. (This is all very well, but there were two more M3 calls to be made that night.)

Mr Draycott puts Nizam's side of the other events of the 1st February; the row in the car, the planting of the paper flowers, and Nizam's coming home soaking wet. 'If Nizam is right he fled from the car because he was not prepared to be a catspaw without knowing what it was about. It was planned that Nizam should be the target for tonight, as it always was when there was something dangerous to be done. Nizam had got away. That's why Nizam was soaking wet when he got home, and Arthur was there.'

Mr Draycott considers the police are right: whoever was in the Volvo must have had the fright of his life—the police missed getting the car by a hairsbreadth. 'If you are a kidnapper and possibly a murderer,' he says, 'that is the time of maximum danger, when you pick up the money.' He pauses. 'That's going to be Nizam's rôle.' The reason for the row was Nizam's asking: 'What's it all about?'

Mr Draycott comes to the 6th February, when Nizam sat around at Gates Garage for twenty minutes '*with no attempt at concealment*'. He repeats Nizam's statement and asks the jury: 'Is it possible that Nizam sat there all that length of time, if he knew all about the crime?'

And after the last scene in The Raven, when Nizam's evidence agrees with that of the police, that he drove Arthur back to look at the suitcases—though Arthur says he's a liar—Mr Draycott asks again: 'If that boy of twenty-two had known of the kidnapping and murder, he'd have known he was wandering into the lion's mouth. Instead of that he goes, blissfully unaware of what it's all about.'

Mr Draycott invites the jury to consider Arthur's attitude to Nizam. 'Isn't it a waste of time to say Nizam was *not* afraid of Arthur, when domination and fear is everybody's evidence?' We hear again about 'the ruler' and 'King Hosein'. 'In my submission the mentality of Arthur is the key to the situation.' He goes on: 'If the Crown case against Arthur is right—and I agree in this instance—Arthur has behaved with considerable unreality in the witness-box and in the preparation of his defence. He has put it forward that Nizam was involved and was being used by a group of figures whose significance is apparent now—*one*, he thought, was Robert Maxwell.' It seemed to Arthur's mind that the jury would accept Mr Maxwell's being connected with the crime because Mrs Murdoch, the wife of his rival, was the intended victim. 'If ever Nizam wanted to get himself convicted,' Mr Draycott says, 'the following up of that story would have put an end to it, because the story is so crazy!' Mr Draycott submits that nobody other than a lunatic could have done it.

(I doubt if anybody in the court seriously disagrees with that. But that's nothing compared with the lunacy of February 6th. The police might have missed taking the Volvo's number the first time, but they really couldn't miss it a second—it is this crucial lunatic episode which sometimes makes one feel it was not so much that the police found the solution to the problem as that the solution came up and hit them on the head.)

Mr Draycott next asks the jury to look at Nizam's attitude to Arthur. 'Put yourselves in *his* position, with a brother who held him in terror and domination!'

There is something the matter among the jury—the eldest of the three jurywomen appears to have fainted. All the jury exit.

(There is a break in which some of us wander out into the lobby. Gossip, speculation. . . . Is Mr Draycott blackguarding Arthur too much to convince? A question I cannot answer. I'm not a juryman, thank goodness!)

The break is over. Mr Draycott develops his case, getting to the police-station scenes. Nizam realised he was involved and that Arthur had done something dreadful. 'He cried and cried,' says Mr Draycott. When he saw the billhook he broke down. (Actually I thought it was when he saw the adhesive tape.) He was *wrong*: he didn't know the billhook was the one from Arthur Road, but thought it was the one he had used for chopping at the Farm.

'If the truth doesn't come out like a gush from a dam,' Mr Draycott says, 'from a boy like this . . .' (Sheer amazement stops me hearing the rest of the sentence.)

'When he cries: "What has Arthur done to me?" doesn't it make more sense to think it is a cry from the heart? Meanwhile, if I am right, Arthur is cock-a-hoop—this is something he had anticipated. Nizam is in trouble: Arthur is in a state of euphoria.' Mr Draycott pauses: 'The people who committed the crime are vile and pitiless. Consider Nizam weeping on the policeman's shoulder! . . .' (I duly consider it—and with unwrung withers am reminded of the peculiar intimacy of connection between the police and the criminal classes. Really they are all *one*. . . . One big warring family, neither side being able to live without the other.)

Mr Draycott is going on to opine with pleasing impartiality that 'The saving grace was when Arthur assailed him and Nizam then had separate advice!' After that Nizam asked to see the police alone and said: 'If I put my cards on the table I'd get out of 90% of this.' Pause. 'Not the attitude of a guilty person,' says Mr Draycott.

'I am not out to convince you by rhetoric or advocacy,' Mr Draycott now tell the jury. 'I am seeking to canalise, to collect evidence.' He returns to Nizam's being Indian—yet in coming clean Nizam has taken an Anglo-Saxon attitude. 'However bad a thing seems, to come out with it and put it in the hands of just persons'—an impartial Judge and a British jury—'is an entirely Anglo-Saxon attitude. Not Indian.' (This makes me feel dizzy for a moment.)

Mr Draycott concedes that there is evidence against Nizam of association; but he warns the jury against being swayed by suspicions, inferences—and also against the luxury of giving way to their feelings when they are charged with impartial weighing up of the evidence.

'I ask no favours,' he says, but he reminds the jury again, apropos Nizam's association with Arthur, of Arthur's having a mind with little grasp of reality. He winds up with a series of most cogent questions. If Nizam were a party to the kidnapping, is it conceivable that he would do a series of things he is known to have done—ring up the police just before the plan was put into operation, hang about at Gates Garage, and so on?

Cogent they are. It really is inconceivable. . . .

His Lordship, he says, will tell them about the necessity for considering each case separately, each defence differently: he gives them a final reminder that Nizam was under no obligation to go into the witness-box. Mr Draycott sits down.

14

The summing up

5th October, *morning*

His Lordship addresses the jury on their duties and their attitude: they have to decide what facts are proved, what inferences they are entitled to draw, applying the same tests to witnesses from whichever direction they come. If in doubt, they must resolve in favour of the accused.

'If you think a view falls from me,' he says, 'you are entitled to disregard it if it's not consonant with your own.' (One wonders if they will, all the same—it must take some nerve to disregard what appears to be the view of the Judge.)

His Lordship begins with two statements.

(i) Nobody could doubt Mrs McKay was abducted—no one has sought to suggest otherwise. There is evidence of false imprisonment, blackmail and threat to murder. Although the jury must consider each count separately, they may feel that Counts 2–7 may stand or fall together; though if they find some distinction to be drawn, they must draw it.

(ii) The charge of murder is on a different footing. Unless and until they come to the conclusion, if they do, that it's proved one or two of the defendants was party to the kidnapping, no charge of murder can be brought. Only if one or the other is concluded to be party must they begin to consider the charge of murder.

His Lordship's advice is that they consider Count 1 last.

He touches on the event of one of two defendants giving evidence which supports the prosecution case against his co-defendant: they should not act on the evidence of one to the detriment of the other unless they are assured that it comes from a *reliable source*. And the evidence as it affects each of them is not the same. This makes it imperative to consider each separately and independently of the other. He stresses the principle of law that it is for the Crown to prove guilt. If the matter might be resolved in two ways, they must adopt that more favourable to the accused, unless there is *compelling* reason to adopt the other.

He now comes to crime. 'The snatching of a woman from her home and family anywhere is a crime which must arouse deep detestation and abhorrence.' Emotional words. 'When such a crime takes place in a quiet suburb or a great metropolis such as ours, it becomes more outrageous and horrific.' (It is these latter words which inadvertently give offence, when quoted later, to people who misinterpreted them to mean that the crime would have been less horrific and outrageous if it had happened behind Paddington to a non-affluent mother.) But they must not let emotion cloud their views, whether it be abhorrence of the crime or sympathy for those who were subjected to torture—they must reject it. They must put indignation and sympathy from their minds, and go only on evidence, where fact is fact—they are not detectives; they are not watchdogs of society.

His Lordship suggests that they may begin with the 2nd Count. (By a Freudian slip he says 1st Count, and corrects it.)

Count 2 is the first charge that they unlawfully carried away Mrs McKay. The event which the prosecution say led up to it —and the jury must decide—took place on the 19th December at the G.L.C., the application that Nizam admits to. The person who used the car was Mr Rupert Murdoch, head of *The News Of The World*. 'To the outside world a man of great substance,' the Judge comments, 'just the sort of man whose pocket is long enough to enable him to pay a substantial ransom if his wife were held hostage.' (This may take a little of the fantasy off the demand for £1,000,000—but not much.)

He goes on to state the theme of Nizam's which has run through the case: 'I am the younger brother. I lived with another brother and after a difference I had to leave. After that I had to live with Arthur, entirely dependent on him. He knocked me about. So when he told me to do things, I had to.' Nizam says that when he went to County Hall he did as he was told.

'I never asked myself why. I did not give it a thought.' His Lordship suggests the jury examine that with great care. 'That note,' he says, 'occurs time and time again. Nizam says: "I did this or that no matter how bizarre, how suspicious, and I never asked the why or wherefore." Mr Draycott has urged with coolness and moderation many points—that Nizam made no attempt to disguise his handwriting. Ponder that!' When Nizam wrote it out perhaps he had no reason to suppose the document would be traced to him. It was not until the 6th February that the police took the number of the Volvo and got a lead to Rook's Farm and the two brothers.

'Ask yourselves,' his Lordship counsels, 'from the beginning, was Nizam so frightened, so stupid, so naif, that he made an application under a false name, a false address, without asking what was behind it?'

Arthur says he was not there. Nizam, now that his handwriting is identified, cannot deny it, but tries to put the responsibility on his brother. It will be for the jury to decide: if other events prove Arthur was there, they may accept that Nizam was not alone and Arthur was there.

On the 26th December there was a row over Liley, and Nizam ran out and fetched the police, who visited Rook's Farm on the morning of the 28th. This is important for the reason—as Mr Hudson, in a persuasive and forceful address, says—Would these two men be inviting the policemen to come to the Farm if they were contemplating the abduction in two days' time and bringing the victim there? His Lordship animadverts on the host of witnesses who said they were invited by Arthur to visit the Farm at this very time. However, the meticulous and comprehensive police search had shown no indication at Rook's Farm that Mrs McKay was ever there, dead or alive.

'The fact that everybody was asked to come there,' says his Lordship, 'may thus lose some of the significance you were asked to attach to it. It is for you to decide.'

(But if Mrs McKay wasn't taken to Rook's Farm, she must have been taken somewhere else—and it then becomes very difficult to believe, as it seems to be accepted by everyone that she heard television somewhere, that other persons were *not* involved. She could not have been murdered, or have died, on the way out from Wimbledon. On this subject the jury have been counselled not to speculate beyond reasonable conjecture, which is all very well: if other persons *were* involved, one is compelled to speculate, and it is very difficult to say, in a fantastic case like this, when reasonable conjecture stops. In this case according to any reasonable conjecture beforehand the crime could never have taken place at all.)

His Lordship comes to the 29th December, the evidence of passers-by in Arthur Road, of Mrs McKay's routine. On the question of the door chain, he offers the explanation that has seemed to me the most likely: 'Persons may have got in and been waiting,' he suggests, 'knowing Mr Alick McKay didn't return till 7.45.'

(I am back, as crypto-juryman, at my difficulty of the Hoseins, if they did it unaided, having only had ten days, including the disruption of the Christmas holiday, to establish the McKays' routine.)

His Lordship is dealing with the copy of *The People*, not the McKays' house-copy, which shows, according to the prosecution, the palmprint of Arthur Hosein. And with the billhook found at Arthur Road, of which Farmer Smith says in his vehement way, 'I defy anyone to say it's not my billhook', giving a demonstration of how he sharpens it in a special way. Arthur denies hearing anything about its being lost at Rook's Farm, but Nizam thinks he remembers Farmer Smith enquiring about it. The farmer may be wrong: he may be mistaken: it has been put to the jury that he is not trustworthy because he falsely signed a form saying he would employ Nizam when he might not to be intending to do so.

'You may think these are coincidences,' says the Judge, 'but when they multiply, when they become a series of coincidences, you may ask yourselves: "Must they have some common factor, some common focus through the activity of some person?"' But perhaps this is an early stage, he concedes, at which to reflect on such matters. They may say to themselves that it is unbelievably unlucky for the fingerprint expert to say 'That is the palmprint of a man at Rook's Farm'; and for Farmer Smith to say 'That is my billhook'. All the same he asks:

'Is there not a procession of things which, tested alone, may be coincidences, but which together make a formidable pattern of relationship?' And he suggests for their consideration the possibility of a human agency, acting from some particular focus, being responsible for the series of coincidences.

His Lordship mentions the Elastoplast tin, 2½ in. wide, found by the police; a minute thing in itself. Yet Arthur said: 'It was never in my house.' There is some basis as more than one officer took the responsibility for not taking it away. Yet the jury may think Mrs Hosein's evidence enables them to dismiss the suggestion of its having been 'planted'.

From the evening of the 29th his Lordship looks back to ten days previously when Nizam went to County Hall. Nizam says that at the end of December or early in January, he saw in a newspaper something about Mrs McKay and *The News Of The World*, but it didn't begin to relate to his enquiry about the user of the car owned by *The News Of The World*. The thought never came into his mind. And it was not until he and his brother were arrested in February that he began to suspect Arthur was implicated.

His Lordship examines Arthur's evidence about what he was doing at the time, about the visit to Farmer Pateman on the afternoon of the 29th, and the telephone call (crucially important) from his solicitor Mr David Coote at 5.30 p.m. But Mr Coote had not been called as a witness. 'You may ask yourselves *why?* Mr Coote may have forgotten about it. You might expect Mr Coote to come into the witness-box and say: "I may well have telephoned Arthur in the afternoon." But Mr Coote didn't come to say that. Is the reason, you may ask yourselves, because he'd have to say he never made the call?' (In the well of the court, sitting at the long table, Mr Coote steadily keeps his head down.)

We then come to Liley's calls, unanswered at 8 p.m. and 9 p.m.—unanswered, the prosecution say, because Arthur and Nizam, maybe with others, were engaged in the abduction of Mrs McKay. (I hadn't realised that the prosecution had conceded to this extent the possibility of 'others'.) Then Liley's call at 10.30 p.m. answered by Arthur—and the explanation of when the bell was audible to Arthur, who says he was in bed all the time with 'flu. There is a conflict of evidence. Nizam says

Arthur went out before he went to bed. Then, Nizam says, he saw Arthur asleep and sneaked the car to go and see Adam, giving the innocent explanation of its being a custom of the Trinidadian Christmas. Nizam and Adam agree that Nizam arrived at Adam's at 11.30 p.m.

'One looks at the map,' says his Lordship. 'Thornton Heath and Norbury Crescent are not far from Wimbledon. If somebody had a part to play at Wimbledon, they might find themselves not far from Wimbledon.' He passes immediately to Nizam's note—in Brixton Prison, six weeks later—held up for Adam to see. 'Why on earth, if the sole purpose of Nizam's presence in South London was the convenient one of visiting his relations, should he be asking Adam to be silent, and not even tell his solicitor about it?' Nizam wants it to be said that he was home, and two farmers to say Arthur was with them. This document, his Lordship points out, is in no way evidence against Arthur: it is only evidence against Nizam, in the way it reflects on his state of mind and knowledge of the affair. Why should Nizam keep silent about the night of the 29th? Nizam's explanation is that if he didn't go along with that story he'd be the odd man out. It was at the time when, Nizam says, Arthur demanded co-operation with the story about the four strange men. The Judge asks the members of the jury to remember the fight after which the brothers separated.

We now go back to the night of the 29th December. Within hours of Mrs McKay's disappearance came the first of a series of telephone calls by which the family was tormented. The Judge reads the transcript beginning: 'This is Mafia, Group 3.' Nizam says that physically he could have made that call.

The Judge reads the transcript of the second call, at 5.30 p.m. on the 30th. 'Your wife has just posted a letter.' And 'Did you get the message'—which may be a slight indication that this was a *different* person. Nizam says that for the whole of that day he was on the Farm.

The following day, the 31st, 'the forlorn messages from that woman'. His Lordship reads: *'I am blindfolded and cold.'* On the envelope the prosecution expert finds fingerprints which he does not doubt are Arthur Hosein's: the defence expert finds not sufficient characteristics to arrive at a *sure* view.

'If those two opposing pieces of evidence stood on their own, in isolation,' his Lordship says, 'who is to decide?' He pauses. 'But they don't stand in isolation. You are entitled to ask yourselves, Is this another coincidence?'

Arthur's explanation is that, if those are indeed his fingerprints, it must be that the stamped envelopes which he had for Christmas cards were abstracted by the four strange men. Nizam says there never were any strange men: it is a story Arthur concocted, and his refusal to go along with it led to the fight in prison.

Mrs McKay's letter, his Lordship points out, was not dated. There was no date on *any* of her letters. A date would indicate when she wrote it, and there was some evidence that other letters were written some days before they were received. *Darling Diane, I heard you on TV*—that was in a letter received on the 22nd January.

On the 31st, the Hoseins say they worked the farm—in the usual way. On the 1st January, when there are the two telephone calls at 7.45 p.m. and 7.40 p.m. to Arthur Road, the caller asks to speak to Diane. He would know her by name as she appeared on TV the evening before. 'You've gone too far.' M3 rings off and then rings again a few minutes later. 'They've gone to the police. Tell them they've got to get a million pounds.' Nizam says he went out to get a cure for tummy-ache before 3 p.m. and denies making the call later. Liley was with Arthur.

The next thing is the letter to the editor of *The News Of The World*. His Lordship discusses the results of investigating the handwriting and the misspelling, and the discovery of the indented sheet of writing-paper in the cardboard box in Nizam's bedroom. Are those more coincidences? He counsels the utmost caution, yet the jury may think the coincidences have become so prolific as to have gone beyond the point of *dis*junction and may be *con*joined by some link.

His Lordship now reads the transcripts of the next telephone calls. To the editor of *The News Of The World*, who thinks he recognises the voice as the same as that recorded at St Mary House. To Mr Alick McKay, on the 14th January, promising him to get his wife to write another letter. To Ian McKay on the 19th—the first talk of a rendezvous; and later talk about The

Boys tracing ULO 18F. Then the next calls to Ian—his Lordship reinforces the Attorney General's references to their 'callousness and bestiality of mind'—one of them referring to his mother's pathetic efforts to get away. Then on the 21st, news that more letters are coming and mention of a piece being clipped off one of them. The letters to Alick and Diane are received in the same envelope together with the first ransom note—posted in N22. His Lordship introduces a new point.

The letters postmarked 21st January were *not* cut. The letter the caller on the 21st was referring to, that *had* been cut, was the one received five days later, postmarked the 26th. He asks the jury to study them.

'Had someone got Mrs McKay to write a whole series of letters, all at the same time, at an earlier stage?' he asks. And the letters of the 21st, and the ransom note, are all written on paper similar to that found in Nizam's bedroom. 'Isn't that another coincidence?'

His Lordship reads extracts from the letters, including Mrs McKay's telling them the gang will give the code name M3. 'By the 21st January,' his Lordship says, 'you may think it was late to be telling Mr McKay what code-number was going to be given by M3.'

Passing to the ransom letter, he summarises the forensic evidence of handwriting and fingerprints: the Crown's expert's opinion that the handwriting, albeit disguised, could not be Nizam's, but there is considerable probability that it is Arthur's. 'You've got to ask yourselves,' he tells the jury, 'if that probability is converted to certainty by the evidence that the palm-print is that of Arthur Hosein.'

He refers briefly to the common view of prosecution and defence experts that the handwriting on the cigarette packet is that of the *same* person, and the defence expert says that if he had to choose, he would say it points to Arthur rather than Nizam.

And with that he glances at the clock and adjourns the court for lunch.

We all pile out, the evening newpaper journalists flying to the telephones, the rest making their way down the marble staircase along with the other regulars. Voices buzz. The first morning of the summing up is over. I don't think there is much disagreement about it—things are looking pretty black for the brothers Hosein.

5th October, *afternoon*

The Judge explains to the jury that he has so far covered *kidnapping*, and whether the defendants were involved in it. The next charge is *intention*—that Mrs McKay was not only abducted, but kept in imprisonment to her detriment. This count is solidly bound up with Count 2.

His Lordship invited the jury to look at the letter received on 22nd January. *Please obey, as no errors must happen. You have no alternative*—together with the instructions which led from the telephone box to another: so that Mr McKay could not know till the last moment where the money was going and, if he played up and went by himself, could not let the police know.

His Lordship invites the jury to look at the topography. All the incidents lie in North London, going out in the direction of Hertfordshire—Bishop's Stortford and so on. 'Not a matter by itself,' he observes, 'possibly another pointer. . . .' All the episodes were in an area easily covered by motor-car, and in places where it was easy to lie in wait and see. He reads more of the ransom note. *Your wife Muriel is with us*, etc. And: *But if you cooperate discretely and we collect the first half million*, etc. There is a palmprint, according to the prosecution expert, of Arthur Hosein. The paper is very like that found in Nizam's bedroom. The handwriting is said to be that of Arthur Hosein.

'How did it come about?' his Lordship asks. 'Unless it is somebody at Rook's Farm who has conducted the telephone conversations?' He warns the jury: 'You must look at the evidence from both sides. Arthur has said: "I didn't know anything of it." He says, moreover, that he doesn't agree it's his palmprint; and if it is, it came there the same way as the fingerprints on Mrs McKay's letter. Because those four men came to Rook's Farm and used his writing-paper.' (I must say 'looking at it from the other side', put this way, sounds pretty thin.)

The Judge now embarks on a detailed reading of the transcripts of the telephone calls, in as much detail, if not more, than the readings by the Attorney General. Ian McKay's demands for proof that his mother is alive. 'You'll have to ask yourselves in another context, Count 1,' his Lordship interpolates, 'if the situation is such that Mrs McKay's captors were no longer in a position to give proof that she was still alive.'

More calls in which Ian argues for proof. 'Ask yourselves,' says his Lordship, 'what was the difficulty in getting that poor woman to write just this: *Help me! I am writing this on . . .* giving the date?'

More calls. Ian: 'You've got a dead person! You're just trying to trick us.' And later M3 saying: 'We haven't murdered anyone as yet, but there's always a first time.' And then M3's remark, the ludicrousness of which is not allowed by his Lordship to pass: 'If we're doing business, we deal with honesty.' And more calls leading up to the letter containing the pieces of clothing—which show that the senders had Mrs McKay in their custody, but it doesn't follow that they had a live body. On this letter the prosecution expert identifies the fingerpint of Arthur Hosein: the defence expert identifies some characteristics but not enough to be clearly recognisable.

'I'm going to take a little time over this,' his Lordship says, and goes over the argument about the validity of totting up the scores from a number of fingerprints on the same document, leading up to the defence expert's agreement that from an academic point of view it is not justifiable, but from a commonsense point of view it is permissible. His Lordship tells the jury they will be guided by *informed commonsense*. Though they must, if they feel any doubt, resolve it in favour of the accused. With more documents and the cigarette packet we come back to the defence expert's saying that if he had to choose, given that the evidence pointed towards Arthur or Nizam, he would choose Arthur.

Then his Lordship comes to Sunday, the 1st February. 'I will digress,' he says, 'to see where Arthur and Nizam were at the time. Arthur says he went to the finishers.' He asks the jury to look at the map of London, and goes step by step through the evidence we have already heard about the first ransom-collecting attempt, beginning with the two brothers being in Tottenham, at one of the finishers, Nizam borrowing 6*d.* for a call he says he did *not* make to Arthur Road, directing 'Ian' and 'the chauffeur' to the telephone box at the corner of Church Street, Tottenham, and the Cambridge Road—'near enough to be observed from the finishers'. Then the conflicting stories ofArthur and Nizam about when, where and why they parted company. The Piccadilly cigarette packet with the thumbprint on it plays its part—his Lordship is inclined to put a favourable interpretation on Mr Rosenthal's evidence; but it doesn't much matter, he tells the jury, as Piccadilly cigarettes are easy to come by. 'But some five hours afterwards it was used as a means of communication,' he points out. 'A cigarette packet probably wouldn't be picked up by anyone, and could reasonably be used for saying where £1,000,000 was!'

So to Dane End at midnight—'The paper flowers were a quite ingenious signal,' his Lordship commented: 'They wouldn't mean very much to anybody except a botanist.' The two police officers, 'Ian' and 'the chauffeur', deposited the black suitcase and drove the Rolls back to Church Street for the call about Mrs McKay that never came. Meanwhile at Dane End other police were watching. 'No doubt the police communicated by radio.' However 'the bait was not taken'. But 'Round about midnight a dark blue Volvo saloon came from the back of the café where the police were parked. It went on to the A10 where it turned right for Dane End. The police had no time to take the number. At that time the Volvo car had no significance.'

His Lordship then goes on to the two policemen who observed the Volvo's nearside obligatory lights not to be functioning, and the note about '2 up'. 'There is no proof that Arthur Hosein was in the car, or Nizam with him,' his Lordship says. 'It could have been.'

After what the forensic experts say, he goes on, about the handwriting, the writing-paper, the paper flowers; each of these things, small though they may be, is circumstantial. 'Tiny brick by tiny brick,' his Lordship calls it. 'The evidence begins to look as if it is shaping against one or the other of the defendants.' He pauses. 'Now what do *they* say? They are not required to prove anything.' The case will be decided from *the totality of the evidence.*

His Lordship outlines Nizam's account first. At the end of it Nizam was asked if he hadn't reflected on his brother's strange requests and he said not. Then he outlines Arthur's story—at the end of which Arthur turned to the jury and said that if Nizam went into the witness-box and said that, they, the jury, could convict him of anything. 'Nizam did say that.'

His Lordship counsels the jury again about the caution with which they are to approach the situation in which, when two people are jointly charged, one goes into the witness-box to inculpate the other. He turns to Mrs Hosein's evidence about that night: 'There is no reason to suppose she's not telling the truth; but sometimes a witness can persuade herself that something has happened.' Mrs Hosein said that Arthur came home at 9.30 p.m.—it was the day the Gordon came and Rosenthal stayed, and it ended with Nizam's arriving at the door, soaking wet, at midnight. His Lordship then produces another fresh point:

'I'm not sure if Mrs Hosein told us if her husband came back to the bedroom they shared. You may ask yourselves: Did Arthur and Nizam go out again? You may think he and his brother may well have been in about midnight, and have gone down to High Cross afterwards.'

(His Lordship appears to be accepting M3's word later that The Boys were hanging around watching—watching for longer than the recorded single trip of the Volvo suggests. That sets another puzzle, sets two puzzles. One: Was it somebody else who was watching? *Was* somebody else involved? Two: if they, somebody else, or one or both of the Hoseins were hanging around all that time, *why*, with swarms of police cars also watching, weren't they noticed—unless it was another case of there being so many plain-clothes police cars that their occupants didn't know which was which?)

The Judge takes up the late series of telephone-call transcripts, reading them *in extenso*. Two calls to Ian McKay on the following Tuesday, the first in which M3 crows over having avoided the police trap. 'What a nice boy you are, aren't you?' he begins. 'I'm on my way to a meeting of the intellectuals. First our business is handled by the intellectuals, the heads. Then there's a meeting of the semi-intellectuals, to be passed on to the ruffians as we call them. This meeting is in consideration of your Mum, whether she's to be executed and what time.' The call lasts eighteen minutes. 'I stood there, Ian, with all The Boys. We saw you when you came in, when you took off the lights, when you stopped and reversed back. . . . We saw when the motor-bikes came in. . . . Police cars parked all over.' And so on.

The Judge interpolates: 'They had watched, and they had realised that anyone who had the temerity to pick up the suitcases would have been taken into custody.'

This is the call where M3 specifies that if she is returned, Mrs McKay must not be interrogated, Mr McKay relying on the apparent seriousness as evidence that she must still be alive.

'Is this,' asks his Lordship, 'another piece of intense hypocrisy?' And finally—for this day—he reads the call in which the meeting is said to have relented, so there is a last chance for handing over the ransom; some arrangement may still be possible. . . .

His Lordship announces to the jury that he expects to complete his summing up tomorrow morning, and the court is adjourned. 'Be upstanding!'

By this time tomorrow we shall either be waiting to know the verdict, or we shall know it.

6th October, *morning*

This, one imagines, is the last day. Three and a half weeks, fourteen and a half working days! The Judge will complete his summing up; the jury will retire, and come back with their verdict. Or will they? Will they be able to make up their minds? Above all, will they be unanimous?

The court is crowded. Journalists swarm. The distinguished visitors' gallery is full. The jury are having their roll of names called. Then everything is ready. 'Be upstanding!' The Judge comes in with a rustle of scarlet robes, seats himself on his additional cushion. Behind him is the long sword in place on the pannelled wall. This might have been a day when, somewhere, a black cap was held in readiness. . . . Thank God those days are over! Although, even at this last moment, my impression of the regular attenders and my confrères in the joint army is that they really doubt if the brothers will be convicted on Count 1—I have spoken to no single one of them who thinks it is certain. Anyway, how can it be, until those twelve men and women, who so far have given no sign of their response, at last divulge it? At the last point of all, so far as we are concerned, there is an incalculable . . .

The brothers are put up, and the Judge immediately resumes his work on the telephone-call transcripts. He begins with the two calls on 5th February, the aftermath of those on the 3rd with which he finished yesterday afternoon. M3 demands to speak to Mr McKay, not Ian, whom he blames for the police presence. Mr McKay is now available again. 'I've stopped mourning my wife,' he says toughly to M3. 'I've got to get back to work.' He agrees to a new rendezvous, but refuses to risk his daughter. A few minutes later M3 rings again, and this time Mr McKay agrees to take Diane. Four o'clock at the telephone box in Church Street, Tottenham, is the instruction. 'Remember any error will be fatal.'

When 'Mr McKay' and 'Diane' went to the box it was three-quarters of an hour before the call came. His Lordship asks: 'Was somebody spending that three-quarters of an hour watching, and seeing that the only persons in the booth were Mr McKay and Diane, unaccompanied?'

The next telephone box is in Bethnal Green, opposite the police station, and in sight of Percy Chaplin's shop, which Arthur and Nizam say they went to between 5 p.m. and 6 p.m. 'The coincidences proliferate,' his Lordship notices. It may be accident; or it may be a pattern, a design pursued by some people.

And so to Epping, then on to Gates Garage and the Minivan, UMH587F. 'Mr McKay' and 'Diane' drop the two white suitcases, M3 having warned 'If you don't drop the money, she'll be dead', and having threatened the use of high-powered, telescopic-sighted rifles if there are any police around. His Lordship turns to the activities of the brothers in the meantime, Nizam circling Gates Garage and Arthur drinking in The Raven. The Volvo comes back at 10.47 p.m., Nizam driving and another man in the passenger seat. Nizam says it was Arthur. His Lordship reiterates: 'In the case of a joint charge, if one defendant gives evidence against the other, don't take it against the other unless it's borne out by other evidence.' The police say it was Arthur.

The Judge retraces some of Nizam's evidence, especially his admission of the note found in his pocket giving the location and number of the Minivan. 'Why *write down* the number and Gates used-car lot?' he asks. 'Of course the person announcing himself as M3, *telling Mr Alick McKay* where to leave the suitcases, gave Gates Garage and the number of the Mini. Such a person would have needed to have these things written down.' He pauses. 'Is Nizam telling the truth?'

The police took the Volvo's number and arrived in force at Rook's Farm on the next day. Inexorably his Lordship lists the objects the police found which provided forensic evidence, down to similarity of the staple marks and tear profile on the ransom letter.

'You may think that by itself it's so very small,' he says to the jury. 'But when added to other things, you find that one reinforces the other.' He pauses. 'You may think it indicates almost certainty, so far as things can be certain.' And then he cautions them as usual. 'You mustn't convict unless you're *sure* of the totality of evidence.'

His Lordship then contrasts the behaviour of the brothers on certain occasions after arrest. He reminds the jury of Mr Draycott's picking up Arthur's description of his brother as 'a stranger in a strange land', and Mr Draycott's further emphasising that Nizam was dependent on Arthur for a roof over his head; therefore Nizam should not be looked at with the same stringency as Arthur. His Lordship cites Nizam's replies to police questions about his whereabouts at certain times. 'Where did Arthur say I was?' When asked: 'Did you go to Wimbledon?' Arthur said 'No'—Nizam said: 'I want to die. I mustn't speak. Let me see Arthur!' His Lordship asks: 'Did Nizam fear for his brother? Or fear that Arthur had already said something?' His Lordship tells the jury they must decide. 'It might be craven, abject fear and alarm,' he suggests, 'or cunning prevarication.'

Keeping his attention on Nizam, his Lordship reminds the jury that Nizam saw Arthur day in day out at Brixton until their fight, in June. Yet when he, the Judge, asked Nizam if he didn't ask Arthur about Mrs McKay during that time—although he had admitted that he thought Arthur had something to do with the Mrs McKay affair—he said no.

'Nizam was there in Brixton, on a charge of a murder. Do you think that in that situation, fear of an elder brother would stifle that question?' His Lordship pauses. 'If Nizam knew the answer, one might understand why he didn't pose the question.'

His Lordship then contrasts the story Nizam told the police about certain events—about 'Susie', and about the paper flowers for instance—with the story he is telling now. When he was first shown the paper flowers, he said: 'I want to die.' He says he was speechless with fear. 'Or was it,' his Lordship asks, 'because there was no other answer, no truthful answer, that would not expose him?'

(One recalls all the other occasions on which Nizam said 'Let me die!' instead of giving an answer to the question.)

After the arrest there were no more messages, no more telephone calls in a West Indian accent to St Mary House. Meanwhile the police find no trace of Mrs McKay at Rook's Farm—the Judge tells the jury they must keep in mind so many witnesses having been invited to come to Rook's Farm. In parenthesis he points out that the bar-help who tried to find the Farm on the Monday afternoon would not have got much hospitality, as Arthur says he was at Farmer Pateman's. Also they must keep in mind that people say Arthur was his normal self at the time.

Lastly, turning again to Nizam, his Lordship refers to the note Nizam held up for Adam to read, five weeks after he'd been taken into custody. 'Five weeks in which he could have pondered his situation, in which, if he'd been a mechanical assistant, he could have decided to tell the truth!' His Lordship repeats Nizam's explanation, and concludes: 'Ask yourself: Is Nizam not a free agent, while in prison—capable of working out "What is the best story I can tell from my point of view?" ' Nizam has admitted the story about 'Susie' was false. 'These,' says his Lordship, 'are matters on which to dwell.'

And now his Lordship comes to Count 1. 'Unless and until you find either or both of the defendants guilty of kidnapping Mrs McKay, there is no vestige of case against them for murder.' He pauses. 'If, however—in order to say what I have to say I have to make an assumption—*if* you find one or other guilty of kidnapping, what are the indications that she is dead?'

One indication is what the kidnappers were saying, but it doesn't follow that each is guilty of killing her. His Lordship tells the jury what murder is, narrowing the definition for the purposes of this case.

'Murder means doing an act which causes death when that act is done with intention to kill.'

His Lordship says the jury may think there is no other possible explanation than that Mrs McKay is dead. He repeats the kidnappers' threats to kill, repeated on several occasions. If the jury finds the defendants guilty of kidnapping, they were making those threats. If the threats of extortion had failed, is it likely she would have been restored? Or would the evil courses have been followed that the telephone calls announced?

'It would be wrong,' he tells the jury, 'to take the facile view that, if there is no body, death cannot be established.'

He gives as an example someone being knifed in the back and the body thrown overboard: the inference of death would be easy. But even where it is more obscure the jury must look at all the facts; and if those facts leave room for *any other* feasible inference, any other possible inferences than that Mrs McKay is dead, they are entitled to infer it. On the other hand, if all the circumstances in combination prove that there is no other rational hypothesis but that she's dead, they will not shrink from making that decision, dreadful and responsible though it is, despite the fact that there are no witnesses to say 'I saw something done to her to cause death. I saw her dead body.'

Mrs McKay was taken away and sent a few notes up to January. M3 was begged to produce proof that she survived. What the McKays got were miserable pieces of her clothing—was it an attempt to provide proof after the body of Mrs McKay had been disposed of?

If, and only if, the jury decide the defendants are the kidnappers, they should ask: Where is she now? Her custodians have been in custody, unless there are others involved. 'What have the others been doing?' his Lordship asks. 'Why are they not sending out some signals or message, if she is alive today, that refutes the dreadful charge hanging over the heads of these two men?' He pauses. 'I fear she is beyond needing the custody of anybody, or you would think there'd be something that showed she still lived.'

And in due course he comes to the final question. And if she's dead, *How?*

Her captors were saying time after time—'She will be executed.' 'Any error will be fatal.' 'This is your last chance.'

'If those two men in the dock are guilty of kidnapping her they have not said anything to show the threats against her life were *not* carried out.' His Lordship then asks: 'Why not?'

He turns to an alternative possibility—that the defendants may have kidnapped her and she died—another horrifying thought—from fear, or by accident. Since they didn't wish to admit to the kidnapping, they didn't say how she died. That would be an act not done with intention to kill.

(This has always struck me as a very important point. They didn't wish to admit to the kidnapping because the number of years' penalty for kidnapping might well be greater than the number that life imprisonment nowadays amounts to.)

However, the jury have to look at the matter against the background of the totality of the evidence. If they decide there is no other rational inference, no other reasonable explanation, then and only then can they return a verdict of Guilty. He reminds them again that it is a case of the greatest gravity.

'You must not convict except on evidence that makes you sure of guilt. Where the evidence falls short, you may say Not Guilty, not as a matter of charity but as a matter of law.'

And lastly: 'You must be unanimous.'

It is 12.35 p.m. and the jury retires to consider its verdict.

15

The verdict

The time while the jury is out is oddly disturbing. One might think everybody would go over to the pub or café, or even to the canteen in the basement of the courts, and pass the time socially if not convivially. People do move to and fro, but in a curiously distracted way, never in fact straying far from the long spacious lobby, with its single benches of back-to-back seats down the middle. In this case nobody could expect the jury to return with their verdict inside several hours, yet even the crime-reporters only go down to the Press-room and work in a desultory way.

Court 1 is meanwhile used for another case and I go in. In the dock two black young men who admit mugging an Italian chef one summer evening in St James's Park. And on the Bench—Mr Justice Sebag Shaw again! *He* is behaving with exactly the same attentiveness and acuteness; but *I* can't help feeling it's a bit of a come-down. Perhaps judges don't have such a wonderful time after all! I steal out.

The trouble is that nobody knows when the jury actually will return; the Old Bailey has no system of bells for indicating imminent crises like the Division bells in the Houses of Parliament. One might expect the policemen to organise a system of runners for themselves at least: but no—Mr Smith and Mr Minors stand chatting seriously with their detective assistants not far from the door of Court 1. On a seat by the window sits Mrs Hosein, attended by two women to look after her. The members of the McKay family, all of them now, are round about. Even I, a mere spectator, feel anxious and oppressed.

After hearing the summing up most people think the Hoseins will go down on Counts 2–7. But on Count 1, murder? Even after hearing the summing up, they mostly still don't know for certain what the jury are going to say. Probably down, yet . . . I try to put myself in a juryman's place. What should *I* say? On Counts 2–7 I think I should feel bound to say that in all probability they did it, though I'm not entirely satisfied with the idea that they did it unaided. They somehow don't look as if they quite could have, though I can't pretend I've got experience of seeing kidnappers and murderers with whom to compare them. Nor have I, after all this, completely fathomed the relationship between them, certainly not what it was twelve months ago.

Granted that the kidnappers were in some ways grossly incompetent and that, as I see it, they were favoured with fantastic luck, their operations were nevertheless in some ways very ingenious and cleverly planned. If the two of them really did it, the way they worked out the whole thing, kidnapping, murdering and disposing of the body, and collecting the ransom, in such a way that they could *apparently be leading normal lives* all the time, seems to me astonishing, to say the least of it. Clever, or cunning, it seems to need a *rapport* between the brothers which has certainly vanished now and which it is hard to visualise then.

Nizam continues to strike me as the odd man out. I go on feeling that his other brothers neither liked him nor wanted him with them—Arthur and Adam say they didn't, and the oldest brother he stabbed can't have. Only clan-loyalty seems to have kept him within the family. That to me is more where the Karamazov-like mystery lies than in Nizam's nature, which seems to have mystified so many people. Once one gets a hold of its schizoid essence, the introverted stillness, the distanced emotions inside their shell, which suddenly cracks in outbursts of weeping or hitting—both curiously *remote*, nonetheless—one is not worried by the idea of his seeming gentleness or even of his really being dominated by Arthur.

Approaching it from a different angle, one can ask if Nizam's is the typical remote kind of nature which takes to exaggerated action in order to break out and come to life. (It's hard to forget the sadistic, taunting, scoring-off-the-McKays note in M3's telephone calls.) Arthur seems much less of a mystery. *Folie de grandeur*, hysteria, paranoia, plus the touchiness about his colour. Can one imagine colossal greed springing from his Napoleonic vitals, and a passionate compulsion to show he is more successful than any white men? *If* the two of them went to 20 Arthur Road, one can imagine Nizam cracking on the edge of suppressed excitement; Arthur—with or without double scotches—in a state of wild euphoria, 'King Hosein' about to lay his hands on limitless riches by his own cleverness. And if I'm right about Nizam feeling above all 'the rejected one', he was at that moment in full association with Arthur—'in it up to the neck', as Mr Draycott said, with Arthur—and in the future no longer to be rejected when he owned half a million. *If* the two of them went . . .

Did they go? I have given my answer; in all probability. But did they afterwards murder Mrs McKay? What, as a juryman, should I have to say to Count 1? As a former juryman at the Old Bailey—as foreman of the jury, as a matter of fact—I have some, if limited, experience of what goes on in the jury-room. It's very like a Whitehall committee-room. Arguments, agreements, disagreements, *quid pro quo*'s; all the convolutions of negotiation that have to be gone through for everyone to consent to be party to the final unanimous decision. In my opinion what brings unanimity from the jury-room is what brings a decision to which everyone is party from a committee-room—stamina: determination not to be worn down. In a jury-room one is worn down—or one wears the others down.

So I put it to myself. In that jury-room now there must be a strong party proposing to find the Hoseins Guilty on Count 1. Should I go along with it, should I consent to be worn down; or not? My answer is as certain as it's immoral. It's immoral because a jury is adjured to find, on the evidence, Guilty or Not Guilty without any reference whatsoever to the punishment. I am affected by the punishment for murder having once been the death penalty, which, apart from its turning my stomach over with its hideous physical nature, appals my mind with its irrevocableness.

So I give my answer, which can only shock any legal person and demonstrate to the world that I am not a fit person to be called for jury service at a murder trial. As the present penalty is life imprisonment, which means that if the doubt which was worn down finally turns out to be justified, at least somebody has not gone to the gallows for it, I might if I were in that jury-room now reconcile myself on the basis of the summing up to being in the end worn down into going along with the rest.

But if the result of saying Yes were for the Hoseins to be forthwith hanged, then I should have to stand out—I *should* stand out, stamina or no stamina—indefinitely. Not, I acknowledge before anyone starts to abuse me, a satisfactory state of affairs. Did they murder Mrs McKay? If it was they who went to Arthur Road that night, I suppose, *I suppose* they must either have murdered her or she must have died on their hands. . . . That's not the basis for a satisfactory state of affairs, is it?

But I am not on the jury. I merely stand and wait to see. . . . And what did M3, whoever he was, say? 'That's why they will never be able to solve this case.' Only if someone who knows how Mrs McKay met her death, who was there at the time, confesses, shall we ever know what actually happened.

Something after half past four the jury are rumoured to have sent for their tea and are consequently thought—don't ask me why!—to be nearing a decision. In fact they are. So after just over four hours we all troop back into the court for the last time. Now it is more than packed. Standing up there is just room for everybody: sitting down it's a squash. One is conscious of bodies all round, breathing, waiting. The accused men are put up. The jury file in, their foreman leading—they have elected the youngest among them to be their foreman, the one who appears to be in his thirties. Suddenly there is silence.

'Are you unanimous?' asks the Clerk of the Court.

'Yes,' says the foreman. He stands, healthy-looking, spectacled, thoroughly in command of himself.

And then the Clerk of the Court reads out again, like a litany, the charges for each defendant, count by count. And count by count comes the answer, each time, for each count, the same answer.

'Guilty.' 'Guilty.' 'Guilty.' 'Guilty.' 'Guilty.' 'Guilty.' 'Guilty.' 'Guilty.' 'Guilty.' 'Guilty.' (Will it never stop?) 'Guilty.' 'Guilty.' 'Guilty.' 'Guilty.'

(I find it peculiarly shocking.)

It is over. But the foreman remains standing. He wishes to say something more. The Judge nods permission. He says the jury unanimously recommend leniency towards Nizamodeen Hosein.

(I suppress the impulse to say 'Good God!' because I have no right to. The twelve men and women drawn from the common public have done what they were adjured to do—for us. At this point it is open to me, metaphorically speaking, only to shut up and bow myself out.)

However there is more to report. The two leading counsel are invited to speak on behalf of their clients before sentence is passed on them. Mr Hudson asks for Arthur's antecedents to be borne in mind: Mr Draycott says the reason for leniency towards Nizam is obvious. The privilege is then extended to the defendants themselves.

Everyone is expecting an explosion from Arthur. The warders surrounding him must be at the ready. He makes a speech. He *would* make a speech, of course. But it begins both bitterly and wittily.

'Injustice has not only been done. It has also been seen and heard by the public gallery'—he waves an arm towards us all—'to be done.'

He addresses himself to the Judge.

'The provocation of your Lordship has shown immense partiality. To his Lordship I would say that from the moment I mentioned Robert Maxwell I knew you were a Jew.' (Not hysteria but paranoia!) He is beginning to work himself up. 'Not that I am anti-Jewish myself,' he adds, thus showing his own absence of partiality. 'This is my privilege,' he says, as the stirring around him seems to be directed towards stopping him. 'You have shown throughout this case,' he tells the Judge, 'that you have directed the jury on only one side, to the Crown. . . . I have produced thirty witnesses, and not once. . .'

His Lordship watches him steadily on the same level over the well of the court. Arthur goes on.

'You have denied me justice!'

Mr Hudson jumps up to intervene. 'Your Lordship, may I have a word . . .'

The Judge: 'He doesn't need your help, Mr Hudson.'

Arthur is now raising his voice in sarcasm to the jury. 'Thank you, members of the jury! It is a grave injustice! . . .'

The warders show signs of crowding in on him and he becomes incoherent and stops. The sentences are to be passed. Nizam has said not a word.

'On the conviction of murder the sentence is life imprisonment.' This is for Arthur. For Nizam the same, with a recommendation of leniency 'from another quarter'.

Now the kidnapping. His Lordship makes a short introductory speech to impart that every right-minded person will expect the punishment to be salutary.

'The kidnapping and confinement of Mrs McKay was cold-blooded and abominable,' he says. 'She was snatched from the security of her home and so long as she remained alive she was reduced to terrified distress. This crime will shock and revolt every right-minded person. The punishment must be such that law-abiding citizens may feel safe in their homes.'

On the count of kidnapping he sentences Arthur Hosein to twenty-five years. To Nizam he says: 'I am not sure whether you are in any degree less culpable, but the jury's view is that you were under the influence of your brother and I have to regard the possibility that this was so.' He sentences him to fifteen years.

Coming to the next count he says: 'There could not be a worse case of blackmail. You put that family on the rack for weeks and months in an attempt to extort money by your monstrous demands.' For this both brothers receive the maximum sentence of fourteen years. For sending threatening letters each gets the maximum of ten years.

The sentences are to run concurrently. In the past, life imprisonment amounted, after remission for good conduct, to an actual ten years or so: but since the abolition of the death penalty the Judge trying the case has power to recommend to the Home Secretary that the prisoner should not be released for a specified length of time, e.g. two particularly dangerous criminals recently were sent down for thirty years. No such recommendation to the Home Secretary was made by Mr Justice Shaw now—so it looks as if his Lordship is sending Arthur down for a certain twenty-five years, and Nizam a certain fifteen years under the kidnapping conviction. As it is the usual practice to remit one-third of a fixed sentence provided the prisoner behaves himself in prison, general opinion among the joint army seems to be that Arthur will serve just under seventeen years and Nizam ten years if they get their remission.

His Lordship has ordered the two brothers to be removed from the dock. Grasped firmly by warders they go downstairs out of sight. (One knows they will appeal, of course!) The Judge then thanks the jury on behalf of the City of London and of society as a whole; and he asks Chief Superintendent Smith, as leader of the investigation and representative of the police, to stand up in court for congratulation. 'It was brilliantly done.'

All is over. For the last time we hear the cry which begins, 'Be upstanding!' and ends—

'God Save The Queen!'

16

The appeal

Both brothers put in applications for leave to appeal, Arthur against the verdict and the sentence, Nizam against the verdict.

On the 29th March 1971, the applications are heard before the Court of Appeal. There is a surprise right at the start—a complete change in Arthur's representation, the result, presumably, of another Napoleonic stroke. Gone are Mr Hudson and his junior, Mr Dunn; in their places are the new incumbents, Mr Edwin Jowitt, Q.C. and Mr A. M. Simpson; also a new solicitor, Mr Aubrey Rose. Nizam's counsel stay the same. For the Crown Mr M. A. Lennox Boyd joins Mr Cussen and Mr Leary.

The application is heard by Lord Justice Edmund Davies, Lord Justice Karminski and Mr Justice Melford Stevenson, presided over by Lord Justice Davies. The proceedings open with Mr Jowitt asking permission for Arthur to attend, admitting that he is a volatile person who may interrupt. Mr Draycott says he had not intended to ask permission for Nizam to appear, but in the cicumstances he claims parity. Their Lordships confer. They grant leave for both to appear.

The brothers are brought in, now handcuffed to warders. There is a marked change in Arthur—he looks terrified, the whites of his eyes showing all round the iris as he glances round. Has such a short time in prison deflated him so far? And Nizam—he looks just as composed as ever. From the general feeling in the court, spoken or unspoken, one gathers Arthur's terror is probably justifiable.

Mr Jowitt outlines his grounds for application, a series of points of which he leaves the first to the end. They consist of details which he claims Mr. Justice Shaw failed to remind the jury of; such things as the conflict of evidence about fingerprints, about the identification of Arthur in the Volvo by not more than one police officer, and so on. But it is the first point that touches the real crux of the case; the possibility that Mrs McKay may never have been taken to Rook's Farm, and that other people may have been involved; and the possibility that actual murder, as distinct from threat of murder, did not fall within the ambit of the enterprise of kidnapping for ransom. Mr Jowitt quotes from the summing up: 'If one of them does it in the pursuance of a design which is common to both and with an intent to kill which they have in common, they are both guilty.' The jury ought to have been asked to consider if there were others involved and if murder was within the ambit of kidnapping: the summing up was defective according to the evidence.

Mr Draycott says he has no separate points on behalf of Nizam. He reiterates that others may have been involved: he considers there was insufficient probing into whether other people may have killed Mrs McKay without Arthur and Nizam being involved.

Their Lordships retire to confer. And they return. Lord Justice Davies begins by announcing that for them in their combined experience at the Bar and on the Bench, this is the most terrible case with which they have had to deal.

(Even granted that judges are emotional men, how can they permit themselves to go on telling us, time after time, that this is the worst case in their experience? Are we to understand that human iniquity is always on the upgrade?)

The brothers' chances are clearly nil.

Lord Justice Davies goes over some of the events of the case again, insisting that the contest between the two groups of witnesses was put fairly and squarely before the jury, in what he and his colleagues all consider was 'an immaculate summing up'. (Before this Jehovianic pronouncement any thoughts about that being a matter of opinion are finally squashed.) He then deals with the points set out by Mr Jowitt and Mr Draycott, introducing a few more of his own. He remarks the depravity as well as the determination of the kidnappers. He reminds us that although no trace of Mrs McKay was found at Rook's Farm, other things were found implicating the brothers. As to the final identification of Arthur in the Volvo: the learned Judge, Lord Justice Davies concedes, did erroneously direct the jury that Arthur's presence was identified by more than one police officer—but the slip could not have misled anyone. With a final word of congratulation for Mr Jowitt, His Lordship dismissed the application.

Nizam's application is dealt with more shortly. His Lordship concedes here that the learned Judge did not make it clear to the jury if the two men were participants in the abduction and other crimes, it did not follow that they were parties to the murder. But the jury were repeatedly told that, unless they were sure, they must not convict of murder. If the kidnappers were saying they would murder Mrs McKay, it does not mean that both would take part and do the same acts. But that is not necessary if murder is done in the pursuance of a crime which both had the intention of committing. It used to be accepted that it was dangerous to convict of murder if no body was found: but the law now is that it is not so if the fact of death is provable by circumstantial evidence, and there is no doubt that Mrs McKay was murdered.

Leave to appeal is refused; and refusing Arthur's application to appeal against the sentence, Lord Davies says the sentences were justly merited. The maximum sentences were right, 'for no more terrible crime could be conjured up'. His voice resounds into a moment's silence. Then he says sharply:

'Take them away!'

Appendix

1. THE LETTERS

Received	*Postmark*	
31 Dec.	Tottenham N.17	From Mrs McKay: *Alick Darling I am blindfolded and cold* . . . (p. 21)
10 Jan.	E.1	M3 to Editor of *The News of The World* (p. 23)
22 Jan.	Wood Green N.22	From Mrs McKay: *Dear Alick I am deteriorating* . . . And: *Darling Diane I heard you on TV* M3's first ransom note (p. 25)
26 Jan.	Wood Green N.22	From Mrs McKay: *Alick Darling If only I* . . . And: *Darling Alick You don't seem* . . . (clipped) M3's second ransom note (p. 27). Three pieces of material.

2. THE TELEPHONE CALLS

Date and time		*Taken by*	*Extract from Message*
30 Dec.	1.15 a.m.	Mr McKay	This is M3. We have got your wife. Find a million!
,,	4.59 p.m.	David Dyer & Mr McKay	Your wife just posted a letter. For heaven's sake don't call the police!
1 Jan.	7.45 p.m.	Diane	It has gone too far.
,,	7.49 p.m.	Diane	Now you tell them they've gone too far.
14 Jan.		Editor of *The News of the World*	Tell McKay I want a million
,,	4.13 p.m.	Ian Burgess and Mr McKay	Did you hear from your editor? When I go back I'll let her write you a letter.
19 Jan.	3 p.m.	Mr McKay	Hello, Alex! (First talk of rendezvous.) Now if you don't co-operate,

Date and time	Taken by	Extract from Message
		you're to be blamed for not seeing your wife again. This is my orders and that is final.
21 Jan. 12.11 p.m.	Ian McKay	She's offering herself. Your Mum wrote you a letter last night. Had to clip a few bits bits off.
,, 12.17 p.m.	Ian	The date is the 1st February. First delivery half a million.
23 Jan. 11.56 a.m.	Ian	Did you get the letters?
,, 1.55 p.m.	Ian	We've never murdered any-one as yet.
,, 2.11 p.m.	Ian	I'm not going to ask her to write.
30 Jan. 11.37 a.m.	Ian	Any error will be fatal.
1 Feb. 7.55 p.m.	Ian	You must give me your solemn word.
,, 9.55 p.m.	'Ian' (Det. Sgt.)	(Instructions at kiosk at A10 and Cambridge Road.)
,, 10.45 p.m.	'Ian'	(Instructions at kiosk down Cambridge Road — Picca-dilly cigarette packet.)
3 Feb. 11.37 a.m.	Ian	Settle the time your Mum will be executed. We saw the police.
,, 1.30 p.m.	Ian	The Boys insist on Diane and your Dad.
5 Feb. 10.25 a.m.	Mr McKay	Any more dealings must be done by you and Diane.
,, 11.17 a.m.	Mr McKay	The day will be tomorrow.
6 Feb. 2.34 p.m.	Ian	This will be the last and final chance.
,, 4.45 p.m.	'Mr McKay' (Inspector Minors)	(Kiosk at Church Street, Tottenham.) If the police are about this time we will execute Muriel.
,, 6 p.m.	'Mr McKay'	(Kiosk at Bethnal Green.) Any error will be fatal.
,, 7.30 p.m.	'Mr McKay'	(Kiosk at Epping.) If you don't drop the money she'll be dead.